FILM FOCUS

Ronald Gottesman and Harry M. Geduld
General Editors

THE FILM FOCUS SERIES PRESENTS THE BEST THAT HAS BEEN
WRITTEN ABOUT THE ART OF FILM AND THE MEN WHO CREATED
IT. COMBINING CRITICISM WITH HISTORY, BIOGRAPHY, AND ANAL-
YSIS OF TECHNIQUE, THE VOLUMES IN THE SERIES EXPLORE THE
MANY DIMENSIONS OF THE FILM MEDIUM AND ITS IMPACT ON
MODERN SOCIETY.

CHARLES W. ECKERT, *editor of this volume in the Film Focus
series, is Associate Professor of English at Indiana University. He has published articles on myth and literature in*
The Classical Journal *and* Comparative Literature.

FOCUS ON

SHAKESPEAREAN FILMS

edited by
CHARLES W. ECKERT

A SPECTRUM BOOK

Prentice-Hall, Inc.
Englewood Cliffs, N. J.

791.4
E19 f

Library of Congress Cataloging in Publication Data

ECKERT, CHARLES W.   comp.
    Focus on Shakespearean films.

    (Film focus)
    1. Shakespeare, William, 1564–1616—Film adaptations.
I. Title.
PR3093.E3   791.43′7   72–4928
ISBN 0–13–807644–8
ISBN 0–13–807636–7 (pbk.)

PRENTICE-HALL INTERNATIONAL, INC. (*London*)
PRENTICE-HALL OF AUSTRALIA, PTY. LTD. (*Sydney*)
PRENTICE-HALL OF CANADA, LTD. (*Toronto*)
PRENTICE-HALL OF INDIA PRIVATE LIMITED (*New Delhi*)
PRENTICE-HALL OF JAPAN, INC. (*Tokyo*)

CONTENTS

Othello (1965)

The Taming of the Shrew (1966)

Chimes at Midnight (1966)

ACKNOWLEDGMENTS

I am especially grateful to Harry Geduld and Ronald Gottesman who helped me with advice and information at all stages of my work, to Robert Hamilton Ball who proofread the filmography, corrected many errors, and graciously shared his original research on Shakespearean films, and to the staff of the British Film Institute who were exceptionally kind and responsive to my many letters.

Introduction
by CHARLES W. ECKERT

Sir Laurence Olivier, as Richard III, turns to look at the audience; from the vast close-up, over ten feet tall, his self-delight, his control, his sense of power over us radiate marvelously. Ronald Colman in *A Double Life* pauses to look at his reflection in a Manhattan shop window and recite Othello's lines, "Haply, for I am black,/ And have not those soft parts of conversation/ That chamberers have . . ."— the camera finding in the reflections and shadows of a tawdry American *mise-en-scène* a metaphor for Othello's darkening, fragmenting world.

To those who have been moved, if only for moments, by the best Shakespearean films and adaptations, and who have returned to the texts with increased affection and insight because of their experience, the legitimacy of film treatments of Shakespeare's plays is not an issue for debate. It is with this premise in mind that I have compiled this anthology. Although many severe criticisms of individual films appear here, I have not included reviews or essays whose argument is solely that Shakespeare's plays should not be filmed. The cinema has long since established itself as one of the new languages of our century; and it was inevitable that Shakespeare would be translated into this still-developing tongue.

One look at the Filmography at the back of this volume will give some sense of the immense domain one enters in investigating filmic treatments of Shakespeare and the reviews and critiques these films have elicited. A pitiful few of the films, however, survive or can be seen. Better than half of the more than 210 films listed come from the silent era; and the vast majority of these are lost, or survive in mutilated copies, or are preserved in archives and private collections. Fewer than twelve of the silent films are available for rental. Of the approximately eighty-six films from the sound era, the average reader will have seen fewer than a dozen; and, again, the number available for rental is small. (When will we be able to see even such a major work as Welles's *Othello?*)

Since relatively few of these films can be seen by present-day audi-

1

ences, I have thought it best to anthologize writings pertaining to only the most important and most available ones. I have deliberately slighted the silent era because we already have in Robert Hamilton Ball's *Shakespeare on Silent Film* a compendium of contemporary reviews, and because criticism in depth only appeared when the advent of sound made it possible to film Shakespeare as spoken drama rather than mime or spectacle intercut with written quotations. As entrancing as Asta Nielsen's *Hamlet* (1920) and Emil Jannings's *Othello* (1922) are, the reviews of these films seem historically curious and anecdotal rather than provocative.

Throughout the reviews and critical pieces presented here certain conflicts of opinion recur. The principal one—it is almost a leitmotiv —is the conflict between those who feel that fidelity to Shakespeare's text is of prime importance and those who are willing to allow the director and adaptor creative authority both in cutting the original and in imposing simplistic or even eccentric interpretations upon it.

The first group is largely composed of academics—teachers and students of Shakespeare whose intimate familiarity with the text inclines them to wince at every cut line, at every omitted character, and at every simplification of Shakespeare's thought. I have not fully represented academic reviewers in this volume because their discussions of the films are too often recitals of the specific passages omitted, of the superiority of one or another stage performance, and so forth. These approaches aid us little in coping with the films themselves.

Opposed to this group are those who, for a variety of reasons, but principally because they have a great love for the cinema, are tolerant of even gross liberties if they feel that the spirit of Shakespeare is retained or his poetry and ideas metamorphosed into cinematic equivalents—into images, editing styles, music, color, and the movements of the camera that comprise the unique language of the cinema. André Bazin's defense of Welles's *Othello* and Paul Jorgensen's sympathetic appraisal of Castellani's *Romeo and Juliet* (an academic critic here) are examples of this approach at its best.

Allegiance to one or the other side in this dispute will probably also incline one to admire the more text-and-theater-oriented, and therefore more academic interpretations of Olivier, Mankiewicz, and Kozintsev as opposed to the more cinematic versions of Welles, Castellani, and Zeffirelli. I have tried to choose critiques that exemplify the whole spectrum of reactions to these important films; but, again, I have included more writers who are sympathetic to the films and to the intentions of the directors and actors.

Max Reinhardt's *A Midsummer Night's Dream* (1935) was one of the first serious attempts to combine the magnificent spoken poetry with images beyond the scope of the stage. Reinhardt's film threw into bold relief the astonishing potential that sound film and the resources of large movie studios held for the mounting of Shakespeare's plays; and it discovered irritating drawbacks from which perhaps no Shakespearean film has been entirely free. Allardyce Nicoll's discussion of this film is still fresh and evocative; he is impressed by the great intimacy with the verse made possible by the use of the close-up, by the relations between Shakespeare's concrete language and the photographic image, and by the ability of the cinema to suggest realms of metaphor beyond the text and yet congruent with it. Conversely, in Richard Watt's essay, we find some chronic problems foreshadowed: casting directed by box-office economics, the need to make Shakespeare popular through whatever Philistine distortion of his thought, and the timidity of producers who, while sensing that Shakespeare will sell, recoil from the notion that he might sell without gimmickry and press-agentry.

Reinhardt's film had its moments of distressing banality, but it was, on the whole, the most sensitive and creative sound-era treatment of Shakespeare prior to Olivier's *Henry V*. In James Agee's review of Olivier's production we relive that moment of electric revelation which those of us who saw the film when it first appeared experienced. Agee's review (or is it really an homage?) still seems to say the right things: the energy that suffused the screen was predominantly Shakespeare's language spoken by actors who deeply loved it and who were inspired by a moment in history (the end of the Battle of Britain). But the film did more than treat Shakespeare with integrity: it suggested that he could repay the substantial investment of a full-length color production, and it inspired others to produce Shakespearean films.

In the films that followed in the forties and fifties, one senses a widening gap between those who wished to produce Shakespeare "faithfully" and those who wished to interpret him or adapt him to the cinema. Mankiewicz's *Julius Caesar* (1952) was motivated by a reverent desire to film the play faithfully. That this attempt should lead to a painstaking reconstruction of Rome in Caesar's time, and to the use of quasi-Roman costume (see P. M. Pasinetti's description of his work as technical adviser) was probably inevitable—and certainly ironic. Obviously, Shakespeare would not have recognized this Rome, and any reconstructed Rome has little in common with the Elizabethan stage. The text, however, as Roy Walker points out, was handled with the deference typical of Olivier's *Henry V* or Cukor's earlier *Romeo and Juliet* (1936).

Welles's *Macbeth* (1948), however, was another kettle of bêtes noires. No other Shakespearean film—not even Zefirelli's much-cut and highly cinematic *Romeo and Juliet* (1968)—has served as so positive a touchstone to discriminate the *cinéaste* from the Bardolater. *Macbeth* came out the same year as Olivier's *Hamlet*. Against *Hamlet*'s labored Elizabethan costumes it pitted a purely Wellesian wardrobe, half barbaric

horde, half science fiction. And against Olivier's stagy but highly realistic Elsinore it pitted a castle of the mind—a dripping, disoriented,
cavelike *space* where a floating dagger seemed commonplace. Bazin,
in his extremely suggestive review of Welles's later *Othello* (1951),
points out that the Venice jury may have given *Othello* the Grand
Prix that they secretly knew was owing to *Macbeth*. Exasperated references to Welles's *Macbeth* will be found throughout this anthology.
English-speaking reviewers in general were—and still are—hostile to
it. But its success among French cinemaphiles was all but inordinate.
Claude Beylie's swelling, effusive, yet keenly calculated review provides insight into this phenomenon—as, in a more oblique way, does
Henri Lemaitre's "Shakespeare, the Imaginary Cinema and the Pre-
cinema." One cannot help wondering if the French are more tolerant
in general of transpositions from one art form to another, or if the
language of Shakespeare is inevitably less sacrosanct to non-English-
speaking people.

Welles's *Othello* (1957) may be the better of the two films, or perhaps it has gained stature through its inaccessibility. Whatever its
distribution problems are, one would like to see it made available in
16-mm film so that criticism of it need not rely upon memory and
hearsay. Micheál MacLiammóir's diary of the making of *Othello, Put
Money in Thy Purse,* is one of the most entertaining—and perceptive
—documents on Welles. I have included a long excerpt from this work,
including all the passages in which Welles's conception of the film is
elaborated. Those who would demythologize Welles will not find an
ally in MacLiammóir; his affectionate but biting portrait of "the
bright-winged old gorilla" convinces one that Welles constructed much
of the mythos that surrounded him at the time he made *Macbeth* and
Othello.

Of the films produced within the last two decades, Olivier's *Richard
III* (1955) and *Othello* (1965), Yutkevich's *Othello* (1955), Kozintsev's
Hamlet (1964), Zefirelli's *Romeo and Juliet* (1968), and Welles's *Chimes
at Midnight* (1966) are doubtless the most significant. (Kozintsev's *King
Lear* and Polanski's *Macbeth,* both made in 1971, have just been released here.) Constance Brown's extended analysis of *Richard III* is
unique in this volume. She attempts the kind of detailed, scene-by-scene
critique that is badly needed for the major Shakespearean films. The
most perceptive review must perforce confine itself to general impressions or, at best, a few sequences of the film. But with the increased use of 16-mm film in schools and colleges we need more in-
depth studies of the films.

For most of the other films I have limited myself to reviews, partly
because of space, partly because extended analyses are not available.
The general impression one receives from working through what has
been written about filmed versions of Shakespeare is that the best criti-

cism—and by best I mean most sensitive to both texts and film—has come from directors, actors, professional film reviewers, and critics sympathetic to the exigencies of film adaptation. Mary McCarthy's reading of Olivier's *Hamlet* seems worth all the reviews that concentrated upon what lines had been cut, how partial Olivier's Freudian interpretation was, and the unconscionable omission of Rosencrantz and Guildenstern. It is also true, however, that much of the former criticism lacks the assiduousness and authority that Shakespearean scholars bring to a discussion of the films.

Certainly we shall continue to have full-length, well-produced films of Shakespeare's plays (we have had five in the past two years). And with the amazing increase in the use of films in schools and colleges—reflected in the burgeoning number of distributors of 16-mm films—we shall see more of them, both in classrooms and film societies. It is inevitable that the quantity and the quality of academic criticism will improve. Perhaps Shakespearean films will even be considered as provocative interpretations of his plays rather than audio-visual guides to the "understanding" of his text. The value of such a libertarian adaptation as Welles's *Macbeth* can be seen if it is compared with one of those short educational dramatizations of individual scenes from the play with their lethargic actors and appalling *mise-en-scènes*.

Outside the academic world, Shakespearean films will continue to perform a function that dramatized versions cannot: they will bring his plays to popular audiences whose appetite for complex emotion, eloquence, and meaning is only increased by the watery dramatic fare set before them on most television programs and in most films. There will probably be more audacious interpretations of the plays, steeped in current cinematic idiom and careless of the text. But Shakespeare's reputation has developed, in part, from his ability to draw life from the very forces that would seem inimical to him—from fashion, changed values, commercialism, and, yes, the ministrations of directors, translators, scholars, and educators. And from no source has he drawn more life in this century than from the cinema.

Merely Players
by IAN JOHNSON

When the credits rolled for Sam Taylor's 1929 *The Taming of the Shrew* critics were aghast at the legend: "Written by William Shakespeare with Additional Dialogue by Sam Taylor." The shock, indignation, and guffaws at that piece of audacity have still not quite died away, but Sam Taylor is still the only director who was bold enough to admit that you can't produce Shakespeare without adapting. A liberal application of truth drug would reveal that since Shakespeare's day there hasn't been a single production which hasn't suffered trims, emendations, or bloody butchery for the sake of presentation, interpretation, or to avoid offending the sensibilities of the age. And that's not to forget that where Shakespeare is concerned even the scholars can't agree. . . .

There was a period, in fact, when Shakespeare was ignored altogether. When the theatres closed in Civil War England in 1642 Shakespeare was relegated to the fairground in comic performances such as *The Merry Conceited Humours of Bottom the Weaver* or *The Gravemakers* or *Imperious Caesar,* and when the theatres reopened his reputation stood not as high as Jonson's and well below that of Beaumont and Fletcher. Pepys liked *Hamlet,* but thought *Twelfth Night* "but a silly play" and *A Midsummer Night's Dream* "the most insipid, ridiculous play that ever I saw in my life." When Davenant reformed the plays, and repopularised them, he expunged the low and vulgar. In his *Macbeth,* Shakespeare's

> *Were such things here as we do speak about?*
> *Or have we eaten on the insane root*
> *That takes the reason prisoner?*

becomes

From Films and Filming, *April 1964, pp. 41–48. Reprinted by permission of the author.*

7

Were such things here as we discours'd of now?
Or have we tasted some infectious herb
That captivates our reason?

But Davenant did his work well, and the public clamoured for more. In 1681 Nathan Tate gave *King Lear* a happy ending, married off Cordelia to Edgar, and sacked the fool. The conventions of the age were that decorum and justice govern human affairs, so Lear was adjusted accordingly. And Tate's version lasted until the mid-nineteenth century. It was Garrick in the eighteenth century who started the nasty habit of extracting episodes from Shakespeare and popping them into tinselly entertainments, and in 1818 appeared Thomas Bowdler's *The Family Shakespeare*. We all know what was missing from that. Liberties with Shakespeare aren't so rife now, but Freud takes his toll, and I still remember the Old Vic production of *The Taming of the Shrew* where Petruchio leaps onto a table, a string of sausages in one hand, proclaiming "What dogs are these?"

In the long view, therefore, it seems a little carping of critics to nag at film-makers for cutting their scripts to one-and-a-half hours, or for not reproducing exactly the version the critics learned at school. So we won't do that here, although we shall compare the originals with the film-versions.

Nobody has ever estimated exactly how many films have been made from Shakespearian plays and plots. Lost copies, bastard versions disguised beneath trumped up names in the early silent years, Shakespearian titles to non-Shakespearian plots, musical versions (George Sidney's *Kiss Me Kate* in 1953, Robert Wise's *West Side Story* in 1960), science fiction versions, Western versions, gangster versions, puppet versions, opera versions, confuse the issue irremediably. In the mid-'fifties Meredith Lillieth (in *Films in Review*) hazarded that 66 films had then been made from 22 of Shakespeare's 33 plays, but apart from the last figure (which is merely questionable) that's certainly an underestimate. The plain fact is that it is simply impossible to make any kind of guess whatsoever. In quantity, at least, Shakespeare, like the Bible, has done well by the cinema.

The producers of the early one-reelers thought Shakespeare an eminently filmable subject, and thought nothing of making verseless versions lasting only a few minutes. Here Robert Hamilton Ball's research in *The Quarterly of Film, Radio, and Television* for 1953, proves invaluable. According to Ball, the first Shakespearian film was almost certainly *King John* with Max Beerbohm Tree, made not long after the play opened at Her Majesty's Theatre on September 20, 1899. Like many of these early films it was most likely made for record purposes, or perhaps for Tree's private amusement. Years later Beerbohm remarked that the film was "entirely without meaning, except to those who were perfectly familiar with the play and could recall the lines appropriate to the action."

The following year the *Duel Scene from Hamlet* was shot by Clément Maurice for Marguerite Chenu's Piano-Cinéma Théâtre at the Paris Exposition. Sarah Bernhardt who had played the rôle of the prince the previous year in a French version of the play labelled, but not enjoyed, by Max Beerbohm as a "preposterous undertaking," took the part again to Pierre Maquier's Laertes. It is said that when the great Sarah saw herself on the screen the shock was so great that she fainted clean away. The film played to five or six audiences a day, with sound effects added—or so it said—by the clashing of kitchen knives and the tramping of feet behind the screen.

Over the next few years there are many titles: *All's Well that Ends Well, A Comedy of Errors, Love's Labours Lost, A Winter's Tale, Much Ado About Nothing,*—but their connection with Shakespeare was, at best, remote. Several were comic burlesques.

Other titles were frank derivations from the Bard: *A Midwinter Night's Dream, Much Ado About, The Taming of the Shrewd, Taming Mrs. Shrew, A Village King Lear, A Jewish King Lear, The Daughters of Shylock, A Modern Shylock, The Vengeance of Iago,* or my favourites, *When Macbeth came to Snakesville,* and *Othello in Jonesville.*

Romeo and Juliet favoured titles: *Romeo and Juliet at the Seaside, A Rural Romeo, Romeo and Juliet in Town, A Would-be Romeo, The Galloping Romeo, A Robust Romeo, Romiet and Julio,* and (take a deep breath) *Romeo of the Coal Waggon* and *Romeo in Pajamas.*

Other titles revealed derivations from Shakespeare: *Seven Ages, Alas! Poor Yorick,* and *Une Drame Judicaiare de Venise.*

An important production of 1905 was Billy Bitzer's *Duel Scene from Hamlet* which he shot for the American Mutoscope and Biograph Company. Bitzer, who was later associated with D. W. Griffith, couldn't have imparted a particularly Shakespearian flavour to his film, however, for some two years later it became an episode in the composite film *Fights of all Nations.*

Another historical landmark was the howling gale, deafening thunder, and flashing lightning which culminated in the collapse of a ship's mast to the deck in Sir Herbert Beerbohm Tree's *The Tempest* performed at His Majesty's Theatre and transferred to film at some date between 1904 and 1910. The film, consisting of three views, each successively a greater distance from the stage, was taken to America in blue moonlight tint and fuller hand colour by George Kleine who sold the prints in 1910 for 13 dollars each.

There is little doubt of the great value of Méliès' two Shakespearian films, both of which have unfortunately been destroyed. However, Méliès' brother Gaston has preserved their memory. He tells us that the 394-foot-long *Shakespeare Writing Julius Caesar* opened with Shakespeare dreaming up the assassination scene in his study. After several false starts the scene he was to write was depicted by double exposure, with Caesar's assassins plotting the murder and Shakespeare remaining an interested spectator. A still survives of Caesar raising his hand defiantly against the rebels in a Rome already falling unto ruins, while Shakespeare sits to the right of frame. The scene changes to Shakespeare's study again and the playwright is by now so worked up that he raises a knife and plunges it straight to the heart of a loaf of bread his servant has just brought in. The film ends rather naively with a dissolve to a bust of Shakespeare "around which," as Gaston puts it, "all the nations wave flags and garlands." This may not have been Shakespeare, but Méliès pursued the wisest course. He avoided bogging himself down in Shakespearian subtitles or vague meaningless mouthing. His film is splendidly visual and offered a lesson his competitors mainly failed to learn. Generally in silent days the closer a film kept to Shakespeare the more ridiculous it became; the more sweeping the adaption to visual imagery the better. Today this problem of how far the cinema and Shakespeare may be reconciled is still one of the most pressing.

Just as cinematic was Méliès' *Hamlet* of 1907. The film opened with the graveyard scene (Hamlet's "manner strongly indicates 'Alas Poor York'" wrote Gaston) and switched to Hamlet's room, where he is confronted with apparitions first of the ghost of his father demanding revenge and then by "his departed sweetheart" whom he attempts to embrace. Ophelia throws flowers on him, he swoons, and is found raving mad by several courtiers. The film ended with the duel scene in which Laertes falls, the Queen drinks from the poison cup and dies, and Hamlet stabs the King and then himself.

Meanwhile on more modest lines Will Barker in England made a *Hamlet* with Charles Raymond as the lead. It was shot in one day with the rest of the cast being paid 10/- at most and being chosen more for their athletic qualities than for any acting talent—the Ghost because he was tall, Ophelia because she could swim, and so on. By now the Shakespearian flood was at full height and so many films were being shot—in America, by Meliès and Pathe in France, and by Cines in Italy (who in 1914 made a *Julius Caesar* with fifteen scenes and a cast of 20,000)—that the details are obscured or lost. Vitagraph had a truly stupendous output. Beginning in April 1908, by the end of the year the company had released no fewer than seven separate films based on Shakespeare plays.

Most of these productions must have paid their way, but money was not the only driving force behind the Shakespeare output. The cinema was striving for respectability and snob value was a way of attracting contemporary writers and actors to the industry. Vulgarity and indecency were raising their ugly heads, too, and fear of censorship or disapproval also encouraged the filming of Shakespeare. Not that the ruse was too successful, for in the States it resulted in an outcry for cuts in Shakespeare films, and in 1908 Chicago's Police Lieutenant Censor disapproved of *Macbeth* as too bloody.

The following years saw the rise and fall of "adaptations" and "cinematograph reproductions." The first were Shakespearian Plots fashioned into vehicles for film stars, films like *Falstaff* (1911), *Shylock* (1913) or *Love in a Wood* from *As You Like It* in 1916. "Cinematograph reproductions" were the stage performances of outstanding Shakespearian actors shot as permanent records of the popular productions of the day. In 1911 Sir Herbert Tree's *Henry VIII* was shot in this way, as was Sir Johnston Forbes-Robertson's five-reel *Hamlet* of 1913, an exact record of the Drury Lane production except for the ghost scene which was shot on the seashore. Of this production *The Times* considered "What cinematography can do was done to perfection," but that though they might be useful to "historians of the drama . . . to suggest that they do justice to the tragedy would be an outrageous absurdity."

Of all the explanations of *Hamlet* the most far-fetched must have been that offered in Asta Nielsen's *Hamlet* of 1921. It was made in Germany but the aroma was undeniably strong Danish. Not only did it have a Danish lead, but it was directed by another Dane (Svend Gade), photographed by Kurt Courant and Axel Graatkjer from a scenario by Erwin Gepard, and embellished with ideas from the twelfth-century Danish historian Saxo Grammaticus and from *Fratricide Punished,* a German drama which was possibly based on a lost edition of Shakespeare. Critics noted it chiefly for its stilted interior shots and its free, natural, outdoor shooting. Its chief merit was Asta Nielsen's "rare ability to mirror the more subtle feelings . . . without any use of gestures." Its surprise ending was in its explanation that Hamlet was in fact—a woman.

Dimitri Buchewetzki's *Othello* of 1922 was perhaps the most successful silent Shakespeare. According to Rene Clair "Emil Jannings as Othello, black, thick-lipped, heavily sensual, is a helpless child driven by Iago. His anxious eyes, reeling gait, trembling hands, everything in him expresses jealousy." As for Werner Krauss' Iago, "Dimitri Buchewetzki the director has not hesitated to present [him] almost as a clown, leaping through the castle, suddenly stopping dead, then darting off again to new misdeeds. Iago's perfidious words—how could they be rendered on the screen—he translates into movement. One gets the impression that he is destroying the castle by his frantic rushing about, much as in Shakespeare's play he did by saying a few words." Variations from Shakespeare occurred in the final act where Othello choked Desdemona instead of smothering her, stabbed

Iago, and finally killed himself and fell on top of the group. Clair thought all this necessary and called the film "a pictorial symphony on a Shakespearian theme . . . not a parasitic feeding on a great work of art. We would show serious lack of understanding of the cinema if we were shocked by the liberties taken with the plot. We can almost see the director steeped in the spirit of the text, shutting the book, and thinking only of the images it has evoked in him. This is the only way to 'adapt.' " . . .

And then came sound and Shakespeare leaped into verse. De Mille saw snob appeal and popped the balcony scene from *Romeo and Juliet* into his sound review *Triumph,* while Warners in their *Show of Shows* plumped for John Barrymore in a scene from *Richard III.* But there was only one full-length Shakespeare film proper for some time.

This was Sam Taylor's adaptation of *The Taming of the Shrew* (1929) and it starred Douglas Fairbanks in his first talkie and Mary Pickford in her second. Contemporary critics were not enthusiastic and the cutting of the original was not approved. They found Miss Pickford "surprisingly violent" while Fairbanks did "not permit any Shakespeare vehicle to stop him." A recent National Film Theatre programme described it as a good attempt at comedy and not an unsuccessful film in its own right. It was vigorous, and good humoured.

In 1935 Max Reinhardt transferred his showy stage methods to the screen in *A Midsummer Night's Dream,* a film which ran for 2¾ hours and cost 1,500,000 dollars to make. It was directed by Reinhardt and William Dieterle, and its leads were calculated box-office successes, although the calculation proved faulty in the event. The critics approved of Joe E. Brown and Hugh Herbert as rustics but were less sure of James Cagney who was considered too urban as Bottom. As Puck Mickey Rooney, then aged 11, was thought "an odd mixture of fawn and street urchin, but close to Shakespeare's fairy land." Least successful were the lovers Dick Powell and Anita Louise, described as "inserts from the world of college comedy." The text of the play was substantially altered and cut and emphasis was placed upon the rustic and fairy scenes with the result that the whole thing was too fairy-like with an over-reliance on chintz and gauze. Reinhardt introduced a goblin orchestra which killed the saccharine a little by its grotesque masques, and critics admired the choreography of Bronislava Nijinska to the Mendelssohn score. In short, as United Artists publicist Tom Waller later remarked: "There was a difference of critical opinion as to whether it was a good film. All critics agreed it was not good Shakespeare."

A Midsummer Night's Dream was a commercial flop. But long before the returns were in, Irving Thalberg had already started *Romeo and Juliet* for MGM. One only has to read of the immense background preparations for this film to have qualms. The film was shot in Hollywood, but two years previously a production crew had gone to Italy for shots and sketches of paintings, architecture, and museum pieces to inspire the sets and decor. Norma Shearer's hair style was taken from Fra Angelico's fresco of the *Annunciation* in Florence and her wedding gown after the one in *The Betrothed* by Michael da Verona. The entrance procession of the Prince of Verona was a duplicate of Gozzoli's *Procession of the Magi* fresco in Florence, while the principals and four hundred extras were instructed in Renaissance fighting methods. The film's publicity claimed "Every Word is Shakespeare's," which was true enough. Only two minor scenes were omitted and the scenes that are narrated in the play (Romeo's flight from Verona, Juliet's funeral procession) visualised with the dialogue patched together from other plays by Shakespeare under the supervision of Professor William Strunk Jr. of the Cornell English Department. Lines containing difficult words were omitted.

After all this preparation the only thing the film lacked was imagination (which was for free). It wasn't the last time the film-makers were to be blinded by middle-brow viewpoints, by elaborate background research, and by cost accounts, only to lose sight of the fact that Shakespeare can be successfully staged for a song—with imagination.

A few crumbs to the film's credit was that the balcony was high enough to provide a genuine obstacle, the tomb sufficiently maze-like to make Romeo's search seem necessary, and a trumpet call announcing the beginning of the film, as in Elizabethan days (followed by the prologue depicted as a worn parchment). The trumpet call frame was also adopted by Olivier in his *Henry V*.

The film was directed by Cukor and Leslie Howard and Norma Shearer played the leads. The part of Romeo had been offered to both Clark Gable and Laurence Olivier who each in turn had turned it down, the latter protesting that "Shakespeare should never be filmed." In the end Howard accepted. One reviewer admitted his "grace, intelligence and flair for lines," but added "the sophomorics of Romeo are too much for him and that sensitive horse's face of his, wrapped in disguises, leads to giggles."

Shearer made a dumpy twelve-year-old and received a mixed critical reception. Perhaps the most perceptive critic was the one who wrote that she was "rather unappetisingly made up . . . neither good nor bad . . . usually content with just being in there trying." In fact, the show was stolen by John Barrymore's Mercutio. Wrote the *New Republic*: "There will never be seen on the boards so much scenery chewing and rubber-faced trickery."

Imagination was lacking, too, in Paul Czinner's *As You Like It* (1936), into which Elizabeth Bergner claimed he put "all his brains and 1,000,000 dollars of his money." Olivier played Orlando in this film, but he went practically unnoticed against Bergner's accent and her "temperamental inability to stop wriggling." One critic, however, did have the courtesy to write: "It is not my Rosalind, I doubt if it is Shakespeare's, but it is a wee bit of personal radiance, an item of joy, an imp of delicate enchantment, an inspirer of son-nets . . ." But the film was admired in England, if not in the States, and it was the last Shakespeare film proper until the end of the war.

In the meantime two trifles. *Men Are Not Gods* was a Korda pro-duction directed by Walter Reisch in 1936, which adapted the *Othello* theme in a rather clever way. Sebastian Shaw is an actor playing Othello, to his wife's Desdemona (Gertrude Lawrence). When Ger-trude becomes jealous of her husband who—unjustly—she believes is having an affair with the secretary of a drama critic, Shaw takes advantage of the mistake and throws himself at the secretary. But Gertrude is found to be pregnant, and Miss Hopkins does the decent thing and throws him back again, only just in the nick of time to stop Shaw's plan to act out the *Othello* scene in real life. It was a tense, melodramatic film, but one of the better British films of the period. *The Boys from Syracuse,* made in 1940, was a version of *The Comedy of Errors.* Classical draperies were shaken to hot jazz, Greeks pressed the keys of cash registers, and chariots were hailed as taxies. The whole was a lively, rather unsuccessful film, shrugged off with disgust by the critics.

And then came Olivier's *Henry V,* and it was magnificent. There are two ways of interpreting Shakespeare's Henry: either as a dry, precise man pushed unwittingly into war by the machinations of his Archbishop, or as a born leader, virile, eloquent, and heaven-sent. With England at the peak and enduring one of the worst periods of the war, this was the way Olivier chose.

For the scenario Olivier collaborated with Alan Dent. The result of their joint efforts was a script neither falsified nor over-simplified and utilising some two-thirds of the text. In addition Olivier directed, played the lead, and nine bit parts, including the youth who sum-mons Mistress Quickly to Falstaff's death bed, the harrassed French court messenger, the sly addressee of the Constable of France the night before battle, and the French knight's attendant the next morning.

From the technical point of view the film provided immense prob-lems. The sets were unrealistic, and the Technicolor was used to keep the perspective flat as in a Mediaeval painting. The outdoor battle sequences were based on Uccello's *Rout of San Romano* and were shot in Southern Ireland owing to the activities of the RAF over Britain and the manpower shortage. So it happened 900 men of the Eirean Home Guard became French and English Knights. A nice touch was the manufacture of the chain mail which is today made only in Germany. For the occasion it was knitted out of wool by girls in an Irish institute for the blind and sprayed with aluminium paint.

Henry V is my favourite Shakespeare film. It was one of the best creations of one of the brightest periods of British film-making, and has the qualities and style which typified that period: solidarity without stageyness, a feeling of enthusiasm and a sweep, a great surge of confidence. Its individual scenes possess a warmth which immediately draws the spectator into intimate attachment to the characters. The opening sequence at the Globe Theatre doesn't quite ring true, maybe, and the Archbishop's description of Salic law tends to tedium. The clash of the realism on the battle front with the frankly flat stagey scenery later is perhaps a mistake. I'm not sure. The switch back from the marriage ceremony in the French court to player king and queen has a double action which shows at twenty-five years space. It is not Shakespeare's player king and queen we are watching any more, but Olivier as film-maker being frightfully clever. But against all this, what moments! Robert Newton's roaring, gloriously over-acted Pistol, Renee Asherson's coy Princess Katherine's English lesson on the battlement, comic yet charming, the battle scenes full of pageantry, the decaying, over-sophisticated picture of the French, the speech "but if the cause be not good" no longer a cynical one but put into the mouth of a simple Devonshire lad to become the voice of a nation at war. And one of the most highly praised sequences: the night before the battle where as Henry walks beneath the black stars the camera tracks "as if it were the wandering king himself among the firelit tents," while Olivier speaks the words.

Later, Olivier gave his views on filming Shakespeare: "You don't need tricky shots . . . up a man's trouser leg or through keyholes," he wrote. "Hollywood developed those techniques to make up for bad acting and weak scripts. In many of our scenes the camera hardly moves. You have to reverse the usual film technique of getting closer to the action as the scene reaches its climax. The photographing of the 1935 *Romeo and Juliet,* for example, was all wrong, because the lines demanded broader acting while the camera compelled Norma Shearer's acting to become smaller."

The next Olivier Shakespeare film was *Hamlet* in 1948. In the meantime, in 1946, C. A. Lejeune, like all the national critics, received a press release about a new British production of *Othello*. "Subsidiary plots have been eliminated," it said, "a complete story being evolved round the thematic treatment of the bloodstained handkerchief. The story is then played out to its tragic finish . . . you are earnestly invited to visit the studios on Thursday or Friday." The release was followed by a terse telegram: "Omit R in Thematic for Bloodstained Read Strawberry Divined stop Earnest Invitation confined to

Friday regrets and regards." All this was for a 45-minute quota production of *Othello* made at Marylebone Studios and produced by Henry Halstead and directed by David McKane. The producer's aims were well-meaning if somewhat condescending and fusty: "To those who are conversant with Shakespeare, our story is well-known. To those who have read or seen little of Shakespeare's plays upon the stage—a few words: this film version is intended for the ordinary filmgoer: it is so edited that all the long and sometimes tedious sections have been eliminated. The story yet remains alive and interesting, for no unreasonable liberties have been taken with the original and exquisite poetic content." Critics were respectful towards this *Othello,* intended as the first of several potted Shakespeares. John Slater made a convincing, if not particularly dynamic, Moor, while *The Times* thought that Sebastian Cabot made "an Iago with the bulk of a Falstaff and something of the mischievous air of a stage Oscar Wilde, a curious reading of a character normally visualised in the terms of lean and sinister energy."

As a follow-up, Marylebone had had in mind a potted *Hamlet,* but instead of Marylebone's we got Olivier's. As long ago as 1940 Leslie Howard had wanted to play *Hamlet* under his own direction in a small budget production using a single castle set. Later Hitchcock had touted around the idea of a modern dress *Hamlet* with Cary Grant in the lead. It could not have failed to have been interesting, but Olivier beat him to it.

Uncut, *Hamlet* plays for four hours, so from the start it was inevitable that Olivier's version could not but be a shadow of its original self. "I see *Hamlet* as an engraving rather than a painting" wrote Olivier, and the film opens with the legend: "This is the tragedy of a man who could not make up his mind," because as Dent said, "one has to choose between making the meaning clear to 20,000,000 cinemagoers and causing 2,000 Shakespearian experts to wince." But it didn't work. In the cutting much of the play's bite vanished, and the Freudian answers provided by Dent and Olivier became too easy, destroyed much of the drama's original intensity. There were several most unkind cuts.

The following characters went: Cornelius, Voltimand, Reynaldo, the second Gravedigger, Fortinbras, and Rosencranz and Guildenstern. This latter was the unkindest cut of all, for though in themselves Rosencranz and Guildenstern would never be missed, they were vital as part of the plot structure. In their endeavours to discover whether Hamlet is really mad they provide a genuine conflict throughout the play. The film is diminished by their absence. In addition Olivier and Dent eliminated many obscure phrases, modernised twenty-five words, omitted the murder of Gonzago but kept the dumb show, and omitted the soliloquies "O what a rogue and peasant slave am I", and "How all occasions do inform against me." A few scenes were transposed, and the device adopted of delivering soliloquies with closed lips in vision, Olivier's voice delivering them over the track.

Olivier also developed the irritating notion of illustrating descriptive passages whilst retaining Shakespeare's original description. He had already essayed this in *Henry V* with "Her vine, the merry cheerer of the heart, Unpruned dies . . ." whilst showing a painted backcloth of the destruction and decay throughout the French countryside. In *Hamlet* the poisoning of the real king was illustrated, together with Hamlet's seafight, Ophelia sewing in the closet, and Ophelia's death. My personal view is that either the illustrative matter or the original verse is all that is required. Used together one or the other is redundant. This device is particularly annoying in *Hamlet* if, like me, you are inclined to believe the Gravediggers' claim that Ophelia committed suicide and that the picturesque description of her death offered by the Queen (and by Olivier) is mere shilly-shally to placate Laertes. But *Hamlet* is so vulnerable to each man's own interpretation that it is almost inevitable that in trying to please everybody, nobody will be pleased. Dent and Olivier foresaw this and published their case in *An Essay on Hamlet*. Their mistake probably lay in their very attempt to simplify. Complexity and contradictions lie at the heart of *Hamlet,* and an attempt to explain these away in Freudian or any other terms is to chase a red-herring. *Hamlet* has a universal appeal; it has something for everyman, which simplification only destroys.

Of Roger Furse's stark set, John Mason Brown complained "at least forty precious minutes are squandered in travelogues up and down Mr. Furse's palace. To sacrifice great language, to have innuendo dispensed with, and to lose key speeches, characters, or scenes merely because so much time is wasted getting the actors from one part of the castle to another, is to be a *Hamlet* dislocated by being on location." Some clever devices were utilised, however. Two sharply pointed arches and repeating arcades were designed to underline "except my life, except my life, except my life." The costumes changed with the changing moods of the play: Hamlet changed from his sombre garb to gold and silver embroidery to suggest his pride in his cleverness, and after her interview the Queen appeared in subdued and undecorated dress (previously, like the King, she had been wearing a design modelled on the playing card). As conclusion, John Mason Brown remarked that Olivier's inventiveness "stopped with the bleaching of his hair," but "no player alive can read Shakespeare as he does."

There is one splendid moment in Andre Cayatte's *Les Amants de Verone,* produced in 1948 as a kind of parallel to the *Romeo and Juliet* story. Angelo (Reggiani) and Georgia (Anouk Aimee), the Romeo and Juliet of this film, are two stand-ins in a film of *Romeo and Juliet.* The stars perform the balcony scene to a crescendo of music and shallow emotions which is just—acting. Then the director calls for the stand-ins to pose on the balcony. Angelo climbs up, and in the blinding glare of the spotlights he meets Georgia. The sounds of the studio dim and vanish. Romeo has met his Juliet; love is born. Cayatte's film was enjoyed by critics for its tender romanticism, and who agreed it had some lovely moments. Then it was forgotten.

No sooner had Orson Welles' *Macbeth* been released in 1948 than it had to be withdrawn. Nobody could understand the Scots dialect which Welles in his meticulous way had insisted on using. Up to this point the production had been a model of economy: a largely unknown cast, shooting finished in twenty-one days, the sound-track finished ahead of time. But rerecording and dubbing in 65 per cent of the dialogue took another nine months and the final version was not released until 1950. The new track had—to say the least—a peculiar quality: part Scots, part Anglicised.

Cinematically, Welles' achievement was magnificent. The costumes were almost Mongolian, the castle a catacomb around which ground mists swirled mysteriously from muddy, thickly puddled, ground. Macbeth first greets his Lady in a vast courtyard where a corpse swings on a gibbet, Duncan rides through the castle gate milling with swine. When Macbeth's mind is "full of scorpions," we do not have to hear the line for his reflection in a distorting mirror is enough; and Macbeth's terror at the banquet scene is first suggested, not by the appearance of Banquo's ghost, but through rows of curious, hostile faces turned at him along the table.

Unfortunately, however, Welles was so intent on making a primal *Citizen Kane,* a story of a man bent on power, that he forgot that Shakespeare's story was not about that at all. *Macbeth* is one of Shakespeare's most simple plays: it is a play about insecurity in a man who commits a crime against his better nature, who is driven on by remorse and conscience. To Welles (as he tells us right from the start) it is a tale of "plotting against Christian law and order" by "agents of chaos, priests of hell and magic" whose "tools are ambitious men," and Welles' explanation of *Macbeth* is as an epic of victorious Christianity (for which purpose he creates a new character, a friar).

All this would be fine if it had anything to do with Shakespeare. But it does not. Moreover, the lines are chopped, scenes are completely rearranged, lines from other plays interpolated, and all—except for the central performance—badly acted. I like Welles' *Macbeth* as a cinematic piece; the visual imagery is superb. But it *is* Welles' *Macbeth,* and not Shakespeare's, and one can only concede to Welles the vanity of genius for departing from the original plot. Unfortunately, though, his own tamperings have only reduced and weakened the drama.

In 1946 a 16mm version of *Macbeth* was produced around Chicago for 5,000 dollars by a young man named David Bradley and directed by an equally young man, Thomas Blair. The costumes (designed by somebody called Charlton Heston) were typical of the economy of this production, so that, for example, Macbeth's jacket was studded with paper fasteners. Non-sync dialogue was utilised and "wide-angle lenses, low-key lighting, and low camera angles were used with great success." Four years later Bradley made another cheap version of Shakespeare, *Julius Caesar*, and shot in a similar manner. Henry Raynor described the film "The film is comparable to Welles' *Macbeth* in its free and often imaginative use of visual imagery and its bold attack; the text is less mangled but indifferently spoken and acted, with the exception of Charlton Heston's vigorous Mark Antony. The best moments—the murder of Caesar, the apparition of Caesar's ghost, the excitingly composed and edited battle scenes—show a strong talent for dramatic narrative in lighting, grouping, cutting; other scenes, notably the dialogue between Cassius and Brutus on the event of battle, are more theatrical than Welles'. An impressive feature of the film is the director's response to natural settings, the tall collonades of huge buildings and the desolate sand dunes near Lake Michigan used for the battle sequences. As in *Macbeth* the fatal flaw is the interpretive; here the conception of the play is less distorted than negative."

In 1953 John Houseman persuaded MGM to allow him to make *Julius Caesar*. Houseman, who had already staged a *Julius Caesar* in New York in modern dress with an implied Fascist parallel, considered black and white better for the play than colour "because there are certain parallels between this play and modern times. People associate dictators with black and white newsreel shots . . . the Mussolini on the balcony sort of thing. With colour, the show becomes a mere spectacle."

Directed by Joseph L. Mankiewicz, Houseman's film showed great fidelity to the script, cutting only where Shakespeare himself had cut in preparing *Quarto* 2 to *Folio* 1, together with some unnecessary lines with no direct relevance to the action. Mob scenes were avoided, close-ups frequent, and the assassination of Caesar conveyed by close-ups of the assassins' reactions, not by a shot of the deed itself. Miklos Rozsa's score was restrained and fitting.

The values of Julius Caesar as a play are more subdued and political than vivid and spectacular. Nevertheless, Mankiewicz' handling of the address to the Roman people was brilliantly edgy, while the performances were consistently good: Louis Calhern an elderly business-man of a Caesar was an easily identifiable statesman, Gielgud with Cassius' "lean and hungry look," James Mason a good combination of "the poetic and prosaic," and Brando handling competently an early rôle.

After the fiasco of Cukor's *Romeo and Juliet,* one would have thought the producers of the 1954 film directed by Renato Castellani would have learned something. But no. The same kind of unnecessary elaborate preparations were embarked upon: the setting for the balcony and ballroom scenes was the Ca d'Oro in Venice, the costumes and props were copies from fifteenth-century Italian paintings, the camera set-ups planned to duplicate actual art works, and so on. Unfortunately, none of this preparation prevented the film becoming a crashing bore. Laurence Harvey gave an incredibly stilted performance as Romeo, Susan Shentall made a very capable Juliet for an inexperienced actress (this is backhanded praise indeed, but well meant), and Mervyn Johns painted a jolly if uninteresting Friar Lawrence. The text was cut and considerably adapted: the Queen Mab speech was dropped, together with some descriptive passages, and some of the heroic couplets at the ends of scenes replaced by dissolves. Some scenes did show imagination: Friar Lawrence was introduced not in a cell, but rather charmingly as he gathered herbs outside the city walls; Romeo's and Benvolio's fight scene is removed from the "public place" to a quiet stream, and the marriage takes place through an iron grill in the monastery as mass is sung in the background. But amongst the uninspired acting and direction these passed almost unnoticed. What a pity that one of Shakespeare's most moving plays should have been so miserably realised by a director who, after all, was one of Italy's most competent.

In the last decade the most filmed of Shakespeare's plays have been *Macbeth* and *Othello.* In 1955 Ken Hughes directed and Philip Yordon scripted, a tough gangster movie called *Joe Macbeth.* The plot is a simple transference: Joe Macbeth is newly wed to an ambitious moll named Lily who plans, no less, for his promotion as King of the Underworld; you take it from there. The idea was ingenious, but insufficiently developed: its style was B-picture grade, it lacked an authentic American background, and the police were omitted altogether, presumably because they would complicate the gimmick.

1955 was a good year for Shakespear. Shortly after *Joe Macbeth,* Delmer Daves' *Jubal* made its appearance, an excellent Western with a couple of ideas borrowed from *Othello.* In this one, Ernest Borgnine suffers the pangs of jealousy, after his gal Valerie French tells him to get him a civilised behaviour. He approaches his suave foreman Glenn Ford who seems to know the inside wrinkles of etiquette, but enter Iago in the form of Pinky (Rod Steiger) to suggest that the only wrinkles Ford might have in mind are designed to entice Miss French into the bunk house. To cut a long story short, the net result of all these machinations is to leave Ford as the sole survivor, but the sole survivor, of the whole affair. In *Films and Filming*, Richard Whitehall commented on the drama: "From the moment Jubal (Glenn Ford) and Pinkham—Pinky (Rod Steiger)—are brought face to face within the first few minutes of the film, it is a basic conflict of good and evil on the plane of *Billy Budd*, with which the story has a number of similarities. The action is as fixed and immutable as Greek tragedy, but Daves avoids the polarity of tragedy by using the background detail of ranch life as an element of spontaneity (the breaking and branding of horses, the washing at the pump before the pay-day ride into town, a poker game around the camp-fire, the working of the small every-day chores into the larger theme, humanise the essentially elemental conflict)."

In 1955 Welles again proved his cinematic brilliance, as well as his scant respect for rival imaginations. Typically, to shoot *Othello* he took a unit to Venice and on and around the battlements of an eighteenth-century Arab Citadel at Mogador in French Morocco. Apart from a fuzzy sound track with sound effects which often completely eclipsed the dialogue, there were several beneficial innovations: the funeral procession for Othello and Desdemona preceded the credits as well as concluding the film, thus acting as a frame for the drama; Cassio is murdered in a mediaeval Turkish bath; Welles puts out the candle in the last scene with his hand, and then—a vivid and ironic touch—smothers Desdemona with the silk handkerchief.

The same year saw the arrival of Olivier's third attempt at filming Shakespeare, *Richard III*, a 2¾ hour spectacle in Vistavision with, again, Olivier playing the lead as well as directing (although Carol Reed made some few suggestions). Olivier discussed the technical difficulties with Roger Manvell in the *Journal of the BFA*. In *Richard III*, said Olivier, he "treated the camera as a person without, I hope, embarrassing it. It's nothing new really; people are seeing it on television all the time. In films it is usually just a gag, but there is a precedent in Shakespeare for it all the time—actors are always coming forward to speak directly to the audience. . . . My make-up and clothing used to take me three hours every day. My nose took an hour. If I had to have my hand on, it took another forty minutes. My wig took half an hour. . . . One of the pre-planning problems was the music for the battle scenes. Sometimes I had cut these scenes and re-cut them, and they were dying for music: but when it came along I found that it didn't fit the rhythm we had set in the original cutting; so we changed and re-changed it until finally the two—music and acting rhythms—came together.

"Another of our problems was to cope with the sets, especially as we often change quickly from Westminster Abbey to the Palace or the Tower. If we had used normal technique, we would have had innumerable dissolves; so we made a kind of composite set. I think people may be surprised to find Westminster Abbey and the Palace and the Tower of London only twenty yards apart: I hope that they will think with me that if they weren't like that—they should have been!"

In all respects the film is brilliant. Richard's confidences to the camera are more satisfying than the thought tricks in *Hamlet*, supplying not only a certain *comedie noire*, but serving a real dramatic purpose as we the audience are increasingly shut off from his confidences and become—as all others—his dupes. Scenes from the film can be remembered vividly: Richard's psychological wooing of Anne, his feigned reluctance to accept the crown from the meagre crowd of Londoners, the impotent sensuality of Cedric Hardwick's Edward V or the scene where the young prince in play cries to Richard: "that you should bear me on your shoulders" to produce in a horrible psychological whip-crack the piercing of Richard's false good humour. And the end, killed not gloriously by young Richmond, but pitifully by an old man, Stanley. Lying on the ground the dying king twitches and kicks and struggles to lift his sword. Olivier omits the line: "There is no creature loves me, and if I die no soul shall pity me." But somehow, despite all, we do pity Richard.

The Wars of the Roses were a familiar subject to Elizabethan audiences and Shakespeare's version had depended precisely upon that familiarity. To get over this and supply the outlines of the conflict briefly and quickly, Olivier cut and rearranged the play borrowing some bits and pieces from *Henry VI*. The film's most vital deficiency in comparison with what Shakespeare actually wrote, is in making Richard a villain among innocents whereas Shakespeare had him a villain among villains. By cutting down Queen Margaret's part, say, or by trimming the conflicts of conscience of the two murderers, Olivier robs the film of the point that Richard is no worse than those he is cheating.

Sergei Yutkevich's *Othello*, also of 1955, with Sergei Bondarchuk as Othello and Irina Skovtseva as Desdemona received high critical praise in this country. Personally, I found it a heavy handed affair, rather hard-going, and over-symbolic (the fishing nets to enmesh Othello in jealousy which are copied from Sternberg, lights flashing in the Moor's eyes to suggest anger, and so on). Bondarchuk made a mild, rather stupid, Othello so that one's interest tended to lie with the sharp and devilish Iago of A. Popov.

There is a place for Shakespeare in *The Magazine of Fantasy and Science Fiction*. The producers of *Forbidden Planet* seem to have thought so too, as Pauline Kael reported in a programme note: "The best of the science-fiction interstellar productions lifts its plot and atmosphere from Shakespeare: the magical island of *The Tempest* becomes the planet Altair-4, where the sky is green and the sand is pink and there are two moons. The magician Prospero becomes the mad scientist Morbius (Walter Pidgeon); the sprite Ariel is combined with Prospero's daughter Miranda, who knows no man except her father, to become Altaira (Anne Francis); and, amusingly, the lumbering Caliban, 'not honoured with a human shape,' becomes Robby, the friendly robot. It's a pity the film-makers didn't lift some of Shakespeare's dialogue; it's hard to believe you're in the heavens when the diction of the hero (Leslie Nielson) and his space-shipmates flattens you down to Kansas. Fred McLeod Wilcox directed. 1956; Cinemascope, color."

I forget who, but one critic once said that the most successful Lady Macbeth was Isuzo Yamada in Kurosawa's *Throne of Blood* (*Kumonoso-Jo, 1957*). One can see what he meant; there is no reason why Lady Macbeth should be the beefy matron she is, and Yamada's frail yet determined Lady is certainly a chilling creature. This Japanese *Macbeth* may not be Shakespeare's but transformed to the aptly named Cobweb Castle the ingredients fit easily into the sixteenth-century Japanese setting. The film made great visual impact, and several scenes are haunting: the witch in her tiny hut crooning over her spinning wheel of time, the terror of the moving forest, or Lord Washizu (the Japanese Macbeth) shot by a hail of arrows from his own men.

In 1950 Jiri Trnka, the Czechoslovak puppet-master, brought off a brilliant *A Midsummer Night's Dream* (*Sen Noci Svatojanske*), achieving with puppets many things not possible in live action: an acorn that falls off a tree to become a little brownie which scurries off into the undergrowth, or Titania gliding through the glade gracefully as becomes a queen—not fluttering as the common sort. But the success of the film was only as good as one's reaction to puppet shows: *A Midsummer Night's Dream* depends on human beings making fools of themselves and not everyone is able to find much impact in the sight of dolls making fools of *themselves*.

There was another Russian *Othello* in 1960, but it relied on Verdi rather than Shakespeare, and in 1959 a German *Hamlet* in the modern manner directed by Helmut Käutner and called *Der Rest ist Schweigen*. In this version Claudius is a wholesale manufacturer in the Rhein-Ruhr area and John (Hamlet) learns of his father's death on his return from Harvard!

The latest *Hamlet* is Chabrol's *Ophelia,* adapted by Chabrol and Martial Matthieu. The histrionics of the actors prove somewhat embarrassing, but again Chabrol reveals his superb visual flair. The film opens with the father's cortege being received into the local church. The doors close, the credits roll. The doors open again—and the widow emerges as the husband's bride. As an opening device this is clever, but unfortunately the *whole* film topples into the realm of the "clever-clever." For example, the hero, Yvan (Andre Jocelyn) only realises that he is paralleling Hamlet's career when he visits the local picture house which is showing Olivier's *Hamlet.* But after that he catches on pretty quickly and stages his own Mousetrap in the form of an amateur film. Thus the play within the play becomes a film within a film. The final twist is that Hamlet Yvan is not the ghost's son after all, but the second husband's son. Masterly as the film's direction is, it leaves an end impression of being over-ingenious and of lacking heart.

The two most recent films with Shakespearian connections have been *All Night Long* (1961), an over-theatrical Ralph Dearden product which transposes *Othello* to an all-night jazz party given by Richard Attenborough, and *A Siberian Lady Macbeth (Sibirska Ladi Macbet)* made by Wajda in 1962. In this version Lady Macbeth kills not for ambition but to safeguard her love after her husband has neglected her. It is a gray, chilly film with a fatalistic philosophy which produces neither tears nor a sense of just retribution at its tragic outcome. It is not really Shakespeare, however, for it is based on one of the better short stories of the Russian author Nikolaj Leskoff: *Lady Macbeth of the Mcenski District.*

As we have seen, there's many a film-maker so awed by the sanctity of the Bard, the Swan of Avon, that he'll a-tremble in his boots so much when it comes to making a Shakespeare film that the end product will be nothing so much as a tepid concession to middle-brow culture. The saddest story I know is connected with this pitiful truth.

The slogan of Hallmark Cards Inc. of Kansas City is "the biggest printers of greeting cards in the world." A few years ago, they decided to sponsor a TV series known as the *Hallmark Hall of Fame,* a series produced by a New York producer named George Schaeffer and as often as not starring a leading American Shakespearian actor called Maurice Evans. In this series Evans and Judith Anderson had appeared in a two-hour *Macbeth* in colour. In fact, it had been the first of the series. But Schaeffer wasn't satisfied. He wanted a more ambitious production, and he wanted it for theatrical distribution. So Hallmark were approached again, and they agreed to sponsor a theatrical production. They hadn't much to lose. The film was to be shot in Technicolor at MGM British Studios, which saved 60 per cent costs over using a Hollywood studio, and what's more qualified as a British quota picture. After another company, Grand Prize, got its share from the theatrical release, all the profits were to go to Hallmark. Finally after cutting the film from two hours to 90 minutes, it could be rerented to television companies, with no additional payment being necessary for actors or technicians.

On the face of it, *Macbeth* had a reasonable technical background. It was produced by Phil Samuel who had previously supervised both Olivier's *Henry V* and *Hamlet*. The music was by Addinsell, and the photography by Fred A. Young, who had been on *Lust for Life*. But the result, which appeared in 1960, was a school's *Macbeth*; well-spoken verse without a scrap of imagination but with an excess of pre-war styles and production. The film lacked terror, was clumsy, and naive. Amongst the crude sets and bloodshot lighting, two new scenes were added (Duncan's funeral and Macbeth's coronation), but neither contributed greatly. The battle scenes were disastrously mishandled, so much so that the editor had obvious difficulties in maintaining any kind of continuity. Of the actors only Ian Bannen emerged with any credit, although Dame Judith did suggest something like dominance of character. Of Maurice Evan's performance as Macbeth, the critics were none too kind. His "struggle to suppress hysteria" when confronting Banquo's ghost in the banquet hall put Philip Gibbs of the *Daily Telegraph* in mind "not inappropriately, of a lion at bay. Alas, this is a momentary impression. Irving is said to have looked in the part like a famished wolf. The animal Mr. Evans finally suggests is a teddy bear."

One would have preferred to have been able to discuss Olivier's *Macbeth*—"shelved" by Rank for reasons of economy a couple of years before Schaeffer went into production.

A few months after I left school, I sneaked into a local fleapit to watch Olivier's *Hamlet*. My entry into the circle was greeted by cries of recognition, and I discovered to my horror that half my old school was being treated to an afternoon's culture. I didn't see much of *Hamlet,* for nobody else was very interested; as far as they were concerned Shakespeare was "culture," a rather unpleasant medicine to be taken for the good of our souls.

This stuffy school text-book attitude is deeply engrained in the Anglo-Saxon. It spreads not only amongst the schools but to the film-makers themselves. It *is* easy to show the wrong sort of respect for Shakespeare: the Schaeffer *Macbeth* was acclaimed by critics as being, if nothing else, at least "reverential" to Shakespeare. It was, in fact, nothing of the sort. The only way to be reverential is to do Shakespeare justice. *West Side Story* is one hundred million times (at least) better than any film of *Romeo and Juliet* yet produced, not only because of Robbins and Bernstein, but because it has the passion, the fire, the imagination, the others don't have. Middle-brow film-makers are too fond of prettifying Shakespeare, of believing the text is enough to carry the film without utilising their own imaginations and the me-

dium of the cinema to complement the words. The old discussion as
to whether Shakespeare and the cinema can be mixed is a phoney.
They not only can be—Olivier proved it twice, and Welles could do
it too—but they have to be if both the audience and the critic are
to be satisfied. It only requires courage and vision from the film-maker.
The writer has done half the work for him.

Shakespeare, the Imaginary Cinema
and the Pre-cinema
by HENRI LEMAITRE

If the Shakespearean bibliography is one of the most abundant, the Shakespearean filmography is no less large: the list of cinematic adaptations of Shakespeare compiled by the British Film Institute comprises no less than sixty-nine items, and it cannot be considered exhaustive. Moreover, of these sixty-nine films, fifty-four were made before 1930; and of the thirty-seven plays written by Shakespeare, eighteen —almost half—have been given filmic treatments.

Even in this bare form, these figures serve to demonstrate how strong, throughout the history of the cinema, the *Shakespearean temptation* was; and, in fact, from its inception, the cinema has presented Shakespeare as if it had in him one of its most prestigious predecessors, and as if it could use that credential to take its place in the tradition of great dramaturgy.

It is obvious that immense problems arise from the encounter between Shakespeare and the cinema, and that what is involved is not just the general relations between theater and cinema, or of the adaptation of literary works to film. There are, in Shakespeare's drama itself, so many perspectives, so many poetic and dramatic potentials, that when the cinema approaches it, it touches upon an entire universe; but it is also true that, by the same token, that universe reveals itself capable of making manifest the permanence or recurrence of certain attributes of cinema, as well as clarifying the spiritual geography of a certain type of dramatic vision which the cinema almost obsessionally conforms to.

Before taking up so difficult a subject, we should say a few words

From Études Cinématographiques 6–7 *(1960): 383–96. Reprinted by permission of* Études Cinématographiques. *Translated by Charles W. Eckert. This is an extract from the first chapter of a work in preparation which will appear in the collection "7ᵐᵉ Art" (Éditions du Cerf) under the title,* Le Cinéma et la tentation shakespearienne.

by way of preamble: my intention was, first of all, to examine some of the Shakespearean adaptations to discover to just what degree film has shown itself capable of "visualizing"—to borrow an English neologism from the language of the great Will—the depth and the extent of the Shakespearean universe; there are also the matters of how the cinema has effected what is not an ordinary kind of adaptation and to what degree it has been led to realize certain of its own potentialities —in which case the study of filmic adaptations of Shakespeare offers the occasion for an important contribution to the aesthetics of cinema.

But, specifically, I propose what I have already alluded to: an inquiry into the exact nature of those secret rapports between the worlds of Shakespeare and, at the least, a portion of the world of cinema, that alone can explain how assiduously, and at times successfully, the cinema has demonstrated its infatuation with Shakespeare—not only in the films directly adapted from Shakespeare, but in all those works that show a manifest Shakespearean influence. And there is, looming beyond this, the two-sided and difficult subject of the Shakespearean affinities of the cinema and the cinematic affinities of Shakespeare, which a study such as this broaches. I do not pretend that one can exhaust this subject—far from it. I intend only to outline its dimensions, and to begin to show how an art of language like Shakespeare's, which triumphs in conferring all the puissant magic of the image upon the word, and an art of the image like the cinema's, which triumphs in conferring all of the allusiveness of the word upon the image, are joined in a communion within the same dramatic aesthetic. In the eternal conflict between *showing* and *seeing,* which has continuously tormented the history of the theater, it seems that Shakespeare and the cinema have succeeded in transcending these two opposed terms, annulling even the dilemma that gave rise to them, and have increased the intensity of the essence of drama in effecting an indissoluble union between *showing* and *seeing.* In this respect Shakespeare and the cinema— at least in the best of his dramatic works—stand in complete opposition to the "Racineian" formula of Thierry Maulnier, "The glory and grandeur of man have ceased to be demonstrated because he has learned to speak." [1] And this is perhaps the right occasion to observe that the cinema has not felt to a similar degree a *Racineian temptation* (a new variation upon the theme *Racine and Shakespeare,* for which we need a *cinéaste* Stendhal of the twentieth century!).

Let us begin by establishing only the pre-cinematic affinities of Shakespearean drama. The cinema has become the organ of a *mise-en-scène* for Shakespeare which, while accentuating certain problems relating to his dramatic vision of the world, throws into relief certain unique capacities of the cinema grounded in the nature of its tech-

[1] Thierry Maulnier, *Racine,* p. 70.

nique, its aesthetic, and its metaphysic. And thus, from Laurence Olivier to Orson Welles, from Mankiewicz to Castellani, through failures and successes, Shakespearean film has earned a significant place in the vast dramatic laboratory that is the cinema: a history both reckless and accomplished that confirms, at least, the ambitions of the seventh art in putting its dramatic aptitudes to the proof.

> . . . the eye itself,
> That most pure spirit of sense. . . .
> (*Troilus and Cressida*. III.iii.105–106)

William Shakespeare is here in agreement with Saint Thomas. In fact, one reads in the *Summa Theologica* that the sense of sight is, of all the senses, the most exalted and worthy, and that it therefore conducts us readily to the knowledge of spiritual realities. In turn, Elizabethan dramatists define the eye as the organ of perfect perception, capable of the purest communication with the mystery of things.[2] This rapport between a theologian and a dramatist is not merely fortuitous, since Shakespeare was himself more impregnated than one supposes with innumerable theological influences. It is, in any case—as the above text bears witness (though the definition of the eye is parenthetical, it is still very significant)—the inheritance of this passion for the visual, of this keen appreciation of the values of the image, that marked medieval culture and that the Renaissance certainly did not repudiate.

In addition, Shakespearean drama, so concise were its material means of production, came to expand the visual values latent in words themselves; which is why dramatic presentation so often owes its power to what the words—their rhythm and their arrangement—are designed to produce. Before the inner eye of the spectator occurs the rich unreeling of an imaginary film: the characters and the very life of their actions, nature with its beauties and its terrors, the decor of cities or of palaces, battlefields, the sea itself, vessels and tempests, human passions stripped of psychological abstraction and given life in suspirations or in dreams, in music or in spectacles—all of this transpiring upon the screen provided by the poetic word in an immense dynamic architecture of forms, arabesques, and colors, enhanced by the fusion or interchange of realism and the marvelous. What director could ever capture on film the wealth of images, of music and movement, latent in the verbal energy of Shakespeare's world! Nevertheless, even if it surpasses in its powers the potentialities of film, that dra-

---

[2] An analogous visual image, one with equally metaphysical implications, is found in *King Lear*: ". . . take upon's the mystery of things,/ As if we were God's spies" (V.iii.16–17).

matic energy makes constant appeal to the eye, the door to the spirit, the soul, and the imagination as well as to other mediators of poetry which are attuned to it.

But, before sounding that universe for at least the most visible signs of its pre-cinematographic nature, let us establish that Shakespeare, in his Elizabethan context, is uniquely *visual*. It is this, one feels, that explains his traditional opposition to Ben Jonson. Couldn't one argue that what characterizes this rivalry is the opposition between a pre-cinematic aesthetic and a theatrical, literary aesthetic? The author of *Volpone,* nourished upon classical literature (so much so that he could not resist saying of Shakespeare, "thou hadst small Latine and less Greeke"),[3] conceived of the theater in accordance with the literary values of the unities, which later inspired French Classicism and led to the pure literature of Racine. And Ben Jonson remains celebrated in the history of English literature for having unequivocally stated, "Shakesperr wanted Arte." [4] The meaning of the word is clear: what Ben Jonson intends by "Arte" is precisely that search for the perfect way of *saying* rather than *seeing,* as he demonstrates in the prologues of *Volpone* and *Everyman Out of His Humour.* The literary aesthetic of Ben Jonson was equally applicable to tragedy or to comedy, as was the pre-cinematic aesthetic of Shakespeare. We should remind ourselves, no doubt, that Ben Jonson was above all a humanist, whereas Shakespeare was above all a man of the theater for whom the word was a tool in the service of a creative enterprise that knew no limits. Ben Jonson aspired to be an *artist* composing in regular numbers in which the linear development of a dramatic action had to be managed as a formal *discourse;* and it was, according to the tradition of Aristotle and Horace, words and their combinations that contributed the highest aesthetic values. Not so with Shakespeare, for whom the word ceased to be the instrument for producing an aesthetic discourse and became instead, like the screen, the door through which crowded into the spectator's imagination the multitude of shapes, beings, and objects of the dramatic universe. The driving force behind Shakespeare was not the Art dear to Ben Jonson but rather a total realism which, by carrying the concrete and sensuous powers of language to their highest degree, forcefully broke through the familiar frontiers of literary language: the genius of Shakespeare resides most, perhaps, in that perpetual metamorphosis of language that usually goes beyond simple symbolism and gives rise to a universe at once vigorous and full, ceaselessly in motion and thoroughly charged with events. Nothing is in this respect more revealing than the Shakespearean *tempo,* fundamentally oriented toward the "compacting of events in time"

---

[3] C. Herford and H. Simpson, *Ben Jonson* (11 vols.; 1925–52), VIII, 391.
[4] Ibid., I, 133.

according to the definition that has been given of cinematic *tempo*.[5]

However, this characteristic *tempo* is far from being solely verbal; it shatters regular rhythms in order to embody that cosmic, spiritual, historical, and musical pulsation that carries the whole drama forward; and, in the case of Shakespeare, it makes sense of his definition of poetry as energy: "powerful rhyme." It defines, moreover, the basic orientation of Elizabethan theater. Shakespeare accomplished, thanks to his unique pre-cinematic *tempo*, the enthusiastic commission which Thomas Kyd placed in the mouth of Hieronimo in *The Spanish Tragedy*: "There you may *show* a passion, there you may *show* a passion." [6] In the entire canon of Shakespeare's works there is perhaps no better example of this energetic *tempo* than in the tragedy that many consider his masterpiece, *Antony and Cleopatra* (Coleridge judged it the most "astonishing"); this play runs the risk, less perhaps than others, of being reduced to a linear development: the dramatic construction is quite complex, both in space and time, and the rhythm of the scenes has the sole purpose of creating an imaginary ubiquity for the spectator. But it is not, as so often in the theater, a simple illusion of ubiquity: it is a dense and dynamic ubiquity that goes beyond rapid changes of place and set and creates a sense of multiplicity that gives the drama the dimensions of that "infinite variety" [7] which makes the *mise-en-scène* of this tragedy so difficult to realise.

Thus Shakespearean tragedy—and it is in this, from a phenomenological viewpoint, that it most closely approaches cinema—enormously develops the spectator's mobility and his capacity for absorption in another world, giving birth to the hyper-realism of the imaginary that is one of the great aspirations of the cinema. Take, for example, the temporary exorcising of Caliban's bestiality in *The Tempest*:

> The isle is full of noises,
> Sounds and sweet airs that give delight and hurt not.
> Sometimes a thousand twangling instruments
> Will hum about mine ears; and sometimes voices
> That, if I then had wak'd after long sleep,
> Will make me sleep again; and then, in dreaming,
> The clouds methought would open and show riches
> Ready to drop upon me, that, when I wak'd,
> I cried to dream again.

---

[5] Etienne Souriau, *L'Univers filmique* (Flammarion, 1953), p. 15.

[6] My italics.

[7] I here borrow from Enobarbus's evocation of Cleopatra (II.ii) a formula that is tempting to apply to Shakespearean drama; on the characters of this drama, particularly in *Antony and Cleopatra*, one can profit from the excellent discussion of Robert Speaight in his *Nature et grâce dans les tragédies de Shakespeare* (Éditions du Cerf, 1957), pp. 153–57.

A pre-cinematic dream of Caliban who saw the clouds "open and show riches/ Ready to drop upon me": isn't this already a presentiment of the dreamlike magic of darkened cinemas? And what was merely a dream to Caliban, provoked by Prospero's magic, is made more significant if one thinks of the general symbolic nature of *The Tempest*; an illusionary magic, like that of every spectacle (for the goal of spectacle is the intensification of the unreal), yet a magic capable of lifting the most obdurate or the most evil soul—and Caliban's is both—into the realm of pure poetic surrealism. This is doubtless the idea that issued from the theater of Shakespeare-Prospero, as it does from the cinema of the most demanding directors and theoreticians.

Thus the pre-cinematic desire to *show,* which explains the visual density and the energetic *tempo* of Shakespearian drama, leads to the use of multiple means of *perfected illusion;* much like those which the cinema achieves with its techniques. This illusion is the opposite of *literary illusion,* which arose from a renunciation of a technique of *showing,* and, through the medium of the word, led to a perfection of the more indirect act of *saying.* The most lucid of our romantics were not mistaken in choosing Shakespeare above Racine in their desire for change and their search for a more direct and perfect means of creating illusion. It was Vigny, for instance, who said of Shakespearean tragedy, "I love it because it exists . . . and for what I respond to in his style, in his language, in his entire manner. . . ." And it was Stendahl who wrote, even more forthrightly: "I feel that these brief moments of perfect illusion are found more often in Shakespeare's tragedies than in those of Racine."

This is the proper place to clear up some ambiguities. If, in the fashion of Stendahl, I have presumed to find in Shakespeare similar episodes of perfect illusion, and have concluded that this demonstrates a pre-cinematic orientation in his work, one could well object that the Elizabethan stage was poor in its means for creating a *mise-en-scène.* How could a theater in which a forest is represented by a placard, which itself confessed—in the prologue to *Henry V*—its scenic poverty, be described as the nearest dramatic ancestor to the cinema, which profusely, even abusively, cultivates a realistic *mise-en-scène?* This also broaches the questions of the psychological mechanisms behind the creation of complete illusion, and of the degree of the audience's receptivity. Illusion, in its technical aspects, depends upon the rapport between the audience and the spectacle: with its placards or with its verbal descriptions, Shakespearean drama attempts to achieve the same goal as the cinema with all of its material realism, although dramatic illusion belongs to a non-materialistic order of experience—a fact that explains certain failures of cinematic realism. In a word, Shakespearean pre-cinema belongs to the order of what

one might term *imaginary cinema* (the term "pre-cinema" pertaining
to the goal of drama, "imaginary cinema" to the technical means employed). The evolution of the technical means does not alter the basic
nature of the dramatic goal, nor the intention to *show;* although one
must emphasize the aesthetic and psychological differences—even if
imaginary—that separate the verbal and the visual methods of *showing* which are typical of Shakespeare and the cinema. One cannot say,
however, that there is not also a poetic dimension to the word in
Shakespeare. I must repeat that if pre-cinema is latent in Shakespeare,
he can in no way be limited to this conception alone.

The fact remains, as Ben Jonson's reaction demonstrates, that Shakespeare's contemporaries saw in him—as did later Vigny or Stendahl—
the master of an aesthetic of illusion quite unlike the intellectual illusion that was the literary ideal. Shakespeare, a man of the theater in
the fullest sense of the phrase, is intimately bound to his audience by
something other than the Art of Ben Jonson: by an illusion of physical
participation, one that the audience ardently desires and naively par-
ticipates in with its own imagination—a condition, we might note,
also typical of movie audiences. Here again the romantics have often
best understood Shakespeare: in a chronicle reprinted in the volume
L'Art moderne under the title "Shakespeare at the Funambules,"
Theophile Gauthier went so far as to state, "What an audience! Here
is a public! If ever one stages Shakespeare's *A Midsummer Night's
Dream, The Tempest,* or *A Winter's Tale* in France, it should be on
this worm-eaten stage, before these tattered spectators." [8] Romantic
exaggeration plays its part here; but it is true that, psychologically
and socially, a completely illusionary drama demands a public that
feels the need for physical contact with the power of a spectacle. Perhaps one can find here the source of the misunderstanding that has led
so many authors to scornfully dismiss cinema *a priori* (somewhat as
Voltaire scorned Shakespeare while envying him), and also of the
error that gives rise to a literary aesthetic of the cinema. Racine and
Shakespeare represent the two radically distinct orders of drama which
may be transposed or translated into each other, but can never be
synthesized.

In fact, while the audience of the literary theater is expected to
have attained a high degree of "culture" and to be utterly denuded
of the trappings of Caliban, the audience of the theater of complete
illusion is Caliban; and the play is that magic by which Caliban was
transformed: Shakespeare *is* Prospero. Thus, as much owing to its
audience as its dramatic nature, the cinema—especially if we don't
restrict it to the French cinema—appears to pertain more to Shakespeare-Prospero than to Ben Jonson and Racine. But let us again

[8] (Paris: Michel Lévy, 1856), p. 167.

dispel some ambiguities: this distinction does not necessarily represent a hierarchy; Shakespeare isn't inferior to Racine, nor the cinema to literature. And, by the same token, when we speak of two types of spectators corresponding to the two kinds of drama, even if these groups are different socially and ethically, the distinction is somewhat contingent: in fact, each of us contains both the aesthetic and psychological characteristics of both types—a reflection of the dual inclination (inherent in human nature) toward what is shown and what is said. Each spectator carries in him, whether he knows it or not, a Caliban attending upon a Prospero.

In few ages has the drama been, as it was in Elizabethan England, addressed to the whole spectator—who is also today the viewer of cinema. We should not forget that Shakespeare is not a "miracle" like Racine but rather the product of a dramatic age described in these terms by an historian of English literature: "We may think of it as a great wave, of which only the topmost crest, luminous and phosphorescent, was the Elizabethan drama proper, that covering the short span of Shakespeare's active career, from about 1587 to about 1612. A quarter of a century in which all that is most wonderful in the English drama was written—perhaps the most remarkable creative moment in the whole history of drama since the similar brief epoch of Athenian tragedy. . . ." [9] Of course, both before and after Shakespeare, there are all of the other Elizabethan authors whose dramatic intentions are similar to his.

When one first encounters the history of the Elizabethan stage, one is struck by the extraordinary dramatic production that arose throughout England: one everywhere encounters companies of actors—usually traveling companies—which remind one of the troupe that appears in *Hamlet*. But one encounters them in universities and the houses of royalty as well as in public houses: the theater is everywhere, as the cinema is today; and it cohabits with both refined and crude manners, for it was an era in which refinement and crudity were joined. As a critic noted, not without humor, the Globe Theater stood next to "Paris Gardens," and the bear- and bull-baitings drew the same spectators that attended *Romeo and Juliet*.[10]

The qualities that the Elizabethan spectator demanded of drama were passion and violence, both in refined and vulgar entertainment; and Shakespeare wrote *Romeo and Juliet* as well as *Titus Andronicus*. The key word used by Elizabethans to define dramatic pleasure is rather significant: *ravished,* a word which suggests a magical spell and contains a presentiment of the fascination produced by the cinema. The dramatic art that can satisfy this need to be "ravished" and to

[9] A. L. Rowse, *Talking of Shakespeare* (London: Max Reinhardt, 1954), p. 173.
[10] Ivor Brown, *Shakespeare* (New York: Doubleday, 1949).

enter into a spell of rapture, had to be, like today's cinema, capable of using all of the means at its disposal. In any case, its principal purpose was to produce that "passionate temperature," [11] the need for which possessed the theater-going Elizabethans as it does present-day movie audiences.

This brings us back to the predominance in drama of a visual obsession, one that is, in the absence of sophisticated technical means, obtained by recourse to the imagination of the spectator. There is, curiously, in Shakespeare a veritable obsession with the eye, an obsession that determines Shakespeare's pre-cinematic tendency to produce a "show," perhaps even that "biggest show on earth" dear to the publicity of American cinema—the Cecil B. DeMille aspect of Shakespeare. This explains how, in the absence of appropriate technical means, Shakespeare sought to satisfy his inclination toward splendor and fullness of effect with what one could call the verbal *mise-en-scène* of his dramas. It was precisely this that shocked his most refined contemporaries, but doubtless fascinated his popular or aristocratic audiences.

But this imaginary cinema is not solely pre-cinematic in relation to *mise-en-scène;* it is also, and perhaps especially, pre-cinematic in structure; and the obsession with the visual, oriented toward creating rapture, leads to the invention of structures that go beyond the orderly processes of the world. To speak of editing and montage in relation to Shakespeare is technically correct; montage and editing were the means used to compact temporal events and to place the spectator in a condition of ubiquity. This is particularly striking in the spatial organization of *Antony and Cleopatra* (which is, according to technicians, the most difficult of the dramas to *"mettre en scène"* in the theatrical sense of the expression). Similarly, the editing of Act II of *As You Like It,* with its juxtaposition of "patches of time" and of completely free and irregularly structured time, could be chosen as a model for cinematic editing. In *King Lear,* from its beginning, isn't unity of action substituted for by the technique of a parallel montage involving two plots, of which one (Gloucester-Edmund-Edgar) is a symbolic reflection of the other (Lear-Regan-Goneril-Cordelia)? One seems never to discover in Shakespeare a clear, linear development based upon a verbal order, but instead "scenes" (or perhaps sequences) consistently organized in a complex, spatial-temporal counterpoint, with constantly shifting points of view. In a word, Shakespeare's technique tends to make the scenes very free. In this respect, the extraordinary hunger for space which Shakespeare's dramas bear witness to is highly significant; and to this one must add the characteristic desire for a temporality that is dense, multiple, infinitely expansive, and

[11] Ibid.

various. It is these two fundamental desires that Shakespeare's technique, in its intentions and its accomplished forms, adheres to.

Of course, only an extended study of the art of editing and montage and of their methods of compacting time and space would reveal what degree of imaginary cinema Shakespeare's drama contains, and would allow us to understand, at the same time, the importance of the Shakespearean temptation for the cinema. But for now it seems apparent, even though our analysis has been partial and fragmentary, that Shakespeare's theater represents an effort directed toward a total *visualization* of mankind and of the world. To place everything that exists in the dimension of a "show," to "openly exhibit," as it was equally well put by Thomas Kyd's Hieronimo and Shakespeare's Caliban—such is the aboriginal and exclusive mission of the theater. And it is from the moment when there appeared, as was the case with Elizabethan dramatists, those techniques and structures most consonant with that mission, that we can appropriately speak of an imaginary cinema. Whole dramas, like *Julius Caesar* (cf., for example, the extraordinary pre-cinematic speech of Casca in Act I, scene 2) and *Antony and Cleopatra* (to which one could also add *A Winter's Tale*) belong to that category, to say nothing of equally characteristic passages like the prologue to *Henry V*.

It remains to be seen if, paradoxically, the imaginary cinema does not run the risk of impoverishing the richness and the power of that drama. It may be that the verbal cinema of Shakespeare is more powerful than the realizations, however admirable in many respects, of Laurence Olivier's *Henry V* and Castellani's *Romeo and Juliet*. But after all, we need not feel scandalized if the same thing happens with the cinema as so often happens to architecture: we know that the masterpieces of architecture often remain visions of the drawing board; but it isn't unusual for these visions to give birth to subsequent works. Why not see Shakespeare and the lessons he can teach us as the unrealized designs of an imaginary cinema capable, at the least, of impregnating today's works of art? Perhaps the most Shakespearean film in the history of the cinema is not one of those drawn from his works, but rather a creation of the most Shakespearean of the masters of the camera, Orson Welles—the film, *The Lady From Shanghai*.

Finding Shakespeare on Film:
From an Interview with Peter Brook
by GEOFFREY REEVES

There are two Shakespeare films which warrant special attention, the Soviet *Hamlet* by Kozintsev (1964) and Kurosawa's *Throne of Blood* (*Macbeth*, 1957) which is a great masterpiece, perhaps the only true masterpiece inspired by Shakespeare, but it cannot properly be considered Shakespeare because it doesn't use the text. Kurosawa follows the plot very closely, but by transposing it into the Japan of the Middle Ages and making Macbeth a Samurai, he is doing another *Seven Samurai*. Where the story comes from doesn't matter; he is doing what every film-maker has always done—constructing a film from an idea and using appropriate dialogue. So that what may be the best Shakespearean film doesn't help us with the problems of filming Shakespeare.

The Russian *Hamlet* has been criticized for being academic, and it is: however, it has one gigantic merit—everything in it is related to the director's search for the sense of the play—his structure is inseparable from his meaning. The strength of the film is in Kozintsev's ability to realize his own conception with clarity. This is the first Shakespeare film to reflect this form of directorial approach: a search for over-all meaning as opposed to the many and varied, sometimes dazzling, attempts to capture on the screen the actor-manager's view of the play as imagery, theatricality, passion, color, effects.

Hamlet is a firm piece of work; Kozintsev knows where he stands politically and socially. He knows what bars and wood and stone and fire mean to him; he knows the relationship of black to white, of full screen to empty screen, *in terms of content*. Moreover, Kozintsev managed to get away from the Russian tradition of operatic theater by using the new Pasternak translation, which is colder, quicker, and more realistic than the nineteenth-century version, and by avoiding conven-

First published in The Tulane Drama Review, *Volume 11, Number 1* (*T33*), *Fall 1966.* © *1966 by* The Tulane Drama Review; © *1967 by* The Drama Review. *Reprinted by permission. All rights reserved.*

tional theater actors. But the limitation lies in its style; when all is said and done, the Soviet *Hamlet* is post-Eisenstein realistic—thus, super-romantic—thus, a far cry from essential Shakespeare—which is neither epic, nor barbaric, nor colorful, nor abstract, nor realistic in any of our uses of the words. The Elizabethan theater had a very complicated yet marvellously free technique, a use of words that was most sophisticated; its blank verse slides in and out of prose, producing texts which continually change gear. If you could extract the mental impression made by the Shakespearean strategy of images, you would get a piece of pop collage. The effect is like a word whose letters are written across three overlapping pictures in the mind. You see the actor as a man standing in the distance and you also see his face, very close to you—perhaps his profile and the back of his head at the same time—and you also see the background. When Hamlet is doing any one of his soliloquies, the background that Shakespeare can conjure in one line evaporates in the next and new images take over. I think that the freedom of the Elizabethan theater is still only partially understood, people having got used to talking in clichés about the non-localized stage. What people do not fully face is that the non-localized stage means that every single thing under the sun is possible, not only quick changes of location: a man can turn into twins, change sex, be his past, his present, his future, be a comic version of himself and a tragic version of himself, and be none of them, *all at the same time.*

Kott's great essay on Gloucester's suicide points out that the act of jumping off an imaginary cliff only takes on its full meaning when performed on a bare stage. Then it becomes a character doing a meaningless jump, and also an actor doing a meaningful jump—both, with full implications both concrete and imaginary, at the same moment. In the cinema, at least in all the films of Shakespeare we have seen, a Gloucester would be forced to stand on a windy heath of some description, although fifty per cent of the extraordinariness of the powerful image is that this is happening on a pretended heath, on the boards of nowhere. A meaning is released by the double nature of the act, a meaning which isn't there if you isolate one aspect of it. A leap on a bare stage can be done by anyone, and a leap on a heath is just as simple. But *Lear* gives you both at once in the theater. So the result is like the idea itself striking you in its purest form. On the other hand, in Kozintsev's *Hamlet* its style is eventually its prison. The film creates a plausible world in which the action can reasonably unfold, but the price we pay for this plausible world is that the complexities I have been talking about cannot be encompassed and demonstrated. That is, the problem of filming Shakespeare is one of finding ways of shifting gears, styles and conventions as lightly and deftly on the screen as within the mental processes reflected by Elizabethan blank verse onto the screen of the mind. The ponderousness of film is that everything about it tends towards consistency within each single image. And we once thought the cinema mobile!

The effect that the invention of sound had on film in general, and on this problem especially, is curious and crucial. Sound stopped the cinema right in its tracks. People thought that sound would deprive the camera of mobility, and so it did—but only for a short time. Then the crane began swinging and gibbing—and for years everyone fondly imagined that the cinema was mobile again. Mobility of *thought*, which the silent film had, is only now being recaptured in post-Godard techniques. In experiment (if not in actual subject matter) Godard is the most important director today. Continually he liberates the picture from its own consistency. At one moment, you are genuinely looking at a photograph of two people in a bar, then you are half alienated, then you are three-quarters alienated, then you are looking at it as a film-maker, then you are reminded that it is made by actors, and then you are thrown right back into believing it. This relates to alienation in the theater and directly with the free theater-free cinema that the original Elizabethan Shakespeare must have been.

A man being objectively recorded sitting in front of a camera does not constitute an objective reality. This particular *cul de sac* has been with us for a number of years. Gradually, we are coming to realize that photography is not objective, is not realistic—the reality of the cinema exists at the time of the projection, at the moment when an image is projected on the screen—if there is a spectator, then the interplay of image and spectator is the only reality. The reality of six weeks or six months before—a man sitting in a room—is no longer real; there is no *virtue* in the so-called "naturalism" of the photographic process. It *would* be real if it gave you total information, but simple recording cannot begin to do that.

We did a very interesting exercise in this connection in the Stratford studio. I seated one of the actors in front of the group and asked him to think up an elaborate situation for himself and then to live, as an actor, all he could of the inner conditions of this situation. Then the group questioned him to find out what was going on. He was not allowed to answer them. This, of course, created a completely absurd situation. One saw a man who was going through something in his mind. That was all. Eventually he revealed his inner novelette—that he was waiting for his girl-friend to see a doctor to discover if she was pregnant, which would mean an abortion and finding the money, and possibly his wife discovering, etc., but of course none of this could possibly be indicated. The exercise simply drove home the fact that what the eye sees is often of no narrative value whatsoever. The actor stayed motionless, deadpan; interpretations of his state varied from the idea that he was waiting for the dentist, to all kinds of wild interpretations. Frustration built as the group couldn't reach the actor and the silent immobile actor couldn't reach them; so, they realized that surface appearances are non-communicative.

It is this realization which leads, to take extremes, both Antonioni and Godard to their (very different) ways of working. Antonioni accepts the stability of the shot and then employs a variety of devices in the attempt to capture the invisible. Godard attacks the stability of the shot, and tries to capture a multiplicity of aspects. What both of them are rejecting is the notion that the frame, by itself or in temporal juxtaposition, carries the meaning—that a single frame is a full unit. The classic theory of cutting, based on the belief that you are juxtaposing units, which in themselves have a certain completeness—the shot is a unit, the shot is a word, the shot is a brick—is false. *Moderato Cantabile* was a personal experiment to discover whether it is possible to photograph an almost invisible reality, whether it is possible in photographing nothing but a surface to get under that surface.

My premise is a greedy one: in the theater, and especially in the cinema, I want to capture all possible information. This leads me to suspect the self-imposed consistency of any consistent style, because this precludes one learning something one might want to know. If you have a purely intimate story about two people, then one wants to know the social reference; if it is an epic subject, one wants to know something of the inner life. It is only in Shakespeare that you find the balance: nothing is sacrificed, nothing is made less. There is no watering down for the sake of cohesion; all aspects are there in full strength without neutralizing each other.

Putting the Gloucester suicide on film would seem to me to involve the use of alienation. Alienation provides infinite possibilities, and is the only device which leads us back to the possibilities of blank verse. The verse image repeatedly puts objects and ideas into fresh perspective, and so does alienation. The freeze frame, caption, sub-title, etc., are all crude examples of filmic alienation. But meeting Shakespeare's requirements poses a problem very different in scope. Godard's films may be leading a search for a new style, but this style cannot cope with the huge resources, the scale and range of action which Shakespeare demands.

A technique with great potential for Shakespeare was used in Francis Thompson's lyrical documentary for Johnson's Wax at the New York World's Fair. People fought to get to see this little study of boys growing up in different parts of the world. The film brilliantly uses the old Abel Gance multiple-screen technique, and shows its extraordinary possibilities. There are three screens side by side, three simultaneous projections. This gives an area as great as a Cinerama screen, but whereas Cinerama pretends that it is all one huge image, one vast window on the world, Thompson's technique is more Brechtian. The thin black gaps between his screens never let you forget that you are looking at three separate frames. Sometimes the screens are used as one, as in the great canoeing sequences on enormous landscapes, the canoes shooting across, jumping the break—it is like sitting behind a pillar in an old movie-house. But those breaks are there as constant reminders that the instant the director no longer needs or wants a full Cinerama scale, he can cut to something quite different. And that is Thompson's strategy: one minute the three screens show traffic flowing in America, a wedding in Italy, an African landscape; then the juxtaposition splinters and one screen shows an African boy while the other two are still in New York; next, there may be three different views of the same thing; next, identical closeups; then, one screen may keep the same view while the others show different angles and aspects, and so on. This is not aesthetically wrenching: Thompson's film makes no greater demands of imaginative effort than standard film-making, but he can make his audience shift from three screens saying the same thing to three saying different things as a natural part of his language, a language potentially as flexible as verse.

The great advantage of this device is that it breaks into the inner consistency of each frame, by opening the range of endless possible permutations. You can show Hamlet in the battlements of Elsinore on the right-hand screen, and the other two screens may just show a rampart and the sea. Or, to return to Gloucester, you can have a heath, and the moment that a soliloquy begins you can drop the heath out of your picture and concentrate on different views of Gloucester. If you like, you can suddenly open one of your screens to a caption, write a line, write a sub-title. If you want, in the middle of a realistic action in color you could have another or the same in black and white, and the third captioned. You could have statistics, or a cartoon parodying the photographic action. This is a film technique which has exactly the possibilities of a Brechtian stage and an Elizabethan one. I believe that this multiple-screen technique is a real opening, a way that Shakespeare might be found on film. But this is just a hunch, and economically hard to realize.

The only thing that matters today is to define the problem. The filmed picture of an actor on a bare stage is a more cramped and constipated statement than the simple face of an actor on a bare stage. But at the start bare stage and blank screen are equal. How can the screen free itself of its own consistencies so as to reflect the mobility of thought that blank verse demands?

A Midsummer Night's Dream
1935

DIRECTION	Max Reinhardt and William Dieterle
SCRIPT	Charles Kenyon and Mary McCall, Jr.
PHOTOGRAPHY	Hal Mohr, Fred Jackman, Byron Haskin and H. F. Koenekamp
MUSIC	Felix Mendelssohn
ORCHESTRA DIRECTION	Erich W. Korngold
ART DIRECTION	Anton Grot
COSTUMES	Max Ree
CHOREOGRAPHY	Bronislava Nijinska and Nina Theilade
EDITING	Ralph Dawson
SOUND	Nathan Levinson

A Warner Brothers Pictures, Inc., Production

CAST

Theseus	IAN HUNTER
Hyppolyta	VEREE TEASDALE
Egeus	GRANT MITCHELL
Oberon	VICTOR JORY
Titania	ANITA LOUISE
Hermia	OLIVIA DE HAVILLAND
Helena	JEAN MUIR
Lysander	DICK POWELL
Demetrius	ROSS ALEXANDER
Bottom	JAMES CAGNEY
Puck	MICKEY ROONEY
Snout	HUGH HERBERT
Flute	JOE E. BROWN
Starveling	OTIS HARLAN
Snug	DEWEY ROBINSON
Quince	FRANK McHUGH

Film Reality: Cinema and the Theatre
ALLARDYCE NICOLL

◆◆◆

Already it has been shown that normally the film does not find re-
strictions in the scope of its material advantageous; so that the typical
film approaches outwardly the extended breadth of a Scott novel. In
dealing with that material, however, it is given the opportunity of
delving more deeply into the human consciousness. By its subjective
method it can display life from the point of view of its protagonists.
Madness on the stage, in spite of Ophelia's pathetic efforts, has always
appeared rather absurd, and Sheridan was perfectly within his rights
when he caricatured the convention in his Tilburina and her address
to all the finches of the grove. On the screen, however, madness may
be made arresting, terrifying, awful. The mania of the lunatic in the
German film, *M*, held the attention precisely because we were enabled
to look within his distracted brain. Seeing for moments the world distorted in eccentric imaginings, we are moved as no objective presentation of a stage Ophelia can move us.

Regarded in this way, the cinema, a form of expression born of our
own age, is seen to bear a distinct relationship to recent developments
within the sphere of general artistic endeavour. While making no pro-
fession to examine this subject, one of the most recent writers on *This
Modern Poetry*, Babette Deutsch, has expressed, *obiter dicta,* judgments
which illustrate clearly the arguments presented above. "The sym-
bolists," she says, "had telescoped images to convey the rapid passage
of sensations and emotions. The metaphysicals had played in a like
fashion with ideas. Both delighted in paradox. The cinema, and ultimately the radio, made such telescopy congenial to the modern poet,
as the grotesqueness of his environment made paradox inevitable for
him." And again:

The cinema studio creates a looking-glass universe where, without
bottles labeled "Drink me" or cakes labeled "Eat me" or keys to im-

From Film and Theatre (*New York: Thomas Y. Crowell Company,*
1936), *pp. 175–81. Reprinted by permission of the author.*

possible gardens, creatures are elongated or telescoped, movements accelerated or slowed up, in a fashion suggesting that the world is made of india-rubber or collapsible tin. The ghost of the future glimmers through the immediate scene, the present dissolves into the past.

Akin to these marvels is the poetry of such a man as Horace Gregory. In his *No Retreat: New York, Cassandra,* "the fluent images, the sudden close-ups, the shifting angle of vision, suggest the technique of the cinema." The method of the film is apparent in such lines as these:

Give Cerberus a non-employment wage, the dog is hungry.
This head served in the war, Cassandra, it lost an eye;
That head spits fire, for it lost its tongue licking the paws
of lions caged in Wall Street and their claws
were merciless.

Follow, O follow him, loam-limbed Apollo, crumbling before
Tiffany's window: he must buy
himself earrings for he meets his love tonight,
(Blossoming Juliet
emptied her love into her true love's lap)
dies in his arms.

If the cinema has thus influenced the poets, we realise that inherently it becomes a form of art through which may be expressed many of the most characteristic tendencies in present-day creative endeavour. That most of the films so far produced have not made use of the peculiar methods inherent in the cinematic approach need not blind us to the fact that here is an instrument capable of expressing through combined visual and vocal means something of that analytical searching of the spirit which has formed the pursuit of modern poets and novelists. Not, of course, that in this analytic and realistic method are to be enclosed the entire boundaries of the cinema. The film has the power of giving an impression of actuality and it can thrill us by its penetrating truth to life: but it may, if we desire, call into existence the strangest of visionary worlds and make these too seem real. The enchanted forest of *A Midsummer Night's Dream* will always on the stage prove a thing of lath and canvas and paint; an enchanted forest in the film might truly seem haunted by a thousand fears and supernatural imaginings. This imaginary world, indeed, is one that our public has cried for and demanded, and our only regret may be that the producers, lacking vision, have compromised and in compromising have descended to banalities. Taking their sets of characters, they thrust these, willy-nilly, into scenes of ornate splendour, exercising their inventiveness, not to create the truly fanciful but to fashion the exaggeratedly and hyperbolically absurd. Hotels more sumptuous than the Waldorf-Astoria or the Ritz; liners outvying the pretentions of the Normandie; speed that sets Malcolm Campbell to shame; melodies inappropriately rich —these have crowded in on us again and yet again. Many spectators are becoming irritated and bored with scenes of this sort, for mere exaggeration of life's luxuries is not creative artistically.

That the cinema has ample opportunities in this direction has been proved by Max Reinhardt's *A Midsummer Night's Dream,* which, if unsatisfactory as a whole and if in many scenes tentative in its approach, demonstrated what may be done with imaginative forms on the screen. Apart from the opportunity offered by Shakespeare's theme for the presentation of the supernatural fairy world, two things were specially to be noted in this film. The first was that certain passages which, spoken in our vast modern theatres with their sharp separation of audience and actors, become mere pieces of rhetoric devoid of true meaning and significance were invested in the film with an intimacy and directness they lacked on the stage. The power of the cinema to draw us near to an action or to a speaker served here an important function, and we could at will watch a group of players from afar or approach to overhear the secrets of a soliloquy. The second feature of interest lay in the ease with which the cinema can present visual symbols to accompany language. At first, we might be prepared to condemn the film on this ground, declaring that the imaginative appeal of Shakespeare's language would thereby be lost. Again, however, second thoughts convince us that much is to be said in its defence; reference once more must be made to a subject already briefly discussed. Shakespeare's dialogue was written for an audience, not only sympathetic to his particular way of thought and feeling, but gifted with certain faculties which today we have lost. Owing to the universal development of reading, certain faculties possessed by men of earlier ages have vanished from us. In the sixteenth century, men's minds were more acutely perceptive of values in words heard, partly because their language was a growing thing with constantly occurring new forms and strange applications of familiar words, but largely because they had to maintain a constant alertness to spoken speech. Newspapers did not exist then; all men's knowledge of the larger world beyond their immediate ken had to come from hearing words uttered by their companions. As a result, the significance of words was more keenly appreciated and certainly was more concrete than it is today. When Macbeth, in four lines, likened life to a brief candle, to a walking shadow and to a poor player, one may believe that the ordinary spectator in the Globe theatre saw in his mind's eye these three objects referred to. The candle, the shadow and the player became for him mental realities.

The same speech uttered on the stage today can hardly hope for such interpretation. Many in the audience will be lulled mentally insensible to its values by the unaccustomed movement of the lines, and others will grasp its import, not by emotional imaginative understanding, but by a painful, rational process of thought. A modern audience, therefore, listening to earlier verse drama, will normally require a direct stimulus to its visual imagination—a thing entirely unnecessary in former times. Thus, for example, on the bare Elizabethan platform stage the words concerning dawn or sunlight or leafy woods were amply sufficient to conjure up an image of these things; latter-day experiments in the production of these dramas in reconstructed "Shakespearian" theatres, interesting as these may be and refreshing in their novelty, must largely fail to achieve the end, so easily and with such little effort reached among sixteenth century audiences. We need, now, all the appurtenances of a decorated stage to approach, even faintly, the dramatist's purpose. This is the justification for the presentation of Shakespeare's tragedies and comedies not in a reconstructed Globe theatre, but according to the current standards of Broadway or of Shaftesbury Avenue.

The theatre, however, can only do so much. It may visually create the setting, but it cannot create the stimulus necessary for a keener appreciation of the imagic value of Shakespeare's lines. No method of stage representation could achieve that end. On the screen, on the other hand, something at least in this direction may be accomplished. In *A Midsummer Night's Dream* Oberon's appearance behind dark bespangled gauze, even although too much dwelt on and emphasised, gave force to lines commonly read or heard uncomprehendingly— "King of Shadows," he is called; but the phrase means little or nothing to us unless our minds are given such a stimulus as was here provided. Critics have complained that in the film nothing is left to the imagination, but we must remember that in the Shakespearean verse is a quality which, because of changed conditions, we may find difficulty in appreciating. Its strangeness to us demands that an attempt be made to render it more intelligible and directly appealing. Such an attempt, through the means of expression granted to the cinema, may merely be supplying something which will bring us nearer to the conditions of the original spectators for whom Shakespeare wrote.

Normally, however, verse forms will be alien to the film. Verse in itself presupposes a certain remoteness from the terms of ordinary life; and the cinema, as we have seen, usually finds its most characteristic expression in the world that immediately surrounds us. The close connection, noted by Babette Deutsch, between cinematic expression and tendencies in present-day poetry will declare itself, not in a utilisation of rhythmic speech but in a psychological penetration rendered manifest through a realistic method.

Films of a Moonstruck World
RICHARD WATTS, JR.

◆◆

The motion-picture producers love to talk about Art, and the surprising thing is that they really mean what they are saying. There is something almost wistful about their anxiety to prove to us that they are missionaries of culture and pioneers of a new aesthetic form. They may go about it pretty clumsily, but they do strive manfully from time to time to provide us with a handsome proof of the earnestness of their intentions. At the same time, they can hardly forget that they are also supposed to be businessmen, concerned with one of the country's greatest industries, which can only succeed when their pictures appeal to widespread audiences and show a neat profit. The result of all this is that the masterminds of Hollywood are driven approximately mad in their grim darting back and forth between Art and Commerce. . . .

The worst result of these warring emotions in the magnate's soul is that it almost inevitably results in the deadening spirit of compromise. It would certainly be much better for the aesthetic quality of the films if the motives could be divided and two definite types of photoplay could be made: the one that frankly was intended as a piece of trade goods and the other that made a thoughtful and complete attempt to be dramatically distinguished, even though forced to appeal to a comparatively limited group. Obviously, the first type of photoplay is manufactured with hearty regularity. *The Informer* comes immediately to mind as an example of the second category. Ordinarily, however, when a film intended to have a certain artistic stature is planned, the spirit of compromise is likely to raise its ugly head, and it is decided that while the picture must, of course, possess aesthetic integrity, there is no reason why a few sops should not be tossed to the less

From The Yale Review *25, no. 2 (December 1935): 311–20.*

earnest-minded spectators. Thus, the magnates argue, all members of the audience will be pleased and the photoplay will be that perfection of miracles, the "artistic" and financial success in one.

The trouble is that in trying to please everyone, they end by satisfying none. Those who would have delighted in the film had it been done with integrity will be alienated by the interpolated shoddiness, while the audiences for whom such interpolations have been made will be annoyed by what they regard as highbrow affectation. At the moment there is a grave possibility that this may be the fate of the elaborate Max Reinhardt version of *A Midsummer Night's Dream*. After making every effort to see that the photoplay was correct in every detail, the producers weakened just long enough to put into the cast, as a popular box-office name, at least one player whose performance is not much short of fatal. If the picture is not a financial success, other factors must be blamed in addition to the presence of a popular crooner in the cast—to his everlasting credit, it should be added that he knew he was the wrong man for the rôle and didn't want to play it —but it is safe to say that his performance hurts the work dramatically without causing the crooner's enthusiasts to revel in the joys of Shakespeare.

Almost every film company makes what it calls its "prestige" pictures. They are certainly not intended to lose money, and almost invariably the process of artistic compromise gets into them, but chiefly they are planned by the magnates in some of their more idealistic moments as proofs that they are artists as well as businessmen. It is their little gesture in the direction of the cinema as the great modern form of dramatic expression. This has been happening ever since the pioneer days of the screen but rarely on so elaborate a scale or so definitely as a challenge as in the case of *A Midsummer Night's Dream*. If the picture is an economic success then we are in for a succession of Shakespearean films. If it is a failure, no matter what the reason, then it is likely that we shall not see *Hamlet* or *Macbeth* or possibly even *Romeo and Juliet* until eventually a fanatical, idealistic gleam appears in the eye of a Hollywood producer and he decides to make another "prestige" picture.

Thereupon, while the success of *A Midsummer Night's Dream* is in considerable doubt, it may be of value to stop and consider whether it really is advisable to "film" Shakespeare. All of us who have at any time theorized about the screen have reserved our finest scorn for the photographed stage play. We have felt that the cinema, if it is ever to become anything more than an imitative stepchild of the drama, must break away from its slavish imitation of the theater and remember once again that it is essentially a visual medium. In the excitement of learning to speak, it did forget that its greatest virtue was the mighty sweep that the camera permitted it. Overnight the films became a succession of stage plays, the action and dialogue of which were photo-graphed scene for scene, with all the limitations that the form of the theater inflicted on them. Gradually it was remembered that the great motion pictures were such works as *The Birth of a Nation, Intolerance, Greed, The Last Laugh, Variety, Potemkin,* and the Lubitsch pan-tomimic comedies, wherein the pictorial image was the essential form of dramatic expression.

There still is an excess of dialogue in the talkies, but the tendency in the better works has been in the direction of minimizing the amount of speech. If, therefore, Shakespeare is to be presented on the screen, will not reaction set in, with a return to the overemphasis on words, rather than pictures? It is my own conviction that, since the cinema, for good or evil, has adopted speech, then it is to the advantage of everyone concerned that the dialogue should be first-rate. The shifting backgrounds and the numerous scenes in the Shakespearean dramas, as well as the very nature of the tales, make them admirable cinema material. Always the screen, at its best, has had a curiously Elizabethan, if not Shakespearean, quality about it. The hearty, farcical low-comedy relief that has been a regularly necessary part of motion-picture drama has belonged definitely to that mood. The highly colored dramatic action, the tendency to believe that heroes really should belong to the upper classes while the lower ranks of society should supply the farcical relief, the disregard of limitations of space—all of these things have tended to present a certain parallel, which, if not startlingly close, is at least enough to suggest that Shakespeare and the films are not altogether alien.

At the same time, there is no denying that numerous objections have been and will be raised against the filming of Shakespeare, not based on the way the filming has been managed, but on the very idea of it. For example, a number of people have objected to the current version of *A Midsummer Night's Dream,* not because of any lack of imagina-tion in the camera work and production—a quite possible cause for complaint—but because the camera did its work too well. The theory was that since the words of Shakespeare created a vision of fairyland that approached perfection, any endeavor to recreate that moonstruck world by mechanical artifice was an intrusion and a sacrilege. Since Shakespeare wrote not for the library, but for the stage, and the stage, even in its simplest forms, cannot escape its visual elements, it seems to me that any such objection should go the whole way and resent the presence of actors, as well as of camera work. The important thing, however, is not the justice of this contention, but that it represents one of the innumerable objections of those who oppose Shakespeare in the films and suggests how far afield the objectors will go in finding arguments. It is a trifle surprising to find one of the cinema's greatest virtues, its camera ingenuity, being brought up against it by its foes.

There is no reason, either, why the matter of the vast amount of dialogue in the plays should upset those who fear too much speech, no matter how magnificent, upon the screen. Since it is the rarest thing in the world to find a Shakespearean acting version that is in any way complete and it is a fact that such eminent actors as Booth, Irving, John Barrymore, and Walter Hampden caused no scandal by using abbreviated scripts, there is no reason why the films should be denied their share of editing. In fact, if Hollywood, without losing its fear of too much dialogue, cannot arrange a more satisfying operation on the words of a full-length, five-act play than the man, say, who cut *King Lear* for Fritz Leiber's stage production of a few seasons ago, then the cinema citadel is losing its customary editorial resourcefulness.

One of the gravest difficulties to be faced in the fairly unlikely event of a Shakespearean outburst in Hollywood lies in the matter of finding actors. That was proved with some conclusiveness in *A Midsummer Night's Dream*. The cinema actor, it is to be feared, simply doesn't possess the sort of voice or voice-training that equips him for the poetic drama. Miss Anita Louise, for example, was as exquisite a Titania visually as a poet could sensibly conceive, yet when she started to recite her lines you were aware of an unhappy feeling of being let down. Her voice was completely unfitted for the ordeal that was thrust upon her; an ordeal that she had been prepared for by nothing in her brief acting career. Definitely more unfortunate was young Mickey Rooney, whose Puck, despite connotations of Tarzan, was admirably conceived pictorially. Here was a Puck to be admired when you watched, but as soon as he opened his mouth and emitted those strange animal outcries, you were aware that much was amiss with the poetic drama.

Offhand it might be thought that this difficulty could be dispensed with by bringing a few more boatloads of English actors to Hollywood. Unfortunately, anyone who saw that brilliant actor, Philip Merivale, and that talented actress, Miss Gladys Cooper, on the New York stage recently in *Othello* and *Macbeth* quickly learned that it was not merely the matter of American vocal peculiarities or lack of histrionic training that resulted in unhappy Shakespearean acting. It is merely that few actors, no matter how expert or how experienced in other fields, have the proper training or the proper instinct for this type of acting. . . .

Despite the problems offered, it would by no means be impossible to cast a number of the plays in Hollywood. When you indulge in the harmless sport of thinking up your own casting, it is surprising to note how often the name of Charles Laughton comes to mind. He would be admirable as Macbeth or Iago or Enobarbus or Falstaff or Dogberry. Edward G. Robinson should make an extremely interesting Richard Third. Miss Jean Muir, who is so lovely as Helena in *A Midsummer Night's Dream*, would be excellently cast as Juliet or Ophelia or

Desdemona. If you saw Miss Katharine Hepburn in *Morning Glory,* you will remember how well she did the balcony scene from *Romeo and Juliet.* There is every reason to think that she would be brilliant in a full-length version of the play, and there are those of us who suspect that she would make a fascinating Lady Macbeth. Leslie Howard, who has talked of doing both Hamlet and Richard Second on the New York stage, would be available for both rôles and many others in the cinema. Of course, only the incomparable Miss Garbo should be Cleopatra, although Cecil De Mille's recent non-Shakespearean version of the story makes it unlikely that the tragic tale will be repeated in the near future.

Whatever may be the fate of *A Midsummer Night's Dream,* it seems likely that we are to have a cinema *Romeo and Juliet* in the near future. Miss Norma Shearer is to be Juliet, and those who might be inclined to suspect that she will not be ideally cast should at least be reminded that we said the same thing when it was announced that she was to be Elizabeth Barrett in *The Barretts of Wimpole Street* and then saw her confute us by giving an excellent performance. More tentative is the announcement that Max Reinhardt's great heart will be broken unless Miss Marion Davies consents to appear in *Twelfth Night.* To skeptical observers it would hardly seem a perfect bit of casting; at least there is nothing in Miss Davies's past career—at times she is a fair minor comedienne—which would suggest that her chance of confuting her critics successfully is nearly so great as that of Miss Shearer.

During the publicity campaign on behalf of *A Midsummer Night's Dream,* Mr. Basil Dean, the London director—who may or may not have been a party to the campaign—announced indignantly that it was an outrage for upstart Americans to desecrate Britain's national poet by attempting to transfer him to the screen. In the midst of his denunciation Mr. Dean seemed to hint that, in the name of the growing English film industry, he himself might consent to rescue the Bard by making a few films of his own. So far, however, there have been no announced plans for filming the national poet on his home ground.

At present, then, the future of Shakespeare in the films seems to rest pretty heavily on the shoulders of *A Midsummer Night's Dream,* or, rather, on the shoulders of the paying spectators. As yet it is too early to tell how the film will do at the box office, but it is giving away no secret to say that business has not been up to anticipations. The reason for this, I should repeat, may be in part that the spirit of compromise made the producers, who were so austere in most respects, weaken long enough to indulge in a bit of box-office casting that turned out to be neither good casting nor good box office. It would be absurd, however, if any such statement made it seem that the hapless Mr. Dick Powell is the one cause for the failure of any vast national stampede to see the Reinhardt spectacle. For one thing, the picture is far too long. Half an hour of the ballets could have come out to admirable effect. A lot less of Puck's boyish screams would have been a great blessing. In addition, there is, upon occasion, a touch of heavy-handedness in the Reinhardt production that seems more Teutonic than cinematic. . . .

In speculating about the cinema's future, it would be a mistake to overlook the new technical possibilities, since technique always has led ideas in the films. Color photography may provide the screen at any moment with one of its periodic revolutions. But since the all-color version of *Becky Sharp* was not a great financial success, the chances are against that happening tomorrow, despite the fact that color has already been successfully used—in one brief episode in an otherwise forgotten photoplay revue, *The Show of Shows,* in which John Barrymore, the best Shakespearean actor of this generation, did a scene from the third part of *Henry Sixth*. Better than any single event in film history, that scene showed the effectiveness not only of color but of Shakespeare in the cinema. There is also the possibility that the technique of voice production and recording may be improved. Whatever may come of the present Shakespearean flurry in Hollywood, it has at least brought up again the matter of voice-training and has reminded us—and, I hope, the magnates—that good speaking is important in any type of motion picture.

Henry V
1944

DIRECTION	Sir Laurence Olivier
SCRIPT	Sir Laurence Olivier, Alan Dent, and Dallas Bower
PHOTOGRAPHY	Robert Krasker and Jack Hildyard
MUSIC	Sir William Walton
ORCHESTRA DIRECTION	Muir Matheson
ART DIRECTION	Paul Sheriff and Carmen Dillon
COSTUMES	Roger Furse
EDITING	Reginald Beck
SOUND	John Dennis and Desmond Dew

A Two-Cities Films, Ltd., Production

CAST

Henry V	SIR LAURENCE OLIVIER
Katherine	RENÉE ASHERSON
Gloucester	MICHAEL WARRE
Exeter	NICHOLAS HANNEN
Salisbury	GRIFFITH JONES
Westmoreland	GERALD CASE
Canterbury	FELIX AYLMER
Ely	ROBERT HELPMAN
Charles VI	HARCOURT WILLIAMS
Queen Isabel	JANET BURNELL
Lewis, the Dauphin	MAX ADRIAN
Burgundy	VALENTINE DYALL
Orleans	FRANCIS LISTER
Bourbon	RUSSELL THORNDIKE
Alice	IVY ST. HELIER
Montjoy	JONATHAN FIELD
Erpingham	MORLAND GRAHAM
Falstaff	GEORGE ROBEY
Dame Quickly	FREDA JACKSON
Pistol	ROBERT NEWTON
Fluellen	ESMOND KNIGHT
Bardolph	ROY EMERTON
Nym	FREDERICK COOPER
Williams	JIMMY HANLEY
MacMorris	NIALL MacGINNIS
Jamy	JOHN LAURIE
Court	BRIAN NISSEN
Bates	ARTHUR HAMBLING
Gower	MICHAEL SHEPLEY
Constable	LEO GENN
Boy	GEORGE COLE
Chorus	LESLIE BANKS

HENRY V
JAMES AGEE

◆◆

It seems impertinent to discuss even briefly the excellence of Laurence Olivier's production of Shakespeare's *Henry V* without saying a few words, at least, about the author. If Shakespeare had been no more gifted with words than, say, I am, the depth and liveliness of his interest in people and predicaments, and his incredible hardness, practicality, and resource as a craftsman and maker of moods, rhythms, and points, could still have made him almost his actual equal as a playwright. I had never realized this so well until I saw this production, in which every nail in sight is so cleanly driven in with one blow; and I could watch the film for all that Shakespeare gave it in these terms alone, and for all that in these terms alone is done with what he gave, with great pleasure and gratitude. But then too, of course, there is the language of a brilliance, vigor, and absoluteness that make the craftsmanship and sometimes the people and their grandest emotions seem almost as negligibly pragmatic as a libretto beside an opera score. Some people, using I wonder what kind of dry ice for comfort, like to insist that *Henry V* is relatively uninteresting Shakespeare. This uninteresting poetry is such that after hearing it, in this production, I find it as hard to judge fairly even the best writing since Shakespeare as it is to see the objects in a room after looking into the sun.

The one great glory of the film is this language. The greatest credit I can assign to those who made the film is that they have loved and served the language so well. I don't feel that much of the delivery is inspired; it is merely so good, so right, that the words set loose in the graciously designed world of the screen, like so many uncaged birds, fully enjoy and take care of themselves. Neither of the grimmest Shakespearian vices, ancient or modern, is indulged: that is to say, none of the text is read in that human, down-to-earth, poetry-is-only-hopped-up-prose manner which is doubtless only proper when a character subscriber to *PM* reads the Lerner editorial to his shop-wise fellow

From Agee on Film: Volume 1 (*New York: Grosset & Dunlap, Inc., 1958*), *pp. 209–12. Copyright 1946 by The James Agee Trust. Reprinted by permission of Grosset & Dunlap, Inc., and Peter Owen, Ltd.*

traveler; nor is any of it intoned in the nobler manner, as if by a spoiled deacon celebrating the Black Mass down a section of sewer-pipe. Most of it is merely spoken by people who know and love poetry as poetry and have spent a lifetime learning how to speak it accordingly. Their voices, faces, and bodies are all in charge of a man who has selected them as shrewdly as a good orchestrator selects and blends his instruments; and he combines and directs them as a good conductor conducts an orchestral piece. It is, in fact, no surprise to learn that Mr. Olivier is fond of music; charming as it is to look at, the film is essentially less visual than musical.

I cannot compare it with many stage productions of Shakespeare; but so far as I can they were, by comparison, just so many slightly tired cultural summer-salads, now and then livened, thanks to an unkilled talent or an unkillable line, by an unexpected rose-petal or the sudden spasm of a rattlesnake: whereas this, down to the last fleeting bit of first-rate poetry in a minor character's mouth, was close to solid gold, almost every word given its own and its largest contextual value. Of course nothing prevents this kind of casting and playing on the stage, except talent and, more seriously, the money to buy enough talent and enough time to use it rightly in; and how often do you see anything to equal it on the Shakespearian stage? The specific advantages of the screen are obvious, but no less important for that. Microphones make possible a much more delicate and immediate use of the voice; reactions, in close-up, can color the lines more subtly and richly than on the stage. Thus it is possible, for instance, to get all the considerable excellence there is out of an aging player like Nicholas Hannen, who seemed weak in most scenes when, on the stage, he had to try to fill and dilate the whole Century Theater with unhappy majesty; and the exquisiteness of Renée Asherson's reactions to Olivier's spate of gallantry, in the wooing scene, did as much as he did toward making that scene, by no means the most inspired as writing, the crown of the film. When so much can be done, through proper understanding of these simple advantages, to open the beauties of poetry as relatively extroverted as this play, it is equally hard to imagine and to wait for the explorations that could be made of subtler, deeper poems like *Hamlet, Troilus and Cressida,* or *The Tempest.*

Speaking still of nothing except the skill with which the poetry is used in this film, I could go on far past the room I have. The sureness and seductive power of the pacing alone and its shifts and contrasts, in scene after scene, has seldom been equaled in a movie; the adjustments and relationships of tone are just as good. For just one example, the difference in tone between Olivier's almost schoolboyish "God-a-mercy" and his "Good old Knight," not long afterward, measures the King's growth in the time between with lovely strength, spaciousness, and cleanness; it earns, as craftsmanship, the triumph of bringing off

the equivalent to an "impossibly" delayed false-rhyme; and psychologically or dramatically, it seems to me—though my guess may be far-
fetched—it fully establishes the King's coming-of-age by raising honor-
able, brave, loyal, and dull old age (in Sir Thomas Erpingham) in the
King's love and esteem to the level of any love he had ever felt for
Falstaff.

Olivier does many other beautiful pieces of reading and playing.
His blood-raising reply to the French Herald's ultimatum is not just
that; it is a frank, bright exploitation of the moment for English ears,
amusedly and desperately honored as such, in a still gallant and
friendly way, by both Herald and King. His Crispin's Day oration is
not just a brilliant bugle-blat; it is the calculated yet self-exceeding
improvisation, at once self-enjoying and selfless, of a young and sleepless leader, rising to a situation wholly dangerous and glamorous, and
wholly new to him. Only one of the many beauties of the speech as he
gives it is the way in which the King seems now to exploit his sincerity,
now to be possessed by it, riding like an unexpectedly mounting wave
the astounding size of his sudden proud awareness of the country
morning, of his moment in history, of his responsibility and compe-
tence, of being full-bloodedly alive, and of being about to die.

This kind of branching, nervous interpretive intelligence, so contemporary in quality except that it always keeps the main lines of its
drive and meaning clear, never spiraling or strangling in awareness,
is vivid in every way during all parts of the film.

It is tantalizing to be able to mention so few of the dozens of large
and hundreds of small excellences which Mr. Olivier and his associ-
ates have developed to sustain Shakespeare's poem. They have done
somewhere near all that talent, cultivation, taste, knowledgeability,
love of one's work—every excellence, in fact, short of genius—can be
expected to do; and that, the picture testifies, is a very great deal.
Lacking space for anything further I would like to suggest that it be
watched for all that it does in playing a hundred kinds of charming
adventurousness against the incalculably responsive sounding-boards
of tradition: for that is still, and will always be, a process essential in
most, though not all, of the best kinds of art, and I have never before
seen so much done with it in a moving picture. I am not a Tory, a
monarchist, a Catholic, a medievalist, an Englishman, or, despite all
the good that it engenders, a lover of war: but the beauty and power
of this traditional exercise was such that, watching it, I wished I
was, thought I was, and was proud of it. I was persuaded, and in part
still am, that every time and place has since been in decline, save one,
in which one Englishman used language better than anyone has before or since, or ever shall; and that nearly the best that our time can
say for itself is that some of us are still capable of paying homage to
the fact.

HENRY V
BOSLEY CROWTHER

◈◈

In the dismal fall and winter of 1943–44, when the people of Britain were enduring the screeching perils of the "little blitz" and their tight little island was sagging under the weight of the growing invasion force, there was quietly being made at Denham, one of London's badly battered studios, a film to which even its director referred cautiously as "an experiment." This was the most that Laurence Olivier would permit himself to say for this war-born and plainly problematic production of Shakespeare's *Henry V.*

A year or so earlier, the brilliant actor had agreed to undertake the job of directing and acting in this picture under the eloquent urging of Filippo del Giudice, the same man who had persuaded Noel Coward to make *In Which We Serve* (which see). Del Giudice had heard Olivier deliver some speeches from the play on the BBC, on one of those patriotic broadcasts that were so popular in Britain during the war, and was excitedly struck with the notion of making the play into a film. What, thought he, could be more appropriate to the British mood and condition at the time than this grandly heroic and triumphant *Chronicle Historie of Henry the Fifth,* in which a stout little band of English soldiers, knights and bowmen fight their way to victory against great odds on the Continent in the fifteenth century!

At first, Olivier was resistant. He felt the film would be too great a risk, that the dramatic verse of Shakespeare was suited only for performance on the stage. Furthermore, he recalled, as did others, that the public had ever shown a discouraging indifference to motion pictures made from plays of the Bard. But del Giudice persisted. He assured Olivier that his renown as a Shakespearean actor with the Old Vic and his popularity as a star in British and American films would insure much attention for the picture, and he confidently proclaimed that the

From The Great Films: Fifty Years of Motion Pictures *by Bosley Crowther (New York: G. P. Putnam's Sons, 1967), pp. 165–68. Copyright © 1967 by Bosley Crowther. Reprinted by permission of G. P. Putnam's Sons and the author.*

intelligence and imagination that Olivier would give it would complete the guarantee of success. The actor was finally taken with the prospect of a bold experiment.

In laying the plans for the production, he faced two major problems. First was the problem of determining the characteristic of the film. Olivier has since told me that he knew "something had to be done to give it a reality that was acceptable to the new audience without outraging the reality of Shakespeare, which can only be conveyed through the medium of the verse and a certain style of address to the matter." In short, he would have to conceive a style or manner of pictorial presentation that would be in accord with the richness of the verse and yet would develop an illusion of reality and credibility.

The second problem was that of the physical production. It was fully recognized and agreed that the film would have to be done on a large, spectacular and expensive scale. The fifteenth century was an age of knights and splendid royal households. Materials would be hard to obtain. Furthermore, shooting schedules would be subject to the uncontrollable inconveniences of war. Personnel might have to be diverted to other more pressing tasks. (Olivier himself had been temporarily borrowed from the Naval Air Arm to make the film.) And since Olivier's concept was that the Battle of Agincourt would have to be staged out in the open, on a full pseudo-realistic scale and not suggested through the eloquence of language, as it inevitably is on the stage, there was the anomalous problem of finding a location in which to perform a medieval battle in a country absorbed in a modern war.

The difficulties were tackled, and scenic designers and costumers performed miracles of ingenuity. The sets and 1,000 or more costumes, including suits of armor that would ordinarily have required vast quantities of metals, brocades, leather, silks, satins and other stuffs, were fabricated from makeshifts. Suits of mail were made from heavy wrapping twine, knit and crocheted by a surprisingly eager group of Irish nuns, then sprayed with aluminum paint to simulate metal. Cheap blankets were dyed splendid colors and used for the hundreds of horse trappings in the great battle scene. Spears, swords and maces were cut from wood and coated with aluminum paint. Even King Henry's delicate crown was made from papier mâché.

The location picked for the battle was the huge estate of Lord Powerscourt at Enniskerry, near Dublin. And there, amid the green and rolling Irish hills, in the late spring and early summer of 1943, while modern armies clashed in distant places, the ancient Battle of Agincourt was staged.

The Eirean Home Guard mustered 500 sturdy young men to don the rough breeches and blouses of the fifteenth century and appear as the English foot soldiers and bowmen who are so crucial in the great battle scene. Close to 200 Irish horsemen came in with their mounts from nearby farms, the only available reservoir of men and horses, to act as the English and French knights. Though Technicolor film was at a premium, del Giudice managed to get hold of enough of this raw stock to shoot the film in color. It would have been folly to do it in black and white.

Midway through production, del Giudice ran out of money and had to sell a majority share of the film to J. Arthur Rank to complete it, but never did he suggest that Olivier should skimp on production or eliminate anything he wanted to do. The total cost was $2,000,000 and it took eighteen months to finish the job. It was the most ambitious and costly picture done in Britain up to that time.

It opened in London in December 1944, with a premiere so brilliant that it seemed to belie the fact of a nation at war. The immediate response of audience and critics was that Olivier's "experiment" had succeeded magnificently. All Britain thrilled to this extraordinary exposition of patriotism and pride, compounded from a less familiar play of Shakespeare and a masterful use of the screen.

In more recent years, some critics have quibblingly complained that the film is no more than an adroitly photographed reproduction of the play, thus consigning it to the shameful status of "noncreative cinema." But it seems to me that this contention misses the crucial point—which is that the film, while beyond question a faithful transcription of the play (considerably pruned of large and tough chunks by Olivier and the literary scholar, Alan Dent), is creative and dynamic precisely because it *does* avail the cinema device to fire the imagination, to sweep the eye over boundaries of time and space in order to give a new dimension of spiritual excitement to a traditionally limited theatrical experience. It is precisely the flow and sweep of poetic drama through a succession of ever-opening pictorial styles that renders this film cinematic, with life and vitality.

If Olivier had been so insensitive as to try to keep the action confined to one stage or even to one style of staging, as it seems about to be at the start, when the camera travels in over a model of seventeenth-century London to the hectagonal Globe Theater, there to pick up the excitement at the world premiere of *The Chronicle Historie of Henry the Fifth,* then there would be full justice in complaining that it is only a photographed play. But he doesn't try that, not by a long shot —or by many long, medium, close or other shots!

The pattern he has given the production is that of a chronicle which evolves through a casual transition out of the stagecraft and age in which it was born into modes of artistic expression and stylization characteristic of the French. Then, when the nature of the action and the intensity of the excitement become so strong that the frame of a formal stage cannot contain them, when the drama demands to be conveyed in the most striking form of illusion, the traditional devices are dismissed and an image of events is presented—something close to reality. When that is over, when the triumph of that illusion has been achieved and the spectator has been tumbled through the midst of the Battle of Agincourt, the progression is reversed. The action and emotion are again subdued as the chronicle is moved back into scenery, into the romantic aura of the Duc de Berri's France, and then back once more and finally into the cozy "wooden O" of the Globe and into the warm and ever-radiant womb of the Elizabethan age.

It is when the action progresses to the night before Agincourt, to the quiet and vigilant camp of the English and, once, to the camp of the French, that the major transition in style and mood is begun. Up to this point, the drama has been tangibly circled by the stage, by the audience's tacit awareness that it is beholding a play. But now, as the scenic structure changes into a vast vault of vague and misty night, with campfires twinkling in the distance, silent tents looming near at hand, and the voice of Chorus speaking softly,

> Now entertain conjecture of a time
> When creeping murmur and the poring dark
> Fills the wide vessel of the universe.
> From camp to camp, through the foul womb of night
>   The hum of either army stilly sounds . . .

we are brought to the point of merging into the illusion of historical actuality.

Here, in this most exquisite passage, as Henry moves quietly through his camp, pausing to salute a fine old warrior who knows well the peril of the morrow, stopping to talk incognito with a group of untried lads who are nervous and frankly doubtful of the necessity and outcome of their cause, Olivier creates a separate philosophical, poetic realm. Now we are in a formless area of subtle intimation and anxious thought, the timeless realm of the lonely soldier who senses that he may soon die. And, as Henry draws aside to engage in his solemn soliloquy,

> Upon the king! Let us our lives, our souls
> . . . Lay on the king! We must bear all! . . .

an almost metaphysical communion with one man, all alone with us, is made.

This soliloquy, shot in medium close-up, with the camera focused on Olivier's face, which does not move but carries a deeply sad expression, as his voice from offscreen speaks the lovely lines, was one of his brilliant devices for acclimatizing Shakespeare to the screen. He continued to use the invention most effectively in his subsequent screen productions of *Hamlet* (1948) and *Richard III* (1955).

And so, with this moving passage, Olivier sweeps us from the stage, blurs the Shakespearean convention with a solely motion-picture device and prepares us for the spiritual breath-taking of a plunge into the real, sunlit outdoors.

Now it is the day of battle, the morning of the moment of truth, when the full majesterial confrontation toward which all has been directed will take place. Here, in the camp of the English, the armorers are busy at work, clanging hammers on their anvils, using derricks to hoist knights aboard their mounts as though they were helpless sea turtles. The bowmen are stretching and flexing their bows, driving stakes in the ground as vicious barriers. And, in the camp of the French, all blue and gold, the armored chevaliers are laughing, clinking glasses, drinking toasts and preparing to sweep to victory in one grand, overwhelming charge.

In the dread pause before battle, Henry, still in tunic and hose, climbs into a haycart and, with his warriors around him, gives the thundering St. Crispin's Day speech, which is, beyond any question, the grandest battle cry in literature. Notably, the camera trucks backward, not forward, during this scene. Instead of closing in on the speaker, as has been done in other Shakespearean films, it draws farther and farther away from him, so that when he hits those final stirring lines

> We few, we happy few, we band of brothers . . .
> . . . That fought with us upon St. Crispin's Day!

the whole array of the English army is envisioned, with Henry but a strong voice in its midst.

Now to the field of battle, as onward across the rolling green hills sweeps the first charge of the French knights, a vast and impressive line of brilliantly caparisoned horsemen, armor rattling, pennants snapping in the breeze, moving forward first at a slow trot then into a canter, then into a thundering charge, as the music of William Walton increases in tempo and sweeps in a grand, martial surge, and the great battle is locked. It runs on for several minutes—a confusion of slaughter, the French knights withdrawing to reform their forces and come back across the body-spotted hills. In this one great sequence, Olivier visions the gist of medieval pageantry, the ageless, romantic, storybook notion of the Battle of Agincourt.

Olivier's direction has forcefulness and sweep, making a rich and flowing fabric of personalities and pageantry. And his own performance of Henry sets a standard of excellence. His majesty and heroic bearing, his full and vibrant use of his voice, create a kingly figure around which the others rightly whirl.

Leslie Banks' Chorus is his equal in vocal eloquence, speaking the English language with appreciation and joy. Harcourt Williams' dotering portrait of the senile King of France, Max Adrian's arrogant mincing as the wholly perfidious Dauphin, Renée Asherson's piquant Princess Katherine, Leo Genn's stalwart Constable of France, Esmond Knight's tricky Welshman, Fluellen, and Robert Newton's braggart, Pistol, are among the multitude of pleasures provided by the brilliant cast. And there are magnificent allusions and intimations in William Walton's musical score.

Within a few months after the opening of this picture in London, the war was over, but the film continued with ever-increasing popularity, a sort of phoenix of the past five bitter years. Such was the unsuspected consequence of a brilliant and brave "experiment." And the reservoir of great films was augmented by this "little touch of Harry in the night."

Hamlet
1948

DIRECTION	Sir Laurence Olivier
SCRIPT	Sir Laurence Olivier and Alan Dent
PHOTOGRAPHY	Desmond Dickinson
MUSIC	Sir William Walton
ART DIRECTION	Carmen Dillon and Roger Furse
EDITING	Helga Cranston
SOUND	John Mitchell and L. E. Overton

A Two Cities Films, Ltd., Production

CAST

Hamlet	SIR LAURENCE OLIVIER
Ophelia	JEAN SIMMONS
Claudius	BASIL SYDNEY
Gertrude	EILEEN HERLIE
Polonius	FELIX AYLMER
Horatio	NORMAN WOOLAND
Laertes	TERENCE MORGAN
Osric	PETER CUSHING
Marcellus	ANTHONY QUAYLE
Bernardo	ESMOND KNIGHT
Gravedigger	STANLEY HOLLOWAY
Francisco	JOHN LAURIE
Priest	RUSSELL THORNDYKE
First Player	HARCOURT WILLIAMS

A Prince of Shreds and Patches
MARY McCARTHY

◆◆◆

"You *liked* the Laurence Olivier *Hamlet?*" breathed a young woman the other day in a shocked undertone, when I mentioned the fact at a party. She herself had not seen the film, the news that it did not employ "the full resources of the cinema" having reached her in time. "And I hear Fortinbras has been cut," she continued, with an inquiring glance into my features, "not to mention Rosencrantz and Guildenstern. And that the Queen is too young, and the Oedipal theme over-emphasized." From these objections one could not wholly dissent. The film is indeed a photographed play, though why a photograph of a play by Shakespeare should be such an inferior article, it is hard to know—would a movie that had "liberated" itself from the text be really preferable? The other objections are more forceful. The Queen, who looks a buxom thirty-five, *is* too well preserved: if the gravedigger's memory does not betray him, Hamlet himself is thirty, middle age to an Elizabethan, a fact, however, which Shakespeare himself seems unmindful of, moved as he is by the poignancy of Hamlet's youth, his blighted studies, and unseasonable death. In the openly erotic scenes between mother and son, the film is all too cinematic— what can the Court be thinking, the audience asks itself; why does no one appear to notice these scandalous goings-on? The omission of Rosencrantz and Guildenstern no one greatly complains of, but Fortinbras is a different thing. He is as necessary to the play as Hotspur to the first *Henry Fourth*. Insofar as *Hamlet* is a study of different kinds of young men, he, Hamlet, and Horatio make a triad of *virtus*, as Osric, Rosencrantz, and Guildenstern make a triad of puerility. The play's frame, moreover, is *the soldier's music and the rites of war;* beginning with an armed watch, it ends on a peal of ordnance. Horatio is unfitted to sound the martial note. Military funerals are not in his line; he is the perennial student, like Raskolnikov's friend, Razu-

From Sights and Spectacles by Mary McCarthy (*New York: Farrar, Straus & Giroux, Inc., 1956*), *pp. 141–45. Copyright* © *1949, 1956 by Mary McCarthy. Reprinted by permission of Farrar, Straus & Giroux, Inc., and William Heinemann, Ltd.*

mikhin, the honest pedant, a little Germanized, the uncouth and good-hearted intellectual. And it is characteristic of the Shakespearean irony and tenderness that peace should descend on the play to the sound of drum and bugle: the simplicities of war, the rules of the field are order and blessed tranquillity when set against the drama of blood and perfidy that has played itself out in the castle. To Fortinbras, the outsider, the man who happens to be passing, the heap of corpses in the hall is a prodigious and unnatural sight. Clean up this mess, he commands, and, touched by something in the dead young prince's aspect, remarks that he might have made a fine soldier, too bad he never had the chance. Without this tonic fresh presence, the dead march at the finale is merely a pageant of woe.

There are other times when the Olivier *Hamlet* is perhaps oversumptuous with the décor of feeling, too interpretive, heavy on the pathos and light on the ethos, as in the bedroom scene, the To be or not to be speech, the drowning of Ophelia, and, above all, in those taffeta glances slid by the camera over the marriage couch. Yet the temptation to the picturesque, the scenic, is in the text itself. There is no tragedy of Shakespeare in which so much play is made with hand-props: Enter Hamlet reading, Hamlet writing in his tables, Hamlet with the mirror, Hamlet with the recorder, Hamlet with the skull. Hamlet's appearances in the play are a succession of pictorial attitudes, as though the glass of fashion were reflecting what was being worn heraldically that year by the model Renaissance man. Reading the uncut *Hamlet,* one cannot fail to be struck by the efficiency with which the hero is put through his paces. Not the least baffling aspect of Hamlet's character is that it often appears to be a mere congeries of "parts": the soliloquies themselves, so disturbing to the line of the action, seem half displays of virtuosity, just as if they had been inserted to show off to best advantage the powers of the principal actor. And the great anomaly, Hamlet's madness, is the actor's supreme opportunity.

What might be called the Mannerist style in which the hero is presented, moreover, is not the only example of a kind of showmanship and professionalism in this otherwise Orestean tragedy. The play is a veritable county fair of attractions. There are the two recitations, Hamlet's and the First Player's, the Dumb Show, the Play, a Danish March, flourish upon flourish of kettledrums, sound of cannon, Fortinbras' army on the Plain of Denmark, Ophelia's flower-strewn mad scenes, the Ghost—a profusion of stage-effects, a mime-show of marvels. In a sense *nothing* happens in *Hamlet* because everything happens on the same level of interest and thus, so to speak, simultaneously. What is seen is a series of pictures, vivid, brief, isolated. Hamlet, his mother, Claudius are so many shivered fragments. "A king of shreds and patches," Hamlet says of Claudius in a line that has been omitted from the Olivier version. He might also have been speaking of himself or of the play which he gives his name to. Hypocrisy, broken faith, play-acting, imposture are the characterological norm of reeling Elsinore. The fissure between *is* and *seems* cracks the world open. *Hamlet* is enigmatic because it is completely histrionic—everybody is playing a part.

This peculiar jerkiness, both in Hamlet's character and in the play as a whole, may be explained by the assumption, put forward by one scholar, that the play is a hasty composite of several earlier lost *Hamlets* pieced together so haphazardly that the discordances were never noticed. The text may have been improvised to serve the needs of an acting company or it may express some interior derangement on the part of the author or, very likely, both. In any case, this unsteadiness, which is the most striking feature of *Hamlet,* is the thing which most acted versions begin by trying to eliminate, either by "interpretation" or by a kind of glaze imparted to the diction that makes it (a) inaudible and (b) all of a piece. Sir Laurence Olivier's is the only *Hamlet* which seizes this inconsecutiveness and makes of it an image of suffering, of the failure to feel steadily, to be able to compose a continuous pattern, which is the most harrowing experience of man. Hamlet, a puzzle to himself, is seen by Olivier as a boy, whose immaturity is both his grace and his frailty. The uncertainty as to what is real, the disgust, the impulsiveness, the arbitrary shifts of mood, the recklessness, the high spirits, all incomprehensible in those middle-aged, speechifying Hamlets to whom our stage is habituated, here become suddenly irradiated. The play appears to be not so much a drama but a kind of initiation ceremony, barbaric like all such rituals, in which the novice is killed.

 Already, in his first scene, Hamlet is grieving for the death of his father, but woodenly, uncomprehendingly, bitterly, as a child grieves who refuses to countenance that such things can happen in the world. The Ghost's appearance is to him almost an adventure. He rushes down from his interview full of jokes and wildness; his boredom is gone—at last he has something to do. But the Ghost's commission is not really quixotic. The enterprise loses its zest with Hamlet's recognition that it is an actual man he must kill, his uncle, whom he knows very well, a sleazy piece of the old, tedious reality. Bored, sullen, and angry, he diverts himself by tormenting Ophelia, whom he suspects of being One of Them. He baits her father, pretends to be mad, and then promptly sloughs his ennui when the players come, gives them a lecture on acting in the patronizing tone that comes easily to precocious, gifted young dilettantes, loses interest shortly, and sends them off for the night. Thoughts of suicide engage him; he wishes himself dead. Meanwhile, a marvelous plan has occurred to him; he will trap his uncle with the play. He draws Horatio into the game, but before the play is over, he has ceased to care about the result. Repelled by the sight of his uncle praying, he lets pass his opportunity and instead makes a row with his mother, kills Polonius and two minutes later has forgotten about *him* in the interests of a new idea—to get his mother to promise not to go to his uncle's bed. At this point, the forces of reality—middle-age, and cunning—themselves take charge of the action, and Hamlet, who has provoked them, is done for.

Whether or not this is the authentic creature of Shakespeare's imagination, it is impossible to say. Behind the gesture and the impulse is there a Hamlet at all? That is the question which in Olivier's unique performance is kept open and aching, like a wound.

From School in Wittenberg
PETER ALEXANDER

❖❖

How far the return to Shakespeare, to the whole Shakespeare, and to nothing but Shakespeare has gone today may be studied conveniently and usefully in Sir Laurence Olivier's film version of *Hamlet*. The convenience lies in our having in the film, since most of us have seen it for ourselves, a common reference point; the utility in this that the production was designed for performance before a larger and more mixed audience than any hitherto envisaged by a producer. By considering the film we might expect to discover what the producer reckoned was the highest common factor, if we can talk of such a thing in the artistic sphere, that he could count on in the various groups that would contribute to its success or failure in the cinema. As the film also happens to illustrate some of the difficulties that will always confront a producer of this play, and no less the relation between the scholarship of a period and its stage production, I propose to comment at some length on the film and refer only briefly to parallel stage productions.

I am not, I may remind you, interested at present in the question

From Hamlet Father and Son *by Peter Alexander (Oxford: Clarendon Press, 1955), pp. 17–23. Reprinted by permission of the Clarendon Press, Oxford.*

whether it was a good or a successful film. It was judged by those who should know it to be both good and successful; and I must say I think that its banning by the Bulgarian Government after a brief but popular run is a testimony to something vital in its appeal that those who would impose an ideology on humanity find disturbing. I am to consider the film only in so far as it professes to offer us an interpretation of Shakespeare, and I try to discount all those features that arise from the play's translation into a medium so different from that for which it was written. I omit all consideration of the propriety of filming Shakespeare; it is enough for me that Shakespeare has been filmed and will be filmed, and that the film we are now to consider may suggest some questions of interpretation that are perhaps worth pondering.

Looking at the film as a help to estimating a common factor in the attitude to Shakespeare today over a wide range of audiences, you will admit, if you remember what has happened in the past, that the result is not discouraging. It is true that *Hamlet* has the power to appeal to all levels of understanding—from that of those who find their thrill in the Ghost or the fencing match to that of those who can see it all of a piece. Perhaps Mr. Alan Dent, in replying to some criticisms of his arrangement of the text, was not justified in arguing that to please 20 million cinema-goers he had to offend some 2,000 Shakespearian experts, unless he felt that in the two thousand there would be no judicious opinion that should outweigh whole cinemas of others; for he might have trusted more than he did to Shakespeare's power especially in *Hamlet* to please all even on the screen of today as on the boards of yesterday.

The film for all its merits yet shows in places the operation of forces that in earlier times made for distortion: the two apparently opposite tensions, the popular and the scholarly, can still be seen each pulling its own way. Let me begin then with a scene in which the producer deliberately as it were turns his back on Shakespeare to solicit popular applause; from there I shall pass to some difficult but crucial places in the management of the action where scholarly and popular opinion may be at cross purposes, and finally come to examine the influence that scholarship has shed over the basic conception of the production.

For the treatment of the nunnery scene in the film I can find no reasonable excuse, since I cannot see that there was anything here, either of time, or of circumstance, to prevent the film's following Shakespeare.

The exchanges between Hamlet and Ophelia that constitute the nunnery scene are prefaced by Hamlet's words, half spoken to himself, on his seeing Ophelia:

Nymph, in thy orisons be all my sins remembered.

The words suggest a very different attitude to her from that displayed
a few moments earlier by her father and the King as they dispose of
her like a bait in a trap; and it is the immediate and emphatic contrast to their purely selfish use of the girl provided by Hamlet's words
that satisfies me that we must reject any suggestion that Hamlet has
overheard in an earlier scene the little plot proposed by Polonius.
Hamlet's words are somewhat out of the ordinary, as critics have
noted, but this is surely because Hamlet sees her for the moment as
something apart from the rottenness infecting the Denmark of his
musings. Ophelia provides the epilogue to the scene—like Hamlet's
prologue a confession drawn from the speaker in the surprise of the
moment—

> O, what a noble mind is here o'erthrown!

Between these two as it were *sotto voce* passages—the inmost ponder-
ings of their respective souls—lie the harsh exchanges, showing to begin with a certain constraint, and passing, as Hamlet gradually discovers the parts the King and Polonius are playing in the scene, into
the unrestrained invective and threats for which Hamlet no longer
hesitates to make Ophelia the vehicle. If you examine Shakespeare's
text at this point, you will, I think, agree that in Shakespeare's presentation of the scene Ophelia is silenced but not overwhelmed by the
torrent of the Prince's denunciation; for, like most women, when men
let themselves rage against conduct that does not square with their
masculine ideas, Ophelia thinks Hamlet is mad.

> O, heavenly powers, restore him!
> O help him, you sweet heavens!

are her well meant but to the recipient of these kindnesses, I fear,
maddening reactions. When at last the Prince gives it up and storms
out Ophelia expresses her feeling in lines in keeping with her earlier
impression, for she now dwells on the pity of Hamlet's condition.
True, she is sorry not only for Hamlet but for herself, as she had
very proper hopes of being his wife. To see so promising a *parti* going
to the bad would doubtless distress any nice girl; Ophelia's reactions
are in the situation as natural as they are humane and becoming.

In the film the episode is managed very differently. As Hamlet de-
parts, Ophelia, instead of speaking Shakespeare's words about

> The glass of fashion and the mould of form,
> The observed of all observers,

instead of translating the fury and invective of the Prince into the music of her own loving comment, without a word, casts herself down on the pavement writhing and howling horribly.

All else apart, this seems to show a sad misunderstanding of the character of Ophelia. Had relief from the pressure of grief and love come so easily to her and found its vent in such simple physical form her reason would not have suffered as it did. By itself, however, the film's treatment of the episode seems unjustifiable, although the device of casting oneself on the floor seems to have been in fashion about the time the film was in the making. This bit of business figured in a stage version of about the same date, but in the scene where Ophelia is distracted. Here too the action seemed uncalled for, though it was not substituted for an important part of the text. Yet in whatever manner Ophelia is played in that scene, the actress should have in mind the words of Laertes:

> Thought and affliction, passion, hell itself,
> She turns to favour and to prettiness.

Such tumblings may be very well in Shaw's *Apple Cart*, where persons and policies are prone to such upsets, but favour and prettiness are not the words we should apply to them.

Macbeth
1948

DIRECTION AND SCRIPT	Orson Welles
PHOTOGRAPHY	John L. Russell
MUSIC	Jacques Ibert
ART DIRECTION	Fred Ritter
COSTUMES	Orson Welles, Fred Ritter, and Adele Palmer
EDITING	Louis Lindsay
SOUND	John Stransky, Jr., and Garry Harris

A Republic Pictures, Mercury Films, Production

CAST

Macbeth	ORSON WELLES
Lady Macbeth	JEANETTE NOLAN
Macduff	DAN O'HERLIHY
Malcolm	RODDY McDOWALL
Banquo	EDGAR BARRIER
Duncan	ERSKINE SANFORD
Lennox	KEENE CURTIS
Ross	JOHN DIERKES
Lady Macduff	PEGGY WEBBER
Siward	LIONEL BRAHAM
Seyton	GEORGE CHIRELLO
Three Witches	LURENE TUTTLE, BRAINERD DUFFIELD, AND CHARLES LEDERER
First Murderer	BRAINERD DUFFIELD
Second Murderer	WILLIAM ALLAND
Priest	ALAN NAPIER
Doctor	MORGAN FARLEY
Fleance	JERRY FARBER
Young Siward	ARCHIE HEUGLEY
Porter	GUS SCHILLING

MACBETH, or the Magical Depths
CLAUDE BEYLIE

◈◈◈

"Since Aeschylus's *Orestes*," wrote A. W. Schlegel apropos of Shakespeare's *Macbeth*, "tragic poetry has produced nothing more grand nor more terrifying." To express *Macbeth*'s violence and formidable energies, what better aural and visual vehicle than a spectacle filled with splendor and barbaric poetry, much like the "theater of cruelty" formerly envisioned by Antonin Artaud? To conduct that march toward hell, both funereal and triumphant, what guide more enlightened than an orchestral conductor holding in his hand, not a baton, but a flaming torch? To give all of the majesty and doleful dignity to the most terrifying Shakespearian fantasms, what decor more hallucinatory, what setting more effective, what style more appropriate, than that of the resounding cinematic adaptation of Orson Welles?

Macbeth is a sanguinary madman, a modern Attila who hears only his own demons and is vanquished by them: he appears, then, on the screen dressed in animal skins or bound in a strange harness redolent of both the paleolithic and the atomic eras—a cuirass reinforced with metal plates that look like hideous blisters, a steel helmet guarded by nightmarish electrodes, horns or antennas. He perspires agony and the fear of death from every pore of what human skin remains. His palace is carved into the rock itself, bored full of shapeless windows like the lair of a cyclops. We are transported with him into "the very bowels of the earth," [1] or perhaps onto some other planet. Since the play is, on the other hand, an image of life itself, "a tale/ Told by an idiot, full of sound and fury,/ Signifying nothing," we experience an orgy of unrealistic images, of demented, low-angle shots, of fantastic lighting suddenly illuminating a landscape as black as a sea of pitch.

Some have protested against what they have termed a "falsification"

From Études Cinématographiques *24–25 (1963): 86–89. Reprinted by permission of* Études Cinématographiques. *Translated by Charles W. Eckert.*

[1] André S. Labarthe, *Cahiers du Cinéma*, No. 117.

of the thought of Shakespeare—although seldom has it seemed more
true, more modern, more *incarnated*. The film has been called "melodramatic," although this might be the highest praise to give it, if it is
true that Shakespeare "never wrote a pure tragedy but rather melo-
dramas that have the stature of tragedy." [2] One critic spoke of the
"gesticulations and howls of an orangutan, crowned with a biscuit-
box and imprisoned in a cardboard Zoo of Vincennes." [3] What in-
comprehension in the face of a decor veritably "telluric," almost sub-
human, a decor that is essentially the pathetic reflection of the consciousness, or rather of the subconscious, of the hero—benighted,
lacerated, cut off from reality—damned. This "prehistoric universe"
to use a phrase employed by André Bazin, implies a predilection for
a total stylization—a game played at the edge of bad taste no doubt—
which only a "re-creator" of the stature of Welles could permit himself. But the wager, as no one now would contest, has been won—and
with what sovereign mastery!

It is not surprising, moreover, that the strict admirers of Shakespeare,
those who dissect him with intelligence but avoid letting themselves
enter that whirlpool arising from the depths, those who follow their
scrupulous (and a bit encumbering) knowledge of the text but not
that primordial enthusiasm that leads one to a kind of fervent *identification*: a Gide, a Salacrou, a Laurence Olivier, for example—it is
not surprising that they have not liked a *Macbeth* so shocking to their
"academic" conceptions. I think it more interesting to report the less
well-known views of an *auteur* of films that are, aesthetically, antipodal
to Orson Welles's; I am speaking of Robert Bresson. On leaving the
film at its showing in France in 1948 he confided to a reporter seeking
his reaction, "I am too fond of real settings and natural light not to
admire the false lights and the cardboard sets of *Macbeth*." [4] We can
go farther: artifice, raised to this degree, unites with the highest form
of realism. *Macbeth* is great art precisely because Welles refuses the
mediocre compromises habitual in attempts at realism (principally in
matters of decor, but also in a certain theatricality in the gestures of
the actors). Can anyone doubt this? Realism is not the surest road to
the real; on the contrary, the royal way is perhaps that of unreality,
of delirium, of the baroque. In any case, Shakespeare cannot gain
from the most literal of transcriptions, those that piously respect each
and every inflection of his text. It is better to begin aggressively, to
invest the text with a vital impulse rather than scholarly compunc-
tions, whatever one's means for production (and certainly Welles's

[2] Orson Welles, *Cahiers du Cinéma*, No. 87.
[3] *Lettres Françaises*, No. 319.
[4] *Le Figaro*, 12 November, 1948.

were, at the time, quite rudimentary—necessity dictated this). And, above all, rather than treasonously seeking cinematic equivalents, what had to be done—and was done—was quite simply to *exaggerate the theatricality.*

Othello is similar in conception, with the sole difference that a kind of sculptural magnificence (the palace of Mogador) is substituted for the *trompe-l'oeil* effects of *Macbeth.* But it is quite obvious that the internal dramatics of the two works necessitated this. On the one hand we have a frenetic world, surging with activity, *rupestral* if I may use the word; on the other hand the subtle refinements of the Italian renaissance: solemnity following upon primitive terror. But aside from this, one readily recognizes, here and there, the same inspiration, the same intuitive and inspired strokes of genius.

Of what help would the trappings of realism be in this domain? Just as the Elizabethan stage director symbolized a forest with a tree bearing a placard, the cinema director with his means at hand—bric-a-brac, cardboard, certain special illusionary techniques—effortlessly discovers the secret substance of literary works, makes them shine forth, and endows them, in our eyes, with his more flamboyant lustre. In like manner the cinema director, instead of being surpassed by his source, forces it to the wall, daring to "materialize," as Guy Dumur notes, "the most cruel, the most audacious metaphors, by carrying them to an absolute extreme." [5] Compared with the *grisaille* of other Shakespearean adaptations for the screen, or even with certain theatrical *mise-en-scènes* (Barrault, for instance, but excepting the remarkable *Macbeth* of Jean Vilar at the T. N. P.), with Orson Welles we are in truth carried to Olympian heights, onto the burning cone of a volcano in full eruption.

And yet, wasn't this the only conceivable landscape? And isn't it remarkable that for this vertiginous ascent the most rudimentary cinematic devices (an hallucinated face, sweating rocks, a few erect spears) sufficed as a springboard? Isn't it best to employ a cosmic vision when one finds oneself torn between Heaven and Earth, between the enchantment of the depths and that of the constellations? Through this means Orson Welles and his *Macbeth* are linked to some of the greats: Rossellini (*Stromboli*), Murnau (*Faust*), Mizoguchi (*Sansho the Bailiff*). And Welles thereby demonstrates, if there is need of it, that realistic art, whether consciously attempting to or not, cannot give birth to a cosmogony.

"Life's but a walking shadow; a poor player,/ That struts and frets his hour upon the stage. . . ." (*Macbeth,* V.v. 25–26). The cinema is only, then, the shadow of a shadow, projected upon the wall of a cave, the ragged garments of a clown ludicrously agitated before the

light of a projector. Given this, *Macbeth*, in the version of Orson
Welles, must be considered one of the most beautiful films ever
created, in that it illustrates, with maximum rigor and simplicity,
this definition (in no way restrictive) of our art. I would venture
to say that, at the least, we know of few films in the history of cinema
which have come so close to what Shakespeare calls "life's fitful fever."

Othello
1951

DIRECTION	Orson Welles
SCRIPT	Orson Welles and Jean Sacha
PHOTOGRAPHY	Anchise Brizzi, George Fanto, Obadan Troania, Roberto Fusi, and G. Araldo
MUSIC	Francesco Lavagnino and Alberto Barberi
ART DIRECTION	Alexander Trauner and Luigi Schiaccianoce
COSTUMES	Maria de Matteis
EDITING	Jean Sacha, Renzo Lucidi, and John Shepridge

A Mogador Films Production

CAST

Othello	ORSON WELLES
Desdemona	SUZANNE CLOUTIER
Iago	MICHEÁL MACLIAMMÓIR
Cassio	MICHAEL LAWRENCE
Emilia	FAY COMPTON
Brabantio	HILTON EDWARDS
Roderigo	ROBERT COOTE
Lodovico	NICHOLAS BRUCE
Montano	JEAN DAVIS
Bianca	DORIS DOWLING

A Review of OTHELLO
ANDRÉ BAZIN

If one must be for or against *Othello,* I am for it. Doniol Valcroze and I were the only ones of this opinion upon emerging from the showing where Welles received both kudos and catcalls. Consequently, I feel free to say that I would not have awarded him the Grand Prix; it is appropriate neither to his failings nor to his strengths. The Special Award of the Jury would have been more appropriate. But I fear that Welles is forever destined to be misunderstood. After the insult in Venice the year *Macbeth* was shown, here we have a jury at Cannes, impressed beyond reason, awarding him the Grand Prix. One can see why they did so, and that this excess of honor is not occasioned by what is best in *Othello.* The same Jury would certainly not have so crowned *Macbeth.* The laurels seemed to be awarded for what was most academic in the audacities of *Othello*—for its Eisensteinian qualities, for instance. But I am putting myself in the place of the members of the Jury who may have liked the film for better reasons, had they been able to resist the enthusiasm shown by those who were discovering Orson Welles's genius *through* Shakespeare.

However that may be, Grand Prix or no, *Othello* seems to me an entrancing work. Before everything else, one must recognize a major achievement of Welles's adaptation: despite certain foolish liberties, it is profoundly faithful to Shakespeare's dramatic poetry. I can think of no other director in the world who could cut so much out of the original written text and replace it with visual spectacle without inviting ridicule. It is absurd to speculate about what Shakespeare himself would have used in place of the written word if he had made films instead of writing tragedies; but one may wonder if Welles's solution is not at least one of the possible answers to this theoretical question. I am convinced that it is, and that it is no small achievement. From this point of view a comparison with *Hamlet* is very damaging to

From Cahiers du Cinéma, *no. 13 (June 1952): 18–19. Copyright ©
1952 by Les Éditions de l'Étoile. Reprinted by permission of Grove
Press and Les Éditions de l'Étoile. Translated by Charles W. Eckert.*

Laurence Olivier. His production was one possible framework for the Shakespeare text, but it could in no way replace that text (it is true that in this respect the production of *Henry V* was far superior).

Having acknowledged such a fundamental asset, one feels more free to mete out both praise and blame. Since I do not want to anticipate the review of Welles's film which I shall presently be writing, I shall limit my remarks here to *Othello*'s greatest strength and its most obvious weakness, as I see them.

Here again I find confirmation of the idea that the problem of adapting theater to the cinema resides not in the choice of actors but in the conception of the decor. The theater stage is a closed centripetal universe spiraling toward its own center, like a seashell. The movie screen is a centrifugal surface, a photographer's mask set up before the limitless universe of nature. The language of the theater is designed to resound within a closed space; in a natural setting it dissolves and disperses irretrievably. In passing from the stage to the screen a play must find a new theatrical locale which will satisfy the two contradictory qualities inherent in cinematographic and theatrical space. In this Welles succeeds brilliantly by re-creating a completely dramatic architecture, but one which is almost solely composed of natural elements taken from Venice and the castle at Mogador. Through the use of montage and unusual camera angles (which effectively prevent the mind from reassembling in space the disparate elements of the set), Welles invents an imaginary architecture adorned with all the salient features, all of the predetermined as well as the unexpected beauties, that only real architecture—natural stone that has been worked by centuries of wind and sun—can possess. *Othello* unfolds, then, in the open sky, but not in nature. These walls, these vaults and corridors echo, reflect and multiply, like so many mirrors, the eloquence of the tragedy.

However, I cannot wholeheartedly praise Welles's editing, for it seems extremely fragmented, shattered like a mirror relentlessly struck with a hammer. Carried to such a degree, this stylistic idiosyncrasy becomes a tiresome device.

But my greatest disappointment is in Welles's own interpretation, which, I admit, sometimes lapses into exhibitionism of the sort which lacks that kind of enormous, cunning naïveté that made the closeups in *Macbeth* something quite different and remarkable.

Still, if there ever was a film that bears a second viewing, it is certainly this one. We shall be talking more about it at some future date.

From PUT MONEY IN THY PURSE
MICHÉAL MacLIAMMÓIR

◆◆

Michéal MacLiammóir was first contacted and offered the role of Iago in Orson Welles's projected Othello *on January 27, 1949. From that date to March 7, 1950, MacLiammóir kept a diary in which he chronicled the hectic casting and producing of* Othello, *the shooting of the film in a number of locales, and the off-camera life of the cast and technicians. The principal members of the company referred to in the following excerpts are: Hilton (Hilton Edwards, who played Brabantio); Rita (Rita Ribolla, Welles's secretary); Bob (Robert Coote, who played Roderigo); Fay (Fay Compton, who played Emilia); and Schnucks (Suzanne Cloutier, who played Desdemona).*

On February 7, 1949, MacLiammóir flew to Paris to meet Welles, whom he found "exactly as he used to be, perhaps larger and more, as it were, tropically Byzantine still. . . ." *After a day of meeting others of the company, his audition began.*

We did some scenes to-day, "First I must tell thee this" and some others; O. sitting with a script in his hand against a window past which rain fell in slanting sheets, and self alternately sitting and pacing up and down past log fire. Overhead some workmen hammered fitfully at something or other. Not relaxed at all. O., however, enthusiastic at intervals that grew shorter and proclaimed loudly that he would now not hear of my making test, as he knew definitely already that Iago and I were just made for each other, and waxed so prophetic of triumph that my mind, grown suspicious through long years spent, however brokenly, in native land, thought this was probably tactful if roundabout way of getting me back to Dublin. Contract, however, immediately discussed in detail, and small army of business men summoned for cocktails and duly warned I was to be treated with care. . . .

From Put Money in Thy Purse *by Michéal MacLiammóir (London: Methuen & Co., Ltd. 1952). Reprinted by permission of Methuen & Co., Ltd.*

Subsequently, Welles assured MacLiammóir that the film would be completed by August at the latest and expanded upon his conception of the costumes they would use.

FEBRUARY 11TH

All is to be Carpaccio, says Orson, lumbering round the room and waving his arms about. (Why do directors always walk about rooms? Is this their only way of getting exercise, or do they expect, on principle of African witch doctor, to find solution hidden somewhere in the furniture? Hilton also has this distracting habit, but he pounds up and down and O. floats, though lumberingly, round and round.) Carpaccio; which means hair falling wispishly to shoulders, small round hats of plummy red felt (though film not to be in colour), very short belted jackets, undershirt pulled in puffs through apertures in sleeves laced with ribbons and leather thongs, long hose, and laced boots. Females also laced, bunched, puffed, slashed, and ribboned and with rather calculating curly hair-do; they won't like any of this if I know them, but like true actresses will, I am convinced, endeavour to look as unlike period as possible and brilliantly succeed.

Shooting, they think, will be in Rome, Venice, and Nice; this will be pleasant, I imagine, though a more adventurous nature might hanker after regions less familiar, but I'm feeling battered and am content with people and places I know. . . .

From February 12 to March 6, Welles continued to search for a Desdemona, an Emilia, and a Roderigo (the latter role successfully filled by Robert Coote). After a brief return to his home in Dublin, MacLiammóir joined Welles in Paris.

MARCH 7TH

Orson, dressed in what appeared to be white serge pyjamas and felt boots, gave me heart-warming welcome in the olive-green suite, and executed superb dance to accompanying song composed by himself at the age of fourteen which goes:

> Everyone loves the fellow who is smiling
> He brightens the day and lightens the way for you—
> He's always making other people happy
> Looking rosy when you're feeling awful blue. . . .

Then changed to dark suit and vanished to conference with financiers. I lunched with Rita and Dr. Giorgio Pappi, the Italian *direttore di produzione,* who has the air of a rosy-cheeked and very startled *stag* and is friendly. . . .

Later. Dinner presided over by Orson (very excitable) in hotel dining-room (also green and gold, but olive gives place to jade). Table set about with young ladies, English, American and French, all of them seemingly convinced they were going to play Desdemona. Orson, rolling his almond eyes hypnotically round the table, explained, in English, his ideas about Cassio, of whom he has a poor opinion, pointing out snobbish attitude to Iago and insufferable treatment of poor Bianca.

"And a nice girl too," he said, "a nice, good girl: now you *know* she was good," and he rolled his eyes more than ever, so all the young ladies hastily assumed expression of Tarts with Golden Hearts in case the quest for Desdemona might prove in vain.

Iago, he went on to say (had heard him on this on last visit and was in agreement), was in his opinion impotent; this secret malady was, in fact, to be the keystone of the actor's approach. Realised, as the talk grew more serious, that I was more in agreement than ever, but felt no necessity to assume appropriate expression so just sat there looking pleasant. (Sudden hideous thought: maybe pleasant, slightly doped expression, habitual with me during meals, *is* the appropriate one for suggestion of impotence and this is why O., who has watched me consume several meals, thinks me so made for the part? Must remember to sound him on this and prove him mistaken.)

"Impotent," he roared in (surely somewhat forced) rich bass baritone, "that's why he hates life so much—they always do," continued he (voice by this time way down in boots). He then gobbled up some sturgeon, ordered some more, and went on to talk about the costumes, which are to be made in Rome.

MARCH 9TH

Rehearsals continue in earnest: we live plunged in atmosphere of violence and alternate settings of Venice and Cyprus in heyday of Carpaccio. Find myself almost entirely in agreement with O.'s ideas of our characters: no single trace of the Mephistophelean Iago is to be used: no conscious villainy; a common man, clever as a waggon-load of monkeys, his thought never on the present moment but always on the move after the move after next: a business man dealing in destruction with neatness, method, and a proper pleasure in his work: the honest honest Iago reputation is accepted because it has become almost the truth.

. . . "And out of her own goodness make the net that shall enmesh them all": to be spoken simply, happily, and logically. One must feel as the cat does with the mouse: think of Rachel—what to her is evil about killing a mouse? And Cyprus is full of mice.

Later. Did bits of jealousy scene all the evening. Careful that this smooth logic doesn't make for monotony. I know Hilton might be afraid of this. O. doesn't seem to think so. Any tendency to passion, even the expression of the onlooker's delight at the spectacle of disaster, makes for open villainy and must be crushed. He must say to Roderigo in discussing the disposal of Cassio, "Why, by making him incapable of his place . . ." Roderigo looks bland, and Iago continues with a pleasant smile as though explaining to a child why it should brush its teeth, "Knocking out his brains."

Monotony may perhaps be avoided by remembering the underlying sickness of the mind, the immemorial hatred of life, the secret isolation of impotence under the soldier's muscles, the flabby solitude gnawing at the groins, the eye's untiring calculation. I like Orson's design for the growing dependence of Othello on Iago's presence, the merging of the two men into one murderous image like a pattern of loving shadows welded. He is speaking many of the lines, especially those in the Emilia cross-examination and in the "What, to kiss in public?" scenes, with a queer breathless rapidity: this treatment, with his great bulk and power, gives an extraordinary feeling of loss, of withering, diminishing, crumbling, toppling over, of a vanishing equilibrium; quite wonderful. Only thing that depresses me is the camera's inability—or unwillingness—to cope with the great organ-stop speeches, the "Othello's occupation's gone" one, for example, which he delivers so far with caution as if afraid of shattering the sound-track. I feel at this apparently inevitable hush-hush and tactful dealing with the matter a return of all my old conviction that Shakespeare, had he written for the screen, would have done his work differently; this feeling accompanied by a longing to see Orson himself, or Gielgud, or Hilton, or any other fine speaker of verse stand up on an honest wooden stage and let us have the stuff from the wild lungs and in the manner intended. This I know Orson tried at various moments in his film *Macbeth* and people didn't like it, a verdict possibly shared by the camera, so there maybe is the answer.

With myself this doesn't apply so much, as he is, for perfectly sound movie reasons, cutting all Iago's explanatory soliloquies and most of the rest is quiet, colloquial, and credible even to the twentieth-century public. . . .

Between March 10 and May 21, while the quest for a Desdemona continued, Welles flew to London in search of financial backing and sent MacLiammóir to Rome for costume fittings. After a considerable wait, MacLiammóir was told to fly to Morocco on the 20th.

Marrakesh. May 21st

Mogador. That is chief and, to me, staggering news item. We are to make *Othello* in Mogador, not Rome at all. Or Nice. Or Paris. Or Venice. Just Mogador. That's the latest.

Mogador: not the Parisian theatre noted for musical shows of the kind known as *light*, but a small town on the west coast of Morocco. No hotel, says Rita, lapping up her rice; der Orson will probably take a villa (the difficulty of that may be the sanitation) where you will all be one happy family. (This Family is disinfected throughout with Jeyes' Fluid). Mogador has a fortress built by the Portuguese (God forgive them) in sixteenth century. Quite perfect, says Rita, but she believes that there is little else. Just a few rocks, some hills—no, not mountains, quite little hills—a palm or two, and possibly an Arab quarter. (Quarter of What, pray, if there's nothing but rocks and a fortress?) There may possibly be, she continues, a funny little *inn* where we can eat kouskous *à l'arabe* and perhaps some fish, and even tea with mint. The sea of course will be *herrlich*, but being also *Atlantisch* it will be far too cold to bathe. Even in Summer. Also, she adds, still lapping her rice, the weather is windy and *foggy*. This too comes from the Atlantic, whose waves dash up over the Portuguese fortress all day and all night, and they cause this fog, which will give, she continues, now waving her spoon at me and looking suddenly deeply unattractive, this impression of mystery, of strangeness, this texture, this *Stimmung, was?*, so coveted by der Velles. . . .

Between May 22 and June 9, numerous complications arose, forcing MacLiammóir to return to Paris and Rome. But finally he was told to come to Mogador where shooting would definitely begin.

Mogador. June 9th

Lee joined me as I unpacked, looking, in spite of his sufferings at Ouarzazate, plump, and, as he was just in the middle of dinner, full of garlic and scandal, strikingly dressed in a yellow sweater and black silk Moorish trousers embroidered in white. After five minutes of sensational news (only half grasped by me as I flung shirts and socks into a tallboy whose drawers either stuck or collapsed as I pulled and pushed them out and in) he escorted me to large stone dining-room on first floor of Beau Rivage next door where, from far end of long table bristling with steaming dishes and bottles of wine, Orson rose thunderously from hordes of tumultuous diners and swept towards me waving his napkin like a flag and crying, "Welcome, welcome, dearest Micheál!" then, folding me in bear-like embrace, stopped dead suddenly to say "Hey! what have you been doing? You've put on about six pounds. God dammit, I engaged you to play Iago and here you come Waddling In To Do It!"

Loyal cries of "he hasn't, he hasn't" from Betsy and the others failed to reassure me, as I remembered the risottos and fettucini consumed at Villa Bottai as well as numerous fell delicacies of highly fattening nature enjoyed so heedlessly with Hilton in Paris. Orson was right, and I dined on eggs, fish, and raw tomatoes in chastened mood. Dinner, however, on orgiastic conversation level in five languages, and the rest of the evening passed by Orson and me visiting (in English and by moonlight) peerless fifteenth-century Portuguese fortress and citadel, with long ramparts over the sea and ancient harbour walls. He has discovered a complete Island of Cyprus with towers, bastions, bells, dungeons, battlements, and green bronze cannons, pointing out, not to the Mediterranean (and what member of the public would know or care about that?) but the Atlantic, frothing and surging over the black rocky coast above which the town lies scattered out like an early Picasso in sharp greenish-white cubes.

Pacing up and down under the moon, I learned of his endless difficulties about money, Italian wardrobe, and cost of labour: everything as I see it is against him before he starts, but his courage, like everything else about him, imagination, egotism, generosity, ruthlessness, forbearance, impatience, sensitivity, grossness and vision, is magnificently out of proportion. His position at the moment is grotesque in its lack of stability and even likelihood, but he will win through and all at the end will fall into his hands, the bright-winged old gorilla.

June 10th

Rehearsal from nine this morning: scene of Iago tempting Cassio to drink. All is far more detailed and down to brass tacks than in Paris: Orson even more Pre-Raphaelite than Hilton in unbelievably inventive detail. Dexterity (not my strongest point) in great demand for business of pouring wine into two goblets from goatskin held by elderly Arab and cheating him over payment while saying, "Here is a brace of gallants that would fain have a measure to the health of black Othello." Complications of this outrivalled in afternoon's rehearsal with Bob Coote (who says he didn't sleep a wink, old boy, owing to infernal shrieking of Arabs below his window).

JUNE 12TH

Finally it is made clear that while my clothes for Iago *may be* in a fit condition to wear in a few days' time, no such hopes are entertained by local tailor about Othello's, Roderigo's, or Cassio's. Orson in despair as sequences for the arrival at Cyprus with which he wanted to start shooting all include, inevitably, these people.

But this is where the winged gorilla is entitled to respect as well as to that jocular interest he can so easily inspire in the ignorant and impressionable public, always more attracted by the glittering bauble in the crown than by the gold of the crown itself. He has decided to open fire with the camera on the attempt on Cassio's life and on the subsequent murder of Roderigo by Iago, and as these incidents usually take place, as the script suggests, in a street, and as this would necessitate clothes for Cassio and Roderigo (no less than their arrival at quayside), he has emerged from a sleepless night with the idea of making the murder happen in a *steam-bath*, with M. and B., God help them, stripped and draped and turbaned in towels. This, as well as dealing with the clothes question until it can be settled, effective and sinister twist of the bloody business of Act Five Scene One with which he is opening.

Roderigo, draped in towels, discovered lying on small straw divan in a rest room after the bath and playing with ears of lapdog (not yet discovered) as he says to Iago (fully clothed and peering playfully round doorway) "Every day thou doffest me with some device, Iago." Action then proceeds through comedy scene of Iago's instructions about the murder of Cassio to series of shots in crooked stone passages and wash-rooms hung with dripping towels and full of vague shapes of bathers and of negro masseurs carrying jars of oil and vats of boiling water through clouds of vapour. Bob (in *négligé*) and me in leather tunic) plotting and peering through ominous gratings and barred windows at Cassio being massaged while I hiss "It makes us or it mars us, think of that"; and we come right down to Roderigo, having made his abortive attempt on Cassio and been himself imprisoned under slatted floor, crying "O damned Iago! O inhuman dog!" During this Iago stabs him through the slats with his sword in the manner of fish-catching in tropical waters, the vapour growing denser as he does it (mercifully for audience, and luckily for myself as my aim none too good; God, let me say it again, help poor Bob!).

JUNE 16TH

Rehearsals still in progress: tailor, by this time, wearing soured expression and afflicted by what seems St. Vitus's Dance, still at work on my costume. Result of this continuous energy is strikingly simple and Relentlessly Unbecoming Effect, but Orson pleased and says daily, "*Now* it's beginning to look like Carpaccio: what I cannot tolerate is that Forest of Arden look. And I don't care how much you desire it, dearest Micheál, because you're not going to get it."

Telegrams arriving daily from Hilton; he hopes to arrive round about the 21st. Had Cassandra-like premonition last night that he had met with some frightful fate: this apparently unfounded as wire again arrived this morning, but cannot rid myself of uneasiness. Premonition was during dinner, not sleep.

JUNE 19TH

Shooting began at 7:30 this morning. Made my début as a voice off (hope this does not turn out to be a prophecy of my film future) saying "It makes us or it mars us, think of that." Bob, draped in towels, did a lot of stuff with a dagger as he wound his way in and out of the labyrinthine ways of the Vapour Bath. This followed by several close-ups, as my tall laced boots, of purest Carpaccio inspiration, not yet finished. Owing to story told by Waschinsky of Pola Negri's first efforts in English on arrival in Hollywood, the close-up, with all its joys and terrors, now known to us all as "One Big Head of Pola."

Orson the soul of patience, and I have an uneasy feeling that, like a tactful dentist with a drill, he is starting me off with a deceptively light and gentle treatment. Made about seven takes, each one from three to fifteen times over.

Find what I have long suspected: (*a*) that one's first job is to forget every single lesson one ever learned on the stage: all projection of the personality, build-up of a speech, and sustaining for more than a few seconds of an emotion are not only unnecessary but superfluous, and (*b*) that the ability to express oneself just *below* the rate of normal behaviour is a primal necessity, especially where Big Heads of Pola are concerned. One single sudden move of eyebrows, mouth or nostrils and all is registered as a grotesque exaggeration. One can feel this as one does it without the humiliation of seeing the result on the screen, which Orson wouldn't allow in any case even if there were a screen to see it on: none of us are to be allowed to witness the showing of the rushes, his theory being that to do so makes one self-conscious. (It would probably make me sick as well, so I raise no protest.)

Such taboos on the favourite activities of the mummer, the dressing up of his personality and the projection of this to the furthest reaches of the cheaper seats, points to what seems an almost conscious trades-union instinct on the part of the camera, whose business it is to perform both these functions. At the same time one discovers that, far from finding one has nothing to do, one is confronted with a complete and bewildering set of new and rigorously negative tasks, the first of which is the stripping from the bones of all the tricks learned in the theatre as if they were rags until nothing is left to one but the naked and shivering ego. . . .

From June 20 to July 7, the company worked ceaselessly but produced few final takes. MacLiammóir found little time to record more than his impression that they were creating nothing but "snippets" and that a movie set, as opposed to a theater stage, was a "meticulous inferno."

JULY 7TH

Fantastic day on the beach at the western side of the town, where we play the scene where Othello (concealed) miraculously misses hearing Iago saying to Cassio "Now if this suit lay in Bianca's power how quickly should you speed" but hears distinctly Cassio's reply, "Alas poor rogue, I think i' faith she loves me," and all the misleading and Desdemona-damning talk that follows, when Bianca joins them from a solitary hike (in long distance) among the rocks. This scene, made so far in three takes, carried on in blazing sunlight in the fangs of smart N.W. gale with the waves leaping mountain high at our feet over stony strand utilised by Arab population as fishing ground and public toilet. So several scouts employed in chasing them away from both these pastimes. Precisely the same uses for this wild and lovely spot are found by multitudes of seagulls, who were at once pressed into service by Orson, boxes of fish being sent for to tempt them to become actors. Obvious results: between the takes the air was thick with white fluttering wings: every time we were ready to shoot they had mysteriously vanished. Morning passed in congealed condition (instead of customary boiling process) and with Orson in dungarees (as takes of the listening Othello are to be made at a later date) jumping up and down on the wall and waving clenched fists in the air as he yelled "Take 13, oh lucky thirteen, come on, Fish, Goddammit! Action! Hey, cut! *Cut!* Can't you hear me, Greaseballs? Look at the silly pronks, all flying away out of the shot! Hey! Come

back, you great big overfed Jezebels—hey! Here they come again!
Action! Fish! Quick, tell those Arab cretins, someone, quick! Action!
Hey! *Fish, Goddammit!*" . . .

*Again, unceasing work for nine days, centering upon the jealousy
scene, with little time for diary-keeping.*

JULY 16TH

Spent all day on ferocious rendering of that portion of the jealousy
scene in which Othello says "Villain, be sure thou prove my love a
whore." Orson, beautifully dressed up and painted a dark chocolate-
brown by Santoli and Vasco, paced to and fro for hours thinking it
all out on the edge of the farthest watch tower, among a thicket of
cannons and anxious shivering technicians, black rocks and leaping
waves below, and a tempest howling overhead. Finally, with warnings
frantically hissed and shrieked at us by everyone, we assume stout
leather belts to which ropes are attached and, held fast by Marc,
Pierrot, and other members of the French crew (the Arabs being
considered too emotional for the job), hang at right angles from the
battlements in order to play the scene, camera at dizzy levels convey-
ing sense of terror and (not wholly unfounded) feeling of physical
danger (thank God for not endowing me with more than rudimentary
height complex). This occupied the morning hours. During lunch
the wind freshened and we passed the time from two to six-thirty
clinging to large cannon on still windier Promontory doing the "I
lay with Cassio lately" speeches culminating with "And sighed and
kissed and then cried 'Curse fate which gave thee to the Moor!'" These
lines, which I have always visualised played quietly into Othello's
ear in atmosphere of sultry stillness with flies hovering in the breathless air (probably because Hilton produced it that way and always
begged me to imagine the flies), these lines, I say, were shouted by
me across some twenty feet of battlemented area at Orson sitting joy-
lessly on the edge of the wall, his burnous flapping up every now and
then to extinguish him completely as the Gale rose higher and higher
in manner worthy of *Lear, Wuthering Heights,* or what you will. As
neither of us could hear the other speak and as we were both continually engaged in pulling portions of our clothes out of our mouths
whither the wild winds had tossed them, intimate and rather spicy
information proffered by Iago was difficult. Finally gave it up and
came home in despair and frustration. He's going to try it another
way when the wind drops a little, but when will that be? . . .

*Work continued through the rest of July with time off for ex-
pansive cast parties and a renewal of the search for a Desdemona. On*

1. Orson Welles as Falstaff in *Chimes at Midnight,* directed by Welles (1966).

2. Welles in *Macbeth,* also directed by himself (1948). Reprinted by permission of IVY FILM/16.

3. Sir Lawrence Olivier (as Hamlet) and Jean Simmons (as Ophelia) in Olivier's 1948 version of *Hamlet*. Reprinted by permission of the Walter Reade Organization.

4. Olivier, shown here with Felix Aylmer as Canterbury, also starred in and directed *Henry V* (1944). Reprinted by permission of the Walter Reade Organization.

5. *Richard III* (1955) with Sir Laurence Olivier and Norman Wooland, directed by Olivier.

6. Micheál MacLiammóir (Iago) and Orson Welles (Othello) in *Othello* (1948), also directed by Welles. Reprinted by permission of United Artists Corporation.

7. Susan Shentall and Laurence Harvey in *Romeo and Juliet* (1954), directed by Renato Castellani. Reprinted by permission of the Walter Reade Organization.

8. A silent version of *Romeo and Juliet* (1916), directed by J. Gordon Edwards, starred Harry Hillyard and Theda Bara.

9. Asta Neilsen as Hamlet in a 1920 version directed by Svend Gade and Heinz Schall.

10. Emil Jannings starred in a German production of *Othello*, directed by Dmitri Bukhovetski (1922).

11. *A Midsummer Night's Dream* (1935) with Victor Jory as Oberon, directed by Max Reinhardt and William Dieterle. Reprinted by permission of UA Sixteen.

12. Joseph Mankiewicz directed the 1953 version of *Julius Caesar* with Louis Calhern as Caesar and James Mason as Brutus. Copyright © 1953 by Metro-Goldwyn-Mayer, Inc. Reprinted by permission of Metro-Goldwyn-Mayer, Inc.

13. Richard Burton (Petruchio), Cyril Cusack (Grumio) and Elizabeth Taylor (Katherina) in *The Taming of the Shrew* (1966), directed by Franco Zeffirelli. Reprinted by permission of Columbia Pictures.

14. A 1955 Russian version of *Othello,* directed by Sergei Yut-kovich, starred Sergei Bondarchuk.

15. Innokenti Smoktunovski (Hamlet) and V. Kopakor (Grave-digger) in *Hamlet* (1964) , directed by Grigori Kozintzev.

August 3 MacLiammóir was back in Paris, uncertain of Welles's whereabouts.

Julien D. rang this morning and made appointment for us to meet at the Dôme. Great excitement, as he brought with him prospective Desdemona. And there is little doubt that Orson's eyes will soon cease to be bloodshot. French-Canadian; experience: French tours and two French films; bi-lingual, a lingering echo of Canada in her English here and there, but voice warm, flexible and soft; her face a Bellini with large grey eyes that bestow lingering and slightly *reproachful* glances, perfect nose and mouth, chin a little too broadly modelled, age just twenty, figure good; a gentle dignity is her authentic hallmark; name Suzanne Cloutier. Manner rather *fin de siècle,* the childish, vague intensity of Mélissande; but Hilton and I agree that this is the merest article of clothing and as easily discarded as the mackintosh she incongruously wore (rain has ceased), and feel sure that somewhere in her There is Steel. Interesting; I smell Ham, Character, Individuality, and above all Indestructible Will, and prophesy that Orson will have trouble with her (as she no doubt with him), but that somehow a Desdemona will emerge. . . .

Suzanne Cloutier proved to be the "right" Desdemona, but Welles was now absorbed in a new search—this time for sufficient finances to continue shooting. Then, unexpectedly, in Venice, an encounter.

AUGUST 8TH

Met Dearest Orson wandering like a thunder-cloud in indigo overalls among the streets behind the Frezzaria. All three of us deeply moved, and he swept us off to lunch at Harry's Bar. Lunch highly succulent. The best paella I have eaten outside Seville and superb and unknown (to us) white wine; must get the name. All chalked up. O. said wasn't it terrible having no money, and we agreed, but it doesn't really make much difference, we'll doubtless have some soon. O. also said why didn't we go and live with him in Torcello? Quiet, fresh, and beautiful with orchards and green fields all round and a perfect country hotel under same management as Harry's Bar, also motor launch to carry one to and fro. Couldn't understand that we enjoyed Venice so much we didn't want to leave it. But in the best form I've seen him since early days at Mogador, and says he hopes we'll be starting work in a day or two. Then invited us to see Suzanne Cloutier's test for Desdemona, to be shown somewhere at dead of night. . . .

But shooting did not begin "in a day or two." MacLiammóir and other cast members languished in Venice for over two weeks before

work was resumed, first at the Grand Canal and then at the Doge's
Palace.

AUGUST 27TH

Location now moved from Grand Canal to Doge's Palace; its magnificence blotched by our yards of cable, standard lamps, boxes, and
baskets overflowing with senators' robes, wigs, hats, shoes, tights,
doublets, and jewelled chains: the extras fight like wild cats as to who
shall wear the grandest. Wardrobe mistresses in despair; all of them
chatter and scream like magpies; Orson is right: Italy is an aviary.
But what a gorgeous aviary, and what gorgeous birds, flapping and
trilling and shaking their wings in their setting of marble and gold
and mosaic under the dazzling violet-coloured sky. We pace up and
down through bars of light and shadow under the colonnades of the
great balcony among the bronze busts of doges, senators, architects,
musicians and poets, and look down, when we are not in action, across
the Piazzetta over the Schiavone and eastward to Salute on one side,
and on the other we watch the Piazza San Marco. Crowds of people
stroll about or sit in the shade outside the cafés, the jangle of string
orchestras play Scarlatti, Irving Berlin, Franz Lehar, Puccini (we'll
have to do a lot of dubbing at some future date, I can see *that* coming),
the pigeons trot about or flap affectedly into the air when the gun
goes off or anyone says "Bo!" to them, the newspaper boys thread
their way through the ranks of yellow chairs collecting cigarette butts.

AUGUST 28TH

Morning passed successfully with scrappy shots between Bob and
me rushing madly up and down sumptuous interior staircase in
Doge's Palace with crowd of senators on our way to listen in to Midnight
Council. We were joined by Joseph Cotten, who's here on a holiday
and walked on as a senator, thus satisfying Orson's superstitious be-
liefs about Joseph C. figuring somehow or other in every picture he
makes and ensuring its good luck. Charming and friendly and accompanied by Joan Fontaine, who appeared as a page-boy.
    This evening a nightmare; Orson as cranky as a dromedary, and
the sun setting much too quickly. Bob Coote, whose face wore that
patient, over-boiled expression that comes from frantic internal com-
bustion, worked away with me at the corner of the balcony on speech
about following Othello "To serve my turn upon him." This was
shot after three halves of a rehearsal which never reached end of
speech, so naturally imagined (was it, on second thoughts is it ever,

natural to imagine things in movie work? Anyway, I'll never do it again) that a cut would come after "In following him I follow but myself," which was as far as rehearsal had ever taken us. Orson in such panic before we shot at all that entire cast and staff, Hilton included, became infected with his mood, lost their heads and yelled at Bob and me, particularly me. Panic spread. I started off; Orson, eyes visibly suffusing with blood, darted rapid glances between sinking sun and my face, expression changing from supplication (for sun) to blank yet pregnant loathing (for me). So I fluffed in the first take and did it again. Got through so nicely with second take that I stopped dead on "follow but myself" and said, beaming with pleasure, "There! was *that* better?," to receive storm of unleashed abuse: I should have finished right down to "I am not what I am."

Mortified, but obviously nothing to do but take it again, and by this time the sun had sunk too low. (Didn't seem too low to me, but confess I am no judge of heights or depths.) So more pandemonium broke forth and Orson bade us all good night and marched away with Trauner. Called my dresser to my side with as much *hauteur* as I could, pulled trousers and coat over Iago clothes, and walked back to the hotel seething. Dined in garden with Fay and Hilton, joined later by Bob, and finally by Orson looking like a dropsical black Panther. Brooding silence followed as he sat down with us and began to devour several lobsters. Then began to abuse Bob. Then me. Then storm broke out. Then we cried and made it up, but only after he'd told me that any other director would have Thrown me into the Canal. (This feasible, but directors not noted for logic, good behaviour, or sense of justice, especially when engaged in racing with sunsets.) Then we both said it was *our* fault. His fault, no my fault, no *his* fault. Nearly rowed again about this but not quite. Now I have to go through it all again to-morrow. Oh, St. Anthony, St. Christopher, St. Michael, and St. Genensius, pray for me.

AUGUST 29TH

Wild orgy of work all over Venice resulted to-night in almost leaving things too late again for setting sun, but I got the long speech, after careful rehearsal, in two takes. Orson jumped up and down and kissed, first me, and then everybody else, on both cheeks and gave complete version (Major Key with Actions) of

Everyone loves the fellow who is smiling.

With the conclusion of work in Venice, the company proceeded to Torcello for a few locale shots and then to Rome for extended studio work.

SEPTEMBER 16TH

Scene of reception to Lodovico devised by Orson as sumptuous
spectacle in pavilion of silks and tapestries: Nicholas looking magnificent. Have worked on this sequence for two days; it leads through
a jungle of cuts, countershots, and general complications to (*a*) a
climax of "Goats and monkeys" and (*b*) to Othello's striking Desdemona across the face. This planned by Orson with hierarchic backgrounds of banquet tables and crowds of distinguished guests, Othello
out of camera but long shot of Desdemona slowly approaching camera
for the lines:

Des. Trust me, I am glad on't.
Oth. (*out of camera*). Indeed!
Des. My Lord?
Oth. (*still out of camera*). I am glad to see you mad.
Des. Why, sweet Othello!
Oth. (*still out*). Devil!

Des. by this time is in Big Head of Pola; black hand of Othello
suddenly strikes her across the face. Cut.

Poor old Schnucks did it countless times, moving beautifully (unlike me, hmph!) towards the camera, but once Big Head of Pola
obtained could not prevent herself flinching before black hand of
Othello appeared, thus ruining the shot. Her lovely face went slowly
numb under this treatment and its constant repetitions, her make-up
repaired and repaired again by Vasco. Hours wore by, we all wilted.
Unfortunate joke on somebody's part that it must be time for lunch
was sternly unheeded. Schnucks did it again. Flinched. Again.
Flinched. And again and again. And at last Orson, his face (un-
made-up) now pale green and hanging in festoons, his hand in its
Renaissance sleeve blacker than ever, said "O.K., Schnucks, you can't
do it. So here's what's going to happen. You just do it once more
and I'm not going to strike you, see, we're going to cut on your line
on your last "Why, sweet Othello!" and we'll take the blow in the
face in another shot and we'll make that to-morrow when you feel
fresh. So here we go, last time; we cut at 'Why, sweet Othello!' and
Remember: *Everyone loves the Fellow who is smiling* . . ."

So off we went again, and Schnucks, reassured and radiant, sailed
into her close-up, no sign of a flinch, and got the best puck in the
face you ever saw and "Cut!" says Orson, and it was all over. "Perfect.
Thank you, Schnucks."

Followed a short silence while Schnucks wiped the salt and smarting tears away, and then deprived us of our breaths by saying very sweetly, "Of course I'm very grateful, Mr. Orson, it was the only way to make me do it, but of course I *did* know all the time you were going to hit me: I guess I'm psychic."

Orson is right and so am I and so are we all; she is everything we accuse her of being, but above all else she is Indestructible. . . .

Then came "a new hitch," unexplained by Welles, but apparently financial and very serious. Hilton Edwards envisioned "doing Othello *for ever," and MacLiammóir mused that they might all develop, in many of the shots, "a sudden and unaccountable maturity, and in my own case, if things continued much longer, the definite stamp of a ripe old Age." Trips to Paris and Dublin occupied a three-week interim.*

DUBLIN. OCTOBER 12TH

Have noticed a not unnatural tendency in Dublin to say "When are we going to see this *Othello*?" or "Isn't that picture finished Yet?" or "Why are you being so Long about it?" and find it impossible to answer these questions except by saying "Well, Orson is continually having to raise some more money, and when he has got what he wants in Italy we're going back there to finish it, but God knows when you'll see it because even the Moroccan sequences aren't done with yet and sooner or later we'll have to go back to Mogador and get down to it, and when we've finished with Italy and Morocco there'll be some dubbing to do in London, and then the music, and then the cutting, and by the time that's done there'll probably be another war and you'll never see it at all."

My God! wouldn't it be ghastly if that were true? Seven months of work and travel without end amen, and nothing to show for it but a lot of rubber stamp-marks in a passport. . . .

On October 17 MacLiammóir was ordered back to Rome where an orgy of work ensued, with side trips to Tuscania and Viterbo for locale shots. During this period the whole company worked at an exhausting pitch, endlessly reshooting scenes until they could not be improved. MacLiammóir found the "energy of both H. and O. quite overwhelming, and capacity for cigars and red wine nothing short of scandalous." He predicted that Welles would collapse if he didn't curb himself, then on October 29 found his prediction realized.

Stout Party No. 1, I mean Orson, has had partial collapse and warned by doctor not to smoke any more, as heart anything but satisfactory. (Red wine not mentioned, but coffee taboo.) I nobly resisted saying, not I told you so, but I told my diary so. Poor O. very dejected, and sinister rumour afloat that a rest of three weeks has been indicated. . . .

ROME. OCTOBER 30TH

Lightning-like and inexplicable decision last night to abandon Viterbo for Rome caused panic-stricken conversation at very late dinner. All methods for the unravelling of problems called into use through metres of spaghetti, from elementary Sherlock Holmes methods to elaborate psychoanalysis of the already absent Orson, who had wisely driven away from us all to Eternal City in full Othello make-up having finished shots of the settling of Schnuck's hash in round church at Viterbo. Schnucks again advanced theory of his Deep, Deep Restlessness of Soul; this scornfully discarded by other members of company, and cynical suggestion made that (a) he was fed up with country life and cooking and with so much running in and out of dazzling metropolis, and (b) that picture had really Collapsed and that Rome was a better centre in which to disperse us all than small country town. Hilton and I, during these impassioned scenes that took the form (and indeed the sound) of a satanic litany, preserved dignified silence as befitted our years, and all were ready this morning at eleven-thirty. . . .

By November 3 Welles and the company were back in Venice, shooting in the Piazza San Marco, the Doge's Palace, and the Ca' d'Oro. Then came another of Welles's departures and a long and inexplicable delay. Between November 20 and December 6, Mac-Lammóir found himself ordered to Marseilles, Paris, Mogador, and again to Paris, where he found Welles filled with plans for a six-weeks' theatrical tour that would raise money for completing Othello. After an enthusiastic discussion, the plan was abandoned as impractical, and MacLiammóir returned to Dublin. Then, on January 20, he was ordered back to Mogador. But Welles was again mysteriously delayed. On January 29 he turned up "looking well but eyes blood-shot." Two days later shooting finally began again.

Find that acting, even for films, is better than not acting at all.
Resumed work on portions of jealousy and epileptic scenes not completed in the summer:

> Marry patience,
> Or shall I say you're all in spleen
> And nothing of a man.

This simple snippet soon rendered inconceivably complicated by Orson, shamelessly aided and abetted by Hilton, who shares passion for Steps and the acrobatic twists and turns they demand. Me in steel greaves too, as legs visible to camera. Shooting was carried out in teeth of gale on flight of malodorous steps by the harbour and took up most of the morning, with addition of counter shots and close-ups of same sequence. The whole place haunted by ghosts of Doris (Bianca) Dowling, Bob (Roderigo) Coote and most of all by Michael (Cassio) Laurence, and by memories of merry laughing sequence between self and Cassio last July with background of unresponsive seagulls and Orson shouting "Fish, Goddammit!" to bevy of shrieking Arabs. . . .

Work proceeded with a proficiency never before experienced, with some exceptional days.

FEBRUARY 5TH

Work has been in progress at port for last two days: link-ups with scenes shot last July and mainly concerned with reactions of Orson and self to arrival of Lodovico. This in complete absence of Nick Bruce calls for much imagination; the eyes, sweeping over the sea, reflecting momentary surprise at beholding advent of entire Venetian fleet, when all they actually see is collection of wooden sheds, decayed fishing smacks, Hilton (returned in great vigour from Mogador and accompanied by Belle of Stockholm) rushing up and down, cigar in mouth, and shouting in English to extras, Gouzy translating, between mouthfuls of sausage sandwiches, and hordes of delighted Arabs.

Before each take Orson goes through now inevitable ritual largely concerning my Carpaccio hat, never quite big enough for outsize head, and in absence of proper mirror invariably ridden up to jaunty angle suggestive neither of super-subtle Italian conspirator or of thwarted impotence. "Now let's have a look. No, your hat's terrible. I'll fix it again. *There.* Now. See if you can hit those—wait a moment, there's a speck on your nose, that's better—see if you can hit those marks. Ready? Don't forget now; momentary surprise at sight of fleet: calculated as to effect on Othello: not too long a pause—none of your hornpipes—and down the steps fast. O.K. Let's shoot. Fanto, if the camera waggles I swear to God I'll strangle you with my own hands, you argumentative Central European. *Vai? Silenzio per favore.* Shut up! Hilton, can't you keep those cretins quiet? *Partito?* 842—Take One. Action!"

Eleven shots (that include O. tripping thrice over train of burnous, camera uncontrollably bouncing as it pans round to follow us, and self falling headlong down steps) finally result in *"Stampiamo con entusiasmo"* and test, during which greaves collapse and have to be borne off to ironmongers to be mended. Then break for lunch, consumed in fierce sunlit gale now blowing in from raging Atlantic and rendering long-waited-for shot of "I lay with Cassio lately" out of question. . . .

Intensive work for over a week again limited the energy Mac-Liammóir had for keeping his diary.

FEBRUARY 15TH

O. again disappeared, this time with Belle of Stockholm, nobody can say where. Not even Schnucks, not even Gouzy. H. and I spend our time talking of future: this complicated by our having no idea of what it is likely to be for at least a year.

FEBRUARY 16TH

Work began this morning in Portugal's Answer to Poe, I mean the Cistern, for Orson has reappeared (looking as mysterious as his surroundings), and shouts directions about lighting for three hours without a single pause. Hilton, wearing immense pair of gum boots, is directing us, and splashes wildly to and fro across the dyed water as he arranges sword-fight between Renzo-Cassio, Dally-Roderigo, and Gigonzac-Montano. Involved and excessively wet work for us all, and the poor devils I have just mentioned get in for the worst of it as the business includes a lot of knocking of swords out of various hands into the water, and much punching and rolling and diving and kicking and plunging in order to regain them. Iago, wise man, contents himself with slipping cat-like behind various pillars, handing swords at odd moments to any of the gentlemen who find themselves without one, and with hissing or shouting such remarks as "Hold ho!" or "God's will, Gentlemen!" or even "Diablo ho!" to anyone within reach. This didn't save me from getting my legs soaked or the rest of myself splashed from endless repetitions of the brawl, done in series of inconceivably short shots, each one of them taking what seemed to be hours and hours, and when the bits including me were finished I changed doublet and greaves with the enthusiastic Jeff, my French double (we have separate pairs of tights and shoes), who, while I am working, sits in a Singlet regardless of the freezing temperature and watches me with fanatical impatience. So he works in all the long-distance shots, and both of us full of gratitude to Hilton, he for artistic and I for despicable reasons. Sensation of getting back into tights and shoes that are dank and stringy with the water, and into a doublet warm from Jeff's body, indescribable. The Mazagan dresser, an absent-minded adolescent of Spanish parentage with a passion for the films so great that he forgets everything I want and has to be yelled at, which causes pained expression, brings me coffee, hot towels, vapour rubs, and talcum, but nothing restores the circulation. Will probably develop rheumatic fever if this continues: the same fate doubtless in store for Dally and the others, to say nothing of the extras, of which there are scores and scores, all of them alternatively splashing and screaming all over the flooded floor and subsequently shivering in corners.

FEBRUARY 19TH

Worked for three days in the Vault but had a change to-day and did the Cage Scene down at the harbour. This Orson's invention and I've been dreading it for months. "The time, the place, the torture; O! enforce it" is to become in the film a visual fact, so into a minute and excessively uncomfortable cage I go, and am hauled up on a dangerously squeaking chain to an immense height by a tower over the sea to have my eyes plucked out by crows, yelling insults as I go. Felt much more inclined to yell "Help, help!" but refrained, and went whirling up about a dozen times, to immense delight of the Arab population who gathered in their hundreds to see the show, their favourite part of it being each descent when the cage with me in it was plumped slowly and unsteadily into the water. Faint applause every time this happened, but respectful silence on my upward flight. Profoundly unpleasant morning.

FEBRUARY 21ST

Back to the Underworld. Frightful series of scenes involving much rushing up and down of steps (in greaves) followed closely by hordes of extras, all of them apparently chosen for gruesome aspect and bird-brains and possessing inordinate passion for tripping me up, treading on my feet, and sticking swords in my backside. What the scenes were about I hadn't the faintest notion and didn't dare ask, as H. and O. both in Wagnerian rages, and in the intervals of screaming at me looked at each other with shaking heads and faint pitying smiles. So spent the day flying obediently up and down stairs brandishing a sword (am strongly convinced it was the wrong one and so is Gouzy, who assures me in panicky mixture of German, French, and English that nobody will notice), also opening and closing doors, gazing camera left with tense expression at nobody at all, turning, twisting, peering through windows, and getting myself kicked, prodded, slapped, pushed, and trodden on by extras till I was black and blue. . . .

After a short slack period, the pace of shooting increased still more, allowing time for only occasional entries.

FEBRUARY 27TH

Repetition of agonising scene with Dog-collar. Dally more solicitous and more shouted at than ever, as he incites band of torturers to drag me up the same long slope where I made the "Lechery, by this hand!" scene with Bob Coote and chased him over the tram tracks to his mark on the wall so many centuries ago. Poor Dally! his face a study of solicitous torment for fear a jerk too strong at the chain should break my neck. Meanwhile the extras behind him were tugging like mad and leaping with sadistic pleasure as they tugged, and being chased away by Micky (Turkish Delight) between the bouts of shooting. All a great success to-day, and scene added of Dally wrenching the dog-collar from my swollen and purple neck and hurling me into the cage, where I consoled myself by yelling, "If she'd been blest she never could have loved the Moor" through the bars.

Afternoon spent on the beach with my discovery of Othello's body (it was the double's) lying prone and epileptic on pile of unspeakable rocks (place as popular for toilet purposes as ever) under tearing Atlantic gale.

Jewish dinner-party to-night at house of rich merchant; we ate strange delicacies and drank strange wines and were waited on by daughters of the house, a chorus of Dazzling Salomés. Citron-yellow walls, black hair, green eyes.

MARCH 1ST

These days have acquired the fly-away pace of a musical coda—not an awfully good composer—a sort of Orpheus in the Underworld gallop to end things up. Dally's wife has arrived from Paris, a tall, quiet, comely creature who, entering the scene at its latest and most abandoned phase, stands aghast at the whirling riot of it all and doubtless wonders what it is about. Orson, Hilton, and the rest of us fly from one location to another, frequently driven by Gouzy in her bumping little car, which is now tied together with string, or else perched on a jeep among gangs of Italian technicians and followed by hooting lorries and mobs of cheering Arabs and Jews (a good half of the male population is in armour and the rest still fighting for jobs), and on arrival at the various destinations a swarming, fluttering activity begins, punctuated by Orson's voice as, mounted on a pile of boxes with Hilton at his side waving his stick and hissing into his ears various diabolical observations, he yells, "No no, not that way, Goddammit, pull that moron's helmet down! No, not down to his chin, you pronk! just over his eyes. Hey! stop waving your hands about, you in green. Hilton, look at that Great Big Piece in green. Oh my God! how did that one get here anyway? Gouzy, tell him in Siamese! Tell that great big Cissy in green to get his ass off the set. Out! Scram, Sister! Now all of you to the left, I said Left! To the Left, Goddammit! Stop that coal-black cretin holding his helmet on! Dally, stop him! Action! I said Action! Cut! Action, Goddammit!"

And all the while the sun beats down and the waves lash up and Vasco says *"Mama mia! Siamo in Africa!"* and Turkish Delight shouts *"Fouttez-moi la paix, vous autres!"* and Schnucks murmurs "I think it's my religion that gets me through, don't you think so too, Mr. Micheál?" and we whirl from quayside to ocean strand and from citadel to dungeon steps under the fish-market, and now at last the film is nearly done. It's nearly over. All that will remain in a few days' time will be the Senate scene, and that, Orson tells us, leaning back in a chair at the Club, and drinking Pernod after the day's madness is checked by the sinking of the sun, will be achieved in a little over a week's work at Perugia at some not far-off date, and will not concern me as Iago, though I am to be invited there for a ten days' Rest.

Can only conclude that if Perugia turns out as the last few days have done in Mogador it might be more restful, though admittedly less exciting, to spend the time in Assisi, or even in Dublin.

MARCH 7TH

Tricky bit of business in the pre-epileptic fit scene, at last achieved, of "Lie with her, lie on her." This taken in a long travelling-shot against a wall by the sea under a broken roof of slats and branches which cast their shadows on us as we walked and paused and walked again over most intricate network of tram-tracks, and when I stumbled on the second take Orson said "Now now, Ireland's Answer to Nijinsky, let's do it again!" So we did, and all was well this time though he insisted on a few more takes and there were seven in all, and to-day is the seventh of March, and Hilton can say what he likes but there *is* something in it, for when it was all over and the sun had gone down once more into the sea, Orson went through the usual kissing ceremony, inevitable when he has got some load off his mind or his chest or wherever he keeps his loads, and said: "Mr. MacLiammóir, I am happy to tell you you are now an out-of-work actor. You have finished Iago."

So after that we drank some champagne at the club and I felt a little sad and a little glad. Glad because it will be a good thing to get back to a week or two in Paris and make our plans for the next film, the Irish one, or the Carmilla one or whatever the hell it's going to be, and to hear of Orson's latest projects, which will probably include another world-tour or two and the squeezing of the last week's Senate scene in Perugia *en route,* and organising a festival in the Vatican if we should happen to pass through Rome. And it will be better still to get back to Ireland and the theatre and Arthur and Rachel, and the garden again, and one's own rhythm and one's own books, and all that goes to make up one's life. And it will be sad because we've emerged from another adventure, Hilton and I, and we both like adventures (within and often without reason, and this has been both). And besides, it's going to be a twisting, searing, wrenching sort of thing to say good-bye to Mogador, where, for me, the film began and ended. And most of all it's going to be sad to see them dwindle into the distance, these friends and fellow-adventurers that have remained to the last.

Already I see them in my mind's eye as if painted on a gauze, through which the back-stage lighting will presently shine, revealing other scenes and other characters, and I will feel that it has only been a painting on a gauze after all. But a very beautiful one, in the manner of a Primitive, I think, with the winged and bodiless cherub heads of Schnucks and Mary and Barbara floating in jocund fashion over a hierarchy of stalwart mail-clad figures of Venetian nobles and soldiers. And Fay with her two angels trumpeting and fiddling. And all three of them cut out in blue and gold against a background of victorious armies and bright painted ships, with the Children of Jehovah and the Children of the Prophet rampant on a field of unravelled celluloid. And then Trauner and Dally and Brizzi and dear Fanto and the rest of them standing in serried ranks, the banners of their trades a-flutter stiffly above their heads. And behind and beyond them all is Orson, mysteriously grimacing as he lolls towards them with hands outstretched, waving Godspeed from his rolling banks of cumulus and thunder-cloud, the Painted Lightning forked ambiguously behind his head.

Julius Caesar
1953

DIRECTION AND SCRIPT	Joseph L. Mankiewicz
PHOTOGRAPHY	Joseph Ruttenberg
MUSIC	Miklos Rozsa
ART DIRECTION	Cedric Gibbons and Edward Carfagno
COSTUMES	Edward Carfagno
EDITING	Herschel MacCoy and John Dunning

A Metro-Goldwyn-Mayer, Inc., Production

CAST

Brutus	JAMES MASON
Caesar	LOUIS CALHERN
Cassius	SIR JOHN GIELGUD
Antony	MARLON BRANDO
Casca	EDMOND O'BRIEN
Calpurnia	GREER GARSON
Portia	DEBORAH KERR
Flavius	MICHAEL PATE
Marullus	GEORGE MACREADY
Cicero	ALAN NAPIER
Soothsayer	RICHARD HALE

The Role of the Technical Adviser
P. M. PASINETTI

◆◆

. . . Why are experts hired? One version is that the producers want to feel "protected": that the historical allusion, the armament detail, the duelist's motion, or whatever, will bear the stamp of specialized approval. This attitude is largely fictitious, unrelated to actuality; for the producer knows very well that his historical reconstruction is not going to be exact and "scholarly" and, which is more important, that there is no reason why it should be so. A film is being made, not a contribution to a journal; the requirements are those of the film as a coherent artistic whole. Therefore also, in order to be of any use at all, the technical adviser should keep thinking that he is, in however minor, indirect, and peripheral a way, contributing to the making of a film.

I admit that my own example—a Roman play by William Shakespeare turned into a motion picture—is a singularly happy one because it offers the most glaring case of art prevailing over historical reconstruction. The moment we stop and think, if nothing else, that those ancient Romans speak English blank verse, we have a wide basis upon which to build as "unhistorical" an edifice as we may wish. This, in fact, could be sufficient artistic excuse for having Shakespeare in modern dress. But here a peculiarity of our own age is felt, of which the very existence of someone called "technical adviser" is a symptom. If ever we adopt modern dress we still do so with the feeling that we are being strange and *avant-garde;* we cannot be casual about it as, for example, Renaissance artists were about dress in the Biblical scenes they painted, or as Garrick was in the balcony scene where he looks like Casanova. The mentality of our time is different. We are under the impact of scientism and the history method.[1]

From Film Quarterly 8, no. 2 (1953): 131–38, © by The Regents of the University of California. Reprinted by permission of The Regents.

[1] Even a novel that had the qualities and intentions of *Forever Amber* was preceded by painstaking "research" in the period. We have in historical works, even more than in ordinary fiction, the phenomenon which Oscar Wilde, in his well-known dialogue by that title, denounced as the "decay of lying."

With MGM's *Julius Caesar,* although I knew that John Houseman, its producer, had staged it once in New York in a "modern" version (with an implied parallel to Fascist situations and emblems), I soon found that the motion picture was going to be in Roman dress. How historical would it have to be? In such a situation it is up to the taste and imagination of those who produce the picture to decide what the function of historical reconstruction should be and to what extent their freedom of choice should be limited. Once it is decided to have the characters look like ancient Romans, I suppose two main dangers have to be avoided: glaring anachronisms on one side and standard film "Romanism" on the other. Possibly the spectator of the film *Julius Caesar* will be so taken by the exceptional quality of the directing and the acting that he will forget about "background," general atmosphere, style, buildings, objects, props. These are the special province of art directors, costume designers, property men: of that score of individual specialists who appear so justly admirable to the layman. It is also mainly here that the technical adviser exercises whatever small functions he has. I would say that in this sense the idea which presided over the making of *Julius Caesar* was that of giving a modern man's vision of ancient Rome and of the feeling of a city alive and functioning. This was what prompted Mr. Houseman to have as "technical adviser" on the picture not an ancient historian or an archeologist but a person of Italian origin and education. The idea was that the atmosphere of Rome in 44 B.C. was closer to that of an Italian city of any period than to anything else, and that a person with such memories could perhaps be less useless than a more conventional kind of expert. One of my favorite pedagogical devices is to invite listeners to transpose the idea of time into terms of space and to imagine, lined up somewhere, about sixty or seventy people: the ones who stand elbow to elbow happen to know each other exceptionally well, usually have lived together for a good portion of their lives. Sixty or seventy is a relatively small number of people; closeness of habits and feelings can be easily assumed. Yet those few people, once we line them up in time instead of space, carry us all the way back to our ancient Roman forefathers.

Nevertheless, the feeling of surprise at finding the many-storied apartment house of Ostia or a Pompeian carpenter's hammer practically identical with the one used now by the upholsterer next door in Rome or Venice, can always be renewed with delight. This was the delight involved in working on research for *Julius Caesar,* and the basic assumptions of the research coincided with those of the producers of the film and with the idea that the city was to be imagined as a "lived-in" place. A brief sampling of introductory notes taken during that time may be appropriate:

. . . Rome was a fast-growing city, but we may assume that the general shape of its central sections had not changed from the time when it had been a small one, in the same manner as downtown Los Angeles doesn't substantially change even though important new buildings are added—especially official ones such as the Federal Building (corresponding to temples, curias, etc., in Rome's center).

The city was inhabited by, and therefore it reflected, an oligarchy of nobles-magistrates on one side, engaged in violent and often vicious struggles for power and office, and in the other by common people like the artisans in the first scene of *Julius Caesar* or like the mutable citizens whom Brutus and Antony address after the murder. . . . The aristocratic dwelling and the slum could be close to one another.

. . . Rome was also a city of narrow streets, slums, dirty little taverns, peddlars, small squares with people yelling across at each other, etc. . . . The temples, theaters, curias, and generally the places like the Forum which were the scenes of the ruling classes' disputations, intriguing, display of pomp, legal fights, and finally of the dictator's murder, must not have looked merely like the official and venerated national sanctuaries but rather like places very much frequented and lived in—like markets, federal court-houses, or stock exchanges.

Books most typically consulted in this respect were the ones that describe the city and the minutiae of its life in that period or in times immediately near. Besides ancient authors like Horace or Martial, useful modern works included those of Friedländer, Carcopino, and the more recent *Vita Romana* by Paoli. For the innumerable questions of detail that might arise, ranging from weapons to specimens of hair-do, from street vendors and shopkeepers to military salutes, there were the standard encyclopedias, Pauly-Wissowa, and, more particularly, Daremberg-Saglio. This sort of research, whatever amount of it might be used, showed one crucial difference between scholarship and film making: while the former can afford to be vague in its results, the latter cannot. However uncertain the evidence, scanty the documents, and numerous the hypotheses, the decision had to be made as to how a piece of garment would be worn, a salute would be given, and so on. Sometimes the "exactly right" detail was found: the sign upon the door of the tavern in the opening scene, for instance, is authentic though probably about eighty years wrong. Sometimes the "expert" indulges in purely Platonic satisfactions: for instance, the words scribbled on the walls in the small Roman square where the film opens were correct in type and legitimate in contents, though the camera hardly caught them. These are only scattered examples. There are problems that come up suddenly during production. "Would senators be wearing beards?" I was once asked urgently over the telephone. Instinctively I said, "No, by no means necessarily." And I started on a study of beard fashions through the Roman centuries—not very useful, but fascinating. (One item: young people would wear beards until white hairs became too numerous for the barber to be able to pluck them out. Vanity, I think, was also one reason for the usual Roman man's way of combing his hair forward: it concealed receding foreheads. Incidentally, in certain quarters in Rome it was fashionable again this year.)

Objects and properties help characterize backgrounds and people. At one point it was considered giving Cicero something that would correspond to a lorgnette. It would have been nonauthentic, but the idea was discarded mainly because the particular object seemed actually superfluous. Shops, street vendors, Forum characters were based on as much literary and archaeological evidence as it was possible to assemble (Roman shop signs in bas-relief are often good pictures of the shops themselves.) Physical authenticity of individual characters was of course not attempted, though a collection of their available portraits was made, and their ages, qualities, ranks, backgrounds were defined. Here again, we have a case where the researcher is tempted to collect material of no direct usefulness but of obviously great fascination, as in the social studies of Rome by F. R. Cowell and L. R. Taylor.

Again, the artistic truth of characters within the drama is what counts, not their relation to history—especially as far as appearance is concerned. Caesar, God knows, was shorter than Mr. Calhern and it would be difficult to find somebody looking less like Cicero than the excellent Mr. Napier. I thought the matter of accents, by the way, turned out to add to characterization: the ultranoble Brutus and Cassius are English; the tougher Antony is American; Cicero, who was provincial middle class but very refined and like Brutus and Cassius much exposed to Greek culture, is English; while Casca is American.

Any result of research is subordinated to dramatic necessities, but sometimes there is a certain happy concomitance of the two. This occurred, for instance, with Brutus' camp at Philippi. The fact that Roman camps were, as is well known, quite elaborate and solid establishments coincided with the possibility of showing that some time had elapsed since the assassination and since Brutus and Cassius' departure from Rome.

A historical piece of information, even if correct and usable at the same time, may not be exploited fully. An example of this may be the question which was raised about some sort of ceremony that would precede the battle. Something like a prayer, a religious sanction, seemed dramatically appropriate; but of the ceremony (called *lustratio*) with slaughtering of animals, etc., which Brutus and Cassius must have held, documented as it is in history and iconography, only a brief visual hint, if anything, could be given.

Dramatic opportunity may even suggest conscious incongruities in minor details. For instance, Brutus was not only a politician but also very much a thinker and reader; at some points he carries with him a book or reads in it. We know, of course, that the Roman book was a scroll (*volumen*); but what with letters and messages of practically the same shape being handled in the play, that book would have been unrecognizable, if it had been a scroll, and therefore ineffective. I suppose I am as responsible as anyone for letting Brutus' book have the appearance of, let us say, a Renaissance small edition of a classic. At least, I confess I refrained from warning anyone about that.

On the other hand, when the question of a common, recognizable emblem for Caesar and his party was raised, and the suggestion was made to use the open hand which appears on top of some of the Roman military standards, that symbol, attractive and recognizable as it might have been, was discarded. It was too special, and had too special a usage on the military *insignia*. The good, fiery, and always serviceable eagle was preferred.

Finally, and most important, there are many situations that need no scholarly consultation because a basic historical truth corresponds to the poetic truth of the text to which the motion picture has strictly adhered. Some of that may be due Shakespeare's use of Plutarch; but one is tempted to credit it also to some sort of divination, the power to interpret the historic event in its essentially human terms. The chance that these characters may look like ancient Romans depends on this rather than on the accuracy of single little items. And the drama in its quality and development will be found to correspond to actual Roman traits. I remember Mr. Mankiewicz remarking once that in directing the big speeches he had kept in mind the conventional motions and style of classic oratory. The coincidence of art and history was perfect there; for in ancient Rome oratory was cultivated as an art, and, like opera now, it had its fans. The dialogue with the crowd is part of the Roman feeling for "life as spectacle," then as now. And the most mournful spectacle, by the way, can be the most thrilling. Horace says that the noisiest affairs in Rome were the funerals. This confirms the main lesson that a technical adviser on a historical picture will, I think, draw from his experience; namely, that history ought to be consulted not in search of alibis but because its suggestions are likely to be more interesting, more usable, and more imaginative than anything we may dare invent in their place.

Romeo and Juliet
1954

DIRECTION AND SCRIPT	Renato Castellani
PHOTOGRAPHY	Robert Krasker
MUSIC	Roman Vlad
ART DIRECTION	Gastone Simonetti
COSTUMES	Leonor Fini
CHOREOGRAPHY	Medy Obolensky
EDITING	Sidney Hayers
SOUND	John S. Dennis and Gordon K. McCallum

A Verona Productions, Ltd./Universalcine Production

CAST

Romeo	LAURENCE HARVEY
Juliet	SUSAN SHENTALL
Mercutio	ALDO ZOLLO
Friar Laurence	MERVYN JOHNS
Nurse	FLORA ROBSON
Capulet	SEBASTIAN CABOT
Lady Capulet	LYDIA SHERWOOD
Montague	GIULIO GARBINETTI
Lady Montague	NIETTA ZOCCHI
Paris	NORMAN WOOLAND
Tybalt	ENZO FIERMONTE
Benvolio	BILL TRAVERS
Prince of Verona	GIOVANNI ROTA
Chorus	SIR JOHN GIELGUD

Castellani's ROMEO AND JULIET
Intention and Response
PAUL A. JORGENSEN

◆◇◆

The old lady crossed over to sit beside me in the Broadway bus. "I see by your program," she said, "that you've been there, too—wasn't it a pity about those two poor young things? I do feel so badly for them." We nodded and as I looked at her, I saw she had tears in her eyes. So had I.

This desirable response to Shakespeare's tragedy of young love was not, as one might suppose, provoked by Renato Castellani's recent motion picture. It was recorded in 1936 (in the October *Catholic World*) after a showing of MGM's film starring Leslie Howard and Norma Shearer—actors whose special distinction did not, as with Castellani's principals, lie in their power to represent "poor young things." Castellani, what is more, was professedly dedicated in his interpretation to the theme of youth struggling against a hostile society. The MGM film, with all its superior fidelity to Shakespeare's poetry, lacked Castellani's poignant concentration on the theme announced in Shakespeare's Prologue:

> From forth the fatal loins of these two foes
> A pair of star-cross'd lovers take their life;
> Whose misadventur'd piteous overthrows
> Doth with their death bury their parents' strife.

It is both sad and puzzling that major critical response to Castellani's dedicated venture has been so perversely neglectful of his emotional intent. Far from coming close to tears, critics have failed to show even the slightest recognition of the piteousness of the misadventured overthrows. Of the reviewers writing for the big weeklies and monthlies—the reviewers, that is to say, who can do the most damage—only

From Film Quarterly *10, no. 1 (Fall 1955): 1–10.* © *by The Regents of the University of California. Reprinted by permission of The Regents.*

Arthur Knight of the *Saturday Review* (December 18, 1954) seems to have been struck by the power as well as the surface beauty of the film; yet the possibility of *pity* did not occur even to him.

To almost all of the major critics the one glory, and yet also the tragic failing, of the film was its scenic brilliance. Emotional message might just as well not have existed. John McCarten of *The New Yorker* (January 1, 1955) ends his elegiac commentary on the picture with "At any rate, the scenery is certainly wonderful." Robert Hatch of *The Nation* (January 8, 1955) observes with a regretful sally, "We had come to see a play; perhaps we should not complain that we were shown a sumptuous travelogue." And he concludes, with a tenderness much like McCarten's, "This 'Romeo and Juliet' is a pretty thing." If there had been only pleasantries of this sort, and a purely facetious interment for the ill-fated venture, one might have reached the easy conclusion that the critics, having found a congenial subject for their wit, were just having a little fun at the expense of a producer notoriously willful in his artistry, or were simply registering their chronic distaste for film spectacle. But many of the reviewers land blows more earnest and solid than these; they point out just where, dramatically speaking, Castellani paid for his spectacle.

Time (December 20, 1954) declares that in his obsession with "the beautiful single frame," the director "has ignored not only the rhythm of Shakespeare's scenes but has even failed to set a rhythm when he cuts from frame to frame." Both Roy Walker of *Twentieth Century* (November, 1954) and Hatch deplore the slowing down of the action by the large, carefully photographed canvas. Walter Goodman of the *New Republic* (January 10, 1955), though inadvertently catching some of the somber poetry which Castellani surely intended in the relationship between the principals and their setting, really means to deplore the fatal effect of scenic richness upon the dramatic action:

> A five-day interlude watched by so many sad-eyed Madonnas from the dusty corners of so many old churches. A nice young English couple reciting poetry to one another while the people of Verona who spawned the tale of feud and love and murder, who seem still close to the seat of it, go about their everyday living.

The many students of Shakespeare's plays who responded favorably (but not, one fears, too confidently or audibly) to the motion picture must have sensed that the magnificent photography of scenes in Verona, Venice, and Siena provided more than a decorative background to a tragic story; that, moreover, the prolonged views of massive Romanesque architecture did not so much slow down the story as comment upon it.

It is true, as Hatch observes, that "it takes time to get around the great chambers and through the narrow, terraced streets"; but it is not true that as a result "the tragedy collapses and is swept away in a visual flood." Motion—painful, frantic motion—is an intentional and basic part of Castellani's interpretation of the play, and it derives from Shakespeare's own intentions. The dramatist had tried to express the mood of driving, futile haste in the content and pace of his poetry. The play abounds in comments upon action—especially swift action contrasted with slow—and in lines in which the lovers express their impatience with a slowly moving world. The lines are sometimes beautiful, as in Juliet's "Gallop apace, you fiery-footed steeds"; at other times, they are mere froth, as in Romeo's early exclamations. Castellani, with characteristic impartiality, cuts the good and the bad and supplies in their place the real thing: frantic running. Both young people seem to run from the beginning to the end of the play. It is a harassed, compulsive, joyless sort of haste, the urgency of something which neither understands. And it is highly relevant that the long corridors, the endless flights of stairs, should forever frustrate them. Extremely effective is Romeo's desperate, baffled running near the end of the film as he tries to reach Juliet in death. The artistic use of both the running and the background seems to imitate comparable sequences in De Sica's *Bicycle Thief,* an Italian neo-realistic film. In both productions, the opposition to the frantically running characters is not in the form of conscious villains, but rather in unwitting landscapes and streets and in the heedless movement and press of people. It is not, therefore, as Goodman asserts, a flaw in dramatic action that the people of Verona "go about their everyday living" as a backdrop to the tragedy. A more alert background of people would be as contrived as the chorus of a musical comedy.

The brilliance of the scenic background, however, does raise a special problem in that Shakespeare's play is not an intrinsically pictorial one. Its language is intense and exclamatory rather than descriptive. And the Italy which Castellani so intimately reveals had probably never been seen by Shakespeare; certainly it does not become part of the verbal texture of his Verona. But neither, one might say in defense of Castellani, does the France of *Henry V,* filmed by Robert Krasker, the cinematographer for *Romeo and Juliet;* and yet critics did not condemn the earlier film for irrelevance to Shakespeare's poetry. It must nevertheless be acknowledged that the problem of relevance in *Romeo and Juliet* is a more complicated one, and may not have been consciously enough grasped by Castellani. The dominant pattern of imagery in this play, as Caroline Spurgeon long ago ascertained, is of a brief, brilliant light (associated with the lovers) against a prevailingly dark background (associated with the hostile world). From the language of the play, one is far more aware of the stark light-darkness contrast than of intermediate colors, or of precise design of buildings, statues, and gardens. In a way, therefore, the very brilliance of Castellani's scene is not merely an irrelevance, but actually a contradiction of Shakespeare's image patterns. Where there should be lusterless gloom as a background, there is breath-taking, compellingly photographed beauty. The young lovers are thus in the very real danger of seeming less attractive than the hostile world which rejects and destroys them.

But somehow the result of this contradiction is not so unhappy as might be supposed. Though some of the poetry does inevitably become less meaningful, the background of irresponsive, age-old sculpture and architecture serves even more poignantly than darkness to set forth the isolation, the temporariness, the fatal passions of the young couple. Castellani's, at any rate, is an interpretation with which John Keats would have sympathized. Both artists make one feel the warm, hurried anguish of living love contrasted with the cold, immobile beauty of art.

In addition, Castellani makes good use of the very massiveness and inpenetrability of the architecture against which the brief, intense struggle is enacted, gaining thereby an emotional quality similar to Shakespeare's image of darkness. Huge walls and forbidding, seemingly windowless exteriors emphasize the difficulty of access from one family to another. The photographic artistry makes one feel, as even Shakespeare's poetry does not, the full significance of a forbidden entrance into the Capulet household. From the interior court one does not see, as in Shakespeare's verse, the open sky and the stars, but long corridors, staircases, arches, and the ever-present walls. Two symbolic functions of the unyielding architecture will forever remain as a part of Shakespeare's play in the minds of those who see Castellani's film. One is the effect of the heavy grille separating Romeo and Juliet during the wedding ceremony. The other is the effect achieved upon Romeo's return from Mantua when he tries (in one of Castellani's invented scenes) to gain entrance to the church of Juliet's funeral. We see his desperate figure dwarfed by the beautifully wrought but adamantly closed door of the Church of San Zeno di Maggiore. Perceptive departures such as these from Shakespeare's text can scarcely be condemned. Unlike the interpolated and rightfully damned scene of Friar John's visit to Mantua, they comment, with all the poetic resources of cinematic art, upon the pitiable separateness of the two young lovers.

Aside from his heavy reliance on photography (as opposed to verbal poetry), the feature of Castellani's willful artistry which has been most singled out for skeptical commentary by the critics is his choice of actors. Upon the young principals, Laurence Harvey and Susan Shentall, the verdict seems to be: authentically youthful and innocent, but dramatically lightweight. Harvey reads his lines "with a kind of empty fervor" and "fails to generate much glandular heat" (*Time*). He is "too light of voice" and "trivial" (Hatch). Miss Shentall plays

Juliet "at a good school level" and seems "very healthy" (Hatch). Neither of the two is "especially adept at delivering poetic lines, and whatever advantage their youth may give visually is offset by their lack of oral fervor" (McCarten). "When they come together, nothing explodes. When they kiss, only the twittering of birds" (Goodman). One is forced to acknowledge a significant agreement among these strictures. And although the judgment—on Harvey in particular— overlooks obvious merits in the interpretation, it is doubtless true that older, more accomplished actors would have given better readings of Shakespeare's poetry. (Sir John Gielgud demonstrated this truth with unintentional clarity in pronouncing the Prologue.) But Castellani was willing to subordinate the actors' command of poetry and passion to what he considered more important: their youthfulness and help-lessness. Stage experience has proved that audiences cannot expect to have the lovers both guileless and experienced; and it must at least be conceded that youthful lovers, inexpert at both self-control and lan-guage, are consonant with Castellani's dominant purpose.

Certain of the other actors are less defensible. The parts of both the Nurse and Mercutio were, in the first place, badly cut; and neither actor was competent enough to make up for the loss. In the role of the bowdlerized Nurse, Flora Robson impressed the critics as "more a nanny than Shakespeare's Rabelaisian nurse" (Hatch), as a "dear old soul" (Walker), and as a "mild cliché" (Leo Lerman, *Mademoiselle,* November, 1954). Aldo Zollo as a Mercutio *sans* both his Queen Mab speech and the chaffing of the Nurse episode brought little to the muti-lated role except a clownishly mischievous face; he was perhaps only a little too harshly recognized as "an ancestor of Chico Marx" (Walker). Castellani would doubtless have done well to make more of both these indispensable roles. Their Shakespearian vigor and coarseness, their decidedly unromantic view of love, are precisely what Castellani needed to set off more emphatically the purer natures of Romeo and Juliet. Equally important, the softening of the Nurse, and the re-sultant loss of the upbraiding scene ("Ancient damnation! O most wicked fiend!") in which Juliet rejects her as a counselor, caused a blurring of Juliet's sense of aloneness and made less intense the follow-ing potion scene, which also was cut.

But there were redeeming aspects of Castellani's casting and char-acter interpretation which almost made up for the distressing botch-ing of Mercutio and the Nurse, and which restored much of the sense of the "piteous overthrows." Above all, the interpretation of Sebastian Cabot as Capulet, though drastically wrenching some of Shakespeare's lines, was perfectly in accord with the dramatist's avowed theme. Cabot's Capulet is no amiable, doddering host at the ball, speaking well of Romeo and trying with rough good cheer to keep the peace. There is a strain and grimness beneath an Italianate smoothness (and a personal plumpness), in his reception of Romeo; and his repressing of Tybalt's anger is less pronounced than the checking of his own. Here—for the first time and contrary to Shakespeare's text—is a very intelligent reason why the marriage of Romeo and Juliet must be clandestine. Guilio Garbinetti as Montague is also, though in a less prominent way, informingly new in the role. Castellani had obviously chosen him, as he chose many another, for his face. (Garbinetti was not an actor but a Venetian gondolier.) The face—angular, gaunt, sad with ancient Italian feuds—is not only a pointed contrast to the round, blandly cruel one of Capulet; it also is sufficiently like Romeo's to suggest the bleak future awaiting this young man if he were not to be immortalized by an early death.

Castellani was justifiably interested in faces. His intuitive way of choosing them is an acknowledged part of his cinematic genius. His camera broods over these interesting faces, singly and in groups. For the stage an interpretation so dependent upon line and mobility of features would never do. Shakespeare, in fact, seldom describes a face in detail. But Castellani was translating for a different medium; and even those of us who affirm the primacy of the human voice speaking dramatic verse must confess that the Italian has caught nuances of facial expression—as in the Capulet ball or the grouping of mourners about the dead lovers—as satisfactory as words. Even when the face is not a mobile one, and Miss Shentall's is not, the cameraman has waited patiently for just the right angle or illumination or suddenly achieved expression to give it eloquence.

To say, finally, that Castellani has done more than critics have given him credit for doing, that he has, indeed, done almost precisely what he intended to do, is not necessarily to say that his *Romeo and Juliet* is an outstanding production or that it should have received more popular support than it apparently has so far done. In all likelihood, it is not so great a film as Olivier's *Henry V* or Mankiewicz's *Julius Caesar,* both of which are faithful to the text as well as the spirit of Shakespeare. But it is certainly a much better film than Orson Welles's *Macbeth* and probably a much better one than Olivier's *Hamlet,* both of which it significantly surpasses in fidelity to Shakespeare's *intentions.*

To a student of Shakespeare it is always pleasant, and usually possible, to make the pious generalization that the only successful way to do Shakespeare is to accept Shakespeare's text as well as his intentions. Mankiewicz did this with brilliant results in *Julius Caesar.* And even the MGM *Romeo and Juliet* succeeded incredibly merely by following Shakespeare with studious humility; it dumbfounded the critics (most of whom were totally unprepared for praise) and forced even the most hostile reviewers into an irritable acquiescence. But actually, when applied to Castellani's noble failure, this pious generalization proves to have a meaning no more profound than that it is safer to keep a stage play a stage play than it is to make it, entirely and profoundly, a motion picture. Castellani wanted, as none of his predecessors had wanted, a motion picture. One cannot deny that he has made one. And no one should deny that it was eminently worth doing.

That the result did not, as he had intended, impress even the sympathetic critics with the poignancy of Romeo and Juliet as lovers in a hostile world, is not mainly attributable to any defects in his translation from stage to screen. Most of the changes he made were conducive, as already noted, to a focus upon the predicament of the young couple; and, for those spectators who could silence Shakespeare's words in their mind long enough to give Castellani a fair hearing, the result was as deeply and beautifully disturbing a love tragedy as film artistry can produce. But most of the critics were not prepared to silence Shakespeare. They waited for the familiar words, and these did not come; they were surprised by climaxes which Castellani achieved not by words but by photographic short cuts; and, above all, they admired with a sense of its disastrous irrelevance the superb setting. No wonder that many people who normally would not miss a Shakespearian play conscientiously avoided this film. Critics had told them that it was "a pretty thing," but not Shakespeare; that it was a "sumptuous travelogue," a well-conducted museum tour, not a drama with a story and message.

What lesson, one wonders, will Castellani himself take from this disappointing experiment? Not, I hope, that it is aesthetically and morally wrong to translate Shakespeare. He need merely look back over seventeenth-, eighteenth-, and nineteenth-century adaptations of *Romeo and Juliet* to recognize that his own liberties with Shakespeare's text have been of the most innocent and moral kind. He is doubtless aware that former-day audiences not only tolerated but acclaimed the most preposterous changes in both the spirit and the letter of Shakespeare's text.

If Castellani submits humbly to any kind of instruction from this failure—and I trust that he will not—the lesson he should learn is a practical rather than an aesthetic one: it is no longer possible, as it had been ever since the seventeenth century, to alter Shakespeare and get away with it. Regardless of how stanch a producer's allegiance to Shakespeare's intentions, he will be judged by his allegiance to Shakespeare's text. The lesson is a hard one, but probably no more unreasonable and no more permanent than the necessity which made seventeenth-century producers supply a happy ending, or which made eighteenth-century producers awaken the lovers for a final farewell in the Capulet vault, or which made nineteenth-century producers bowdlerize the play.

Regardless of the justice of Castellani's painful lesson, it is sad to step from the sparsely filled theater into the fully populated American city streets. For almost three hours, one had come to accept as normal a quietly passionate ancient world in which every physical shape, texture, and color was incredibly beautiful; in which all faces were worthy of long and anxious scrutiny; in which there were few words, but these the quintessence of Shakespeare's poetry; and in which two young people, who seemed to belong more to the story than to stage or screen, fled through brief sequences of Shakespeare's play. So immersed in Castellani's wonderfully hybrid world, one carries out into the heedless street throngs some of the proselytizing fervor that the Italian himself had brought to the venture. Critics who carried no absorbing emotion, none of the intended pity, from the experience are surely fit for treasons, stratagems, and spoils.

In Fair Verona
ROY WALKER

❖❖

The stage should show a synthesis of speech and spectacle. Too often it has been a battlefield over which first one and then the other element has flaunted its temporary triumph. The Elizabethan stage was by no means the austere affair of bare boards and a passion that our more puritanical reformers pretend, and it affords no legitimate precedent for skeletal Shakespeare. But it was a theatre in which the spoken word was predominant, the poetry painted the picture and the actor dominated the scene. Towards the end of the last century, however, the spectacular element had so far gained the upper hand that Shakespeare's texts were slaughtered to suit the scene-shifters. The very proper reaction to this has, like most reactions, gone careering towards the opposite extreme. To hear some enthusiasts talk, and managements who need to economize on production costs are unlikely to discourage them, you might suppose that there was something immoral about sumptuous settings for Shakespeare. In fact, the only sane objective for Shakespearian producers in the twentieth century is to create a new synthesis of speech and spectacle. To do this it is necessary

From The Twentieth Century *156, no. 933 (November 1954): 464–71.*
Reprinted by permission of The Twentieth Century.

to reinterpret the second term. The nineteenth century notion that the true end of scenic art was to lend an air of verisimilitude to an otherwise bald and unconvincing narrative by a precise archæological and chronological pedantry was possible only in a time of dramatic decadence. The ultimate objective is nothing less than the visual equivalent of the dramatic poem itself. Only an artist who has had a clear vision of the values, the dominant symbols and the inner movement of a Shakespearian play can hope to create a setting for it that is not, in the last analysis, a nuisance. Even on the modern stage the technical difficulties of doing so may be virtually insuperable.

The stage's extremity is the screen's opportunity. Comparatively speaking, the camera has no visual obstacles to overcome, it need never face a producer with the choice between continuity of speech and action and the fullest variety of illustrative or interpretative scenery. What an opportunity; and at the same time, what a temptation. Every art has not only its true centre, but the bias it was born with. Drama, as the art of the spoken word, tends to look down on decor as an incidental trimming. The original mute cinema habitually regards dialogue as a mere auxiliary to photogenic action, and like the fidgety adolescent it is cannot keep still for a moment without feeling uncomfortable. If, in the popular poll, the eyes have it—and to see what ugly rubbish they will put up with rather than read or listen it is only necessary to look in on the average television play, which seems to attain the visual standards of a poor supporting film of some fifteen or twenty years ago—that is because our shallowly extroverted age seems to have no philosophy of the relative importance and right relationship of the inner and outer aspects of experience, and what is worse no real sense of it. This sense, quite as much as the particular facilities offered by various artistic media, should guide our use of verbal and visual resources in the performing arts. However much it may have surprised the sort of theorists who are really only talkative technicians, the most completely successful stage productions of Shakespeare in recent years have been those in which the visual patterns partly translated the verbal ones into their own medium. Conversely, the best Shakespearian films have not been those of Orson Welles, who at least interpreted them in what were regarded as the more cinematic terms, but those of Olivier and Mankiewicz, where the characters were allowed to pause and think aloud without having their soliloquies sliced or spoken against a background that was constantly calling attention to itself by showing itself off from different angles every other moment.

If, as I think cannot be too often repeated, the film can never compete with the stage as a medium of dramatic art, of which the essence lies in the relationship that can be established between the actor and the audience in whose actual presence he is performing, it could, in my opinion, produce more complete integrations of verbal and visual image than any stage production, though there is always the danger of overinterpretation, of providing a sort of strip-cartoon equivalent to the rising tide of footnotes on which Shakespeare's lines float uneasily in the more learned modern editions. Renato Castellani's film of *Romeo and Juliet* is, however, the modern equivalent to the Irving or Tree stage production of half a century ago. Spectacle comes first and foremost, and the text is cut and altered to fit. The formula for this film is most eloquently, though perhaps not intentionally, expressed in the omission from the programme of Shakespeare's name. We are told that *Romeo and Juliet* has been "adapted for the Screen and Directed by Renato Castellani." We are told the names of the actors and of the photographers, costumiers, recording staff and musicians. But nobody thought of mentioning the Mr. W. S. who wrote most of the dialogue, though not all of it, and whose rather wordy shooting script was pretty drastically pruned and amended. "Shakespeare's play," Castellani explained in London to a reporter, "was not real enough for the vast cinema audiences. Certain dialogue written by Shakespeare was too theatrical. I want the public to believe that Romeo and Juliet really existed." There is, of course, a pleasant irony about all this. The story that Shakespeare derived from Luigi da Porto and Matteo Bandello has simply been reclaimed as Italian property by their countryman who has made as free use of the English version as Shakespeare, and Arthur Brooke before him, did of the Italian tales.

At any rate the motto of this beautiful film might well be that of the second line of the prologue: "In fair Verona where we lay our scene." Castellani lays his scene there to such effect that fair Verona is the indubitable star of the film. That is what one remembers first and last. Not a line that is spoken, not anything the actors do, but the sheer loveliness of Verona. From the first scene, where we mingle with the crowd thronging through the high gate of the city to the market square, down the great cascades of stone steps where the factions clatter in pursuit of each other, in the majestic court of justice and the chambers and terraces of the Capulet palace, through the cool cloisters and chapels of the Franciscan friars to the great cathedral aisles and funeral vaults in which the tragedy culminates, this is the story of Verona, a symphony in stone. Costumes and colours and the art of the camera combine to people this superb setting with something of the glow and splendour of Italian Renaissance painting. The richness is so overwhelming that, after nearly two and a half hours of it, a critic may find himself echoing Macbeth's "mine eyes are made the fools o' th' other senses, or else worth all the rest." Will people really go on squinting at Shakespeare through the fish tanks of television, or sitting through the ghastly vulgarities of Hollywood Biblical epics,

after seeing this film? No doubt they will, but they will no longer be
without a standard by which to know that they are putting up with
something less than second best.

But that is to salute spectacle in its own right. There is still the
question of interpreting Shakespeare's tragedy. The illuminating comparison, I think, is with the superb scenes in colour photography in
the Russian film that gave us excerpts of the Prokofiev ballet *Romeo
and Juliet,* danced with incomparable grace by Galina Ulanova. Here
a breath-taking stage spectacle actually accelerated the swift dramatic
movement of the story. Castellani's spectacle slows it down at every
turn. More than that, he dismembers Shakespeare's scenes as he goes
along, thereby robbing them of meaning. Take the first scene of the
play, for example. The direction is: *Enter Sampson and Gregory, with
swords and bucklers.* Their skirmish is, in fact, the forerunner of the
fatal fight in which Mercutio and Tybalt are later slain. But in Castellani's film neither man is armed. Sampson is a servant carrying a basket
of logs, and with one of these he kills Abraham, of the house of
Montague. This links visually not with the death of Tybalt but with
Romeo's killing of Paris, done in the film by one blow with a huge
candlestick. And it is not a significant link, for the death of Paris is
not part of the feud and the death of Tybalt is. Nor do Benvolio and
Tybalt join in this first brawl, followed by Capulet and Montague
with their wives and parted, temporarily at least, by the intervention
of the Duke himself. Instead there is a pursuit to the Capulets' house,
where the second fight takes place, and we first see the Duke in his
own court, where he is warning Montague and Capulet against further
violence. Finally, Romeo does not enter on the very scene of the fight,
but is discovered in yet another place, the fields outside the city,
thus substituting pastoral for the ominous prelude to tragedy.

With not only the Queen Mab speech but the chaffing of the Nurse
cut, Mercutio hardly lives at all before he dies. The glimpses we do
get of him, as played by an Italian actor, suggest an ancestor of Chico
Marx. There are no masquers either to be welcomed to the Capulet
ball; Romeo gate-crashes by the side door. Rosaline is there to hand
Romeo a visor and tell him in very blank verse to "Put on the mask
and leave this place at once." Juliet, whose mother calls her away before Romeo can kiss her, returns asking rather peevishly "Where's
he gone?" and shows no apparent interest in the other departing
gentlemen. Most of the foreboding notes have disappeared from the
text, there is no glimpse of starry sky in the balcony scene, Juliet pours
out the drug from the vial into a glass as though taking medicine, and
—another dramatic balance missed—Romeo buys no poison from an
apothecary, but is content to stab himself in the tomb. On the other
hand, Castellani has expanded to an episode the misadventure of Friar
John that causes the letter to go astray. Some of these points, and it

would be possible to make as many more, are not alterations made in
the interests of spectacle, and I am afraid they therefore show that
the adapter's failure to grasp the pattern of the tragedy goes deeper.
Some of his inventions are, however, excellent. A massive iron grille
separates Romeo and Juliet as the Friar marries them, a visible symbol
of the barrier between their loves. And Juliet's wedding dress is hung
on a basket-work lay figure which somehow looks like a hollow mock-
ery, a sinister forewarning of the young bride dead and shrunken to
a skeleton.

Not much acting has been called for, and not much supplied. The
camera is almost a substitute for it, so rich are the visual impressions.
Repose, certain angles of the head and occasional pleasure or agitation
are almost all that the director seems to have required of his players.
When one recalls John Barrymore's crazy delivery of the Queen Mab
lines, in the American film of *Romeo and Juliet* twenty years ago,
and the superly sharp speech that matched the skilled swordsmanship
of Basil Rathbone's Tybalt—I am interested to see from a recent book
that these are the performances that remain fresh in Paul Dehn's
memory too—one realizes how much is missing from Castellani's film.
To be sure there is Sir John Gielgud to speak the prologue. Unfortunately nothing in the subsequent film comes anywhere near that
masterly miniature. Susan Shentall speaks Juliet sensibly and sensi-
tively, but her voice is breathy and apparently limited in range. Among
other cuts she loses her denunciation of the Nurse—Pandar's indubitable predecessor—"Ancient damnation!" No one could say that of Flora
Robson's Nurse, anyway, who is a dear old soul. So is Mervyn Johns's
Friar Laurence, what with starting lines three times over, having a
little Latin back-chat with the brothers and keeping a pet rabbit.
Norman Wooland plays Paris as though he were still playing Horatio
in Olivier's film, and that is about all except for Sebastian Cabot's
Capulet, an inflated Philip Harben. There is still Romeo to be considered, or what Mercutio called (though not in this version) Romeo
without a roe. Laurence Harvey is not exactly fishified, but he never
suggests a grand passion. Indeed both lovers fail to generate the creative ecstasy that, even in death, brings together the sundered families.
This is traditionally suggested by allowing the dead lovers to lie one
across the other in what is half an embrace. In the film they both die
on the floor and are neatly laid out side by side in the cathedral when
the reconciliation of their fathers takes place. No wonder nobody says
anything about putting up solid gold statues to them. Even Oscars
would scarcely be deserved.

The limitations of Mr. Harvey's Romeo have been underlined by
his stage performance of the same part at Stratford this year. He
quite simply failed to fill it. It is time the Old Vic dropped its emer-
gency measure of giving leading roles to film stars because they have

the largest following; and perhaps the failure of Laurence Harvey's Romeo will warn the Stratford Governors in time. The real and very considerable virtues of the Stratford *Romeo and Juliet* lay mainly in the production rather than the acting. So do the real qualities of Castellani's film. But in the significant use of spectacle Glen Byam Shaw with much more limited visual resources makes rings round the Italian. He employs a single permanent setting with slight variations for such scenes as the bedroom and the tomb. This structure in light wood drew various sallies from the critics. It was like a bathing pool in the Home Counties, they said, it was the utility furniture centre of Renaissance Italy. That it embodied any particular conception of the action of the tragedy was not suggested in any of the notices that came my way. Yet unless I am very much mistaken there was such an idea, not just about the stage mechanics, but of the pattern of the play. It could be argued that if the idea did not get over, it was a failure. But many things affect the experience of an audience of which they are not conscious. A spectator, other than a very observant professional critic or an electrician, who noted every lighting change in a production would almost certainly not be living in the performance as, fortunately, it is possible for most of us to do most of the time.

The Stratford setting consisted of two-storey buildings, one at either side of the stage and set well back. These were made to suggest the "two houses" whose factions immediately swarmed on to the stage from either side. The Prince made an effective central entrance to part them—temporarily at least. But, of course, the real problem is not to part the Montagues and the Capulets, but to bring them together. The setting hinted how this might be done. For over the heads of the fighting and quarrelling men the gulf between the houses *was* bridged by a curved balcony supported on light pillars so that there was a clear view of the sky above and below the balcony. This, to labour the point, was the level of love, where humanity was already in heaven. The problem that was insoluble on the lower level of violence did not exist on the level of love. But there was no raising one weight without lowering another as sacrificial counterbalance. At first Juliet came down to the lower level and danced in the ball. How cleverly Mr. Byam Shaw made the dispute between Capulet and Tybalt over Romeo's presence flare across the forestage, drowning the harmonies of the dance, hiding the graceful wheel of girls. Then in the orchard, with two stars showing briefly below the balcony, Romeo strained upwards to where Juliet stood on the balcony over his head. He climbed up to that balcony to descend with her to the bedchamber that would also be the tomb, and there the marriage of love and death was consummated. And so the pattern filled out to its inevitable end. On the level of violence Mercutio and Tybalt were killed and presently Romeo and Juliet lay there self-slaughtered with the Friar kneeling beside them. He had gone to and fro across the lower fore-stage like an old mole in the ground trying to make a clandestine marriage into a happy reconciliation. Above, on the level of love for the first time, Montagues and Capulets gazed down on their dead children and joined their hands in reconciliation. I cannot recall ever having seen this concentration of characters on the equivalent of the upper stage in any other production of *Romeo and Juliet*. But I was interested to learn from Nugent Monck the other day that he used this device in his productions of the tragedy at the Maddermarket Theatre in Norwich. If this is not a great conception of *Romeo and Juliet* and a truly poetic and Shakespearian vision of the play that Byam Shaw presented to us, then I think we might as well forget about the synthesis of speech and spectacle and make the most of Verona with Renato Castellani, whose film might almost have ended with the ubiquitous James A. Fitzpatrick bidding a soulful farewell to old Verona, city of riot—and romance.

But in fact it is surely an impressive instance of a production Shakespearian in spirit and not only in text. It has been slowly dawning on me for some years that Glen Byam Shaw is probably the greatest living producer of Shakespeare. That it has taken me a long time to realize it is not entirely due to critical obtuseness. Byam Shaw is the rarest kind of artist in the theatre, the producer who has the humility to let the Shakespearian work of art control him, rather than impress his own personality on it. The outward sign of this is that when Byam Shaw invents a little piece of stage business we don't say "that's good, I've never seen that done before"—we say "of course" and as likely as not suppose that this detail has always been there where it obviously belongs.

There are further Shakespeare films on the way of which fairly high hopes may be reasonably entertained. Sir Laurence Olivier has conscripted virtually all the theatrical nobility for *Richard III*, Robert Helpmann is to tackle *The Tempest,* and Michael Redgrave presumably still hopes to film *Antony and Cleopatra* in Italy. One can sympathize with the determination of some of our leading Shakespearian actors not to fall into the hands of the ordinary commercial film producer. But it is unlikely that the completely satisfying Shakespeare film will be made by an actor who is starring in it. When are the studios going to send for Glen Byam Shaw?

Romeo and Juliet

1954

DIRECTION	Lev Arnshtam and Leonid Lavrovski
PHOTOGRAPHY	Alexander Shelenkov
MUSIC	Sergei Prokofieff
ART DIRECTION	Peter Williams and K. Jefimov
CHOREOGRAPHY	Leonid Lavrovski
EDITING	T. Lichatchova
SOUND	Boris Volski

A Mosfilm Production

CAST

Romeo	YURI ZHDANOV
Juliet	GALINA ULANOVA
Mercutio	SERGEI KOREN
Nurse	I. OLENINA
Friar Laurence	L. LOSCHILIN
Capulet	A. RADUNSKI
Lady Capulet	E. ILYUTSHENKO
Montague	S. UVAROV
Paris	A. LAPAURI
Tybalt	ALEXEI YERMOLAYEV
Benvolio	W. KUDRAYASHOV

ROMEO AND JULIET
GAVIN LAMBERT

❖❖

The new Russian ballet film of *Romeo and Juliet* (Gala), to be shown in London soon, is fascinating from many points of view. As the presentation of a full-length ballet on the screen, with music by Prokofiev, choreography by Lavrovsky, and Ulanova as Juliet, it is a transposition with impressive credentials—not "cinematic" (in the Powell-Pressburger sense) but unusually resourceful in its deployment of camera and cutting, often in its sets, to extend and heighten theatrical effects. The original work, apparently nearly an hour longer on the stage, suffers from a few disadvantages inherent in its tradition: there are some episodes of plot, such as the wedding, Friar Laurence's explanation of the "poison" when Juliet comes to beg for his help, that cannot be satisfactorily expressed by dancing, and are reduced to dumb-show—reinforced, in the film, by a commentary. The final scene on the tomb is also a formidable challenge to a choreographer's invention, and Lavrovsky has met it disappointingly. On the screen perhaps, the limitations of ballet as narrative art show up more immediately: and while the directors, Lev Arnstam[1] and Lavrovsky himself, have been content to accept these limitations, they have created a film often rich in beautiful and exciting movement.

The Verona is not Italianate, but has its own legendary quality. In its exteriors, the ancient town with its wide market square, colonnades,

From Sight and Sound *25, no. 2 (Autumn 1955): 85–86. Reprinted by permission of* Sight and Sound.

[1] Arnstam is an interesting lesser-known personality of the Soviet cinema. Born in 1905, he was an outstanding concert pianist in his 20's, then turned to writing. With the arrival of sound, he became interested in the cinema, and wrote the scenario for the Ermler-Youtkevich *Counterplan* (1932), an important early Soviet sound film. In 1935 his *Girl Friends* made the actress Zoya Federova famous, and in 1944 his war story *Zoya* was shown in this country. His biography *Glinka* (1947) was highly praised in Russia, but never exported. Arnstam has usually written and directed his own films; no doubt his broad cultural background, especially his musicianship, is vital to the superiority of *Romeo and Juliet* over other recent Russian ballet films (*Trio Ballet, Concert of Stars,* etc.).

flights of steps, oriental-looking streets lined with stalls, and a huge, rugged range of mountains encircling it, is distinctly Caucasian in atmosphere. The townspeople in the crowd scenes remind one of *Sadko*. While the costumes at the Capulet ball are courtly and elaborate, their subdued, sombre tints of dark red and brown have no Renaissance glow but a fascinating, wintry remoteness. (It is a pity that the interior settings do not achieve consistency of style; while the palace ballroom is strikingly successful in its sober but dramatic colour and design, Juliet's bedroom looks too like a faded theatrical print.) At their best, the images finely match Prokofiev's music—which, in its opulence of orchestral texture, its rhythmic variety (the heavy, insistent, almost dirge-like theme for the "Cushion Dance" at the ball is an extraordinary *tour de force*) and its occasionally unexpected use of solo instruments, notably the saxophone, seems to have all the ideal qualities of a ballet score: sensuous appeal and subtle dramatic instinct.

The crowd scenes are spectacularly inventive and brilliant. The duels in the market square, the death of Mercutio, the introduction of a carnival element—clowns, tumblers, a jesting Death, performing some characteristic Russian leaps—the sudden vengeful fury of Lady Capulet over Tybalt's body, are staged with exhilarating force and some virtuoso crane movements by the camera; and the whole ballroom sequence—the "Cushion Dance," the masked entry of Romeo, his pursuit of Juliet, her unwilling dance with Paris—is beautifully composed. While the lovers' passages are uneven, there are moments of exquisite delicacy, most of all in the ecstatic flight of imagination during the balcony scene, when their figures are dissolved through to a *pas de deux* against a vague nocturnal backdrop, dim shapes of mountains in the distance and soft oases of light on the grey expanse of floor. The camera records this dance with perfect fluidity. The film also creates an imaginative moment in its own right: Juliet's terror on the night before her wedding to Paris, her sudden flight through the palace, her white figure hurrying through dark corridors and down shadowed flights of steps.

There remains Ulanova. At her first appearance—rather sexlessly, unflatteringly dressed in white, and an unfortunately choreographed scene with the Nurse in which her skittish movements only serve to emphasize a lack of youth—one is disconcerted. But when the choreography ceases to pretend that she is a young girl, the marvellous lyric power of the dancer takes over, and one is continually held by her lovely poetic grace. The Romeo (Y. Jdanov) is excellent, sympathetic, if a little heavy in appearance, and there is a superb, captivating Mercutio (S. Koren).

Othello

1955

DIRECTION AND SCRIPT	Sergei Youtkevich
PHOTOGRAPHY	Evgeni Adrikanis
MUSIC	Aram Khachaturian
ART DIRECTION	A. Vaisfeld, W. Dorrer, and M. Kariakin
COSTUMES	O. Krotschinina
EDITING	K. Aleyeva
SOUND	B. Volski

A Mosfilm Production

CAST

Othello	SERGEI BONDARCHUK
Desdemona	IRINA SKOBZEVA
Iago	ANDREI POPOV
Cassio	VLADIMIR SOSCHALSKI
Emilia	A. MAXIMOVA
Brabantio	E. TETERIN
Roderigo	E. VESNIK
Lodovico	N. BRILLING
Montano	A. KELBERER
Duke of Venice	M. TROYANOVSKI
Bianca	L. ASHRAFOVA

OTHELLO
DEREK PROUSE

◆◆◆

Sergei Youtkevich has defined his interpretation of Othello's tragedy not primarily as one of love and jealousy but of misplaced trust. Othello's murderous act is committed in defence of truth and justice, out of the violation of his faith in man's noble and harmonious destiny. For many years Youtkevich has cherished his dream of bringing *Othello* to the screen (*Cinema 56* recently published an article on his conception written by the director as early as 1938), and now the final result, meaningful and mature, carries the weight of a subject profoundly felt and understood.

The first quality that strikes one in the film is the authority and confident ease with which it takes to the open air. Here is no calculated transference of a stage classic to the screen, but a total reconsideration of the subject from first to last in terms of cinema.

Othello himself is first seen through the eyes of Desdemona. She spins an ornamental globe dreamily, and the scene fades. We see Othello, hero of the countless exploits which have fired her romantic imagination—the valiant warrior, the shipwrecked galley slave, the natural candidate for the highest honour and renown. The dream fades . . . into the credit titles. (Welles' pre-credits action was the funeral cortege; "He began with death, I began with life," Youtkevich is reported impartially to have observed at Cannes.) We next see Othello in his time of full contentment. His noble conception of life has proved an attainable ideal. To Desdemona he is the tenderest of lovers, and in the Senate he speaks from a deep, certain and rapturous self-fulfilment. After the marriage (it is Cassio who guides the swift and secret gondola along the night canal), when Brabantio strides, dismayed and angry, from the Senate, it is almost as an afterthought that he turns to hurl back his warning: "Look to her, Moor, if thou hast eyes to see; she has deceived her father, and may thee." As Othello and Desdemona move down the wide, sunlit steps to the square be-

From Sight and Sound *26, no. 1 (Summer, 1956): 30. Reprinted by permission of the author and* Sight and Sound.

low, Desdemona drops her handkerchief. Iago, hovering and alert, darts forward to retrieve it and thereby to earn his first "honest Iago." A masterly ironic stroke, and a brilliantly casual strengthening of the incidents to come.

Passions, both secret and open, bind the central characters together and inform their every action. A provocative and sexually eager Emilia buys Iago's kisses rather than his good-humour with the purloined handkerchief. Her arm twists across the screen as she coquettishly teases her husband with the handkerchief; later, Othello's hand will be seen in an arresting close-up as he desperately demands the handkerchief from Desdemona. And in the final scene the same handkerchief is raised to Cassio's lips. Was Desdemona urged to plead for him by an almost unconscious awareness of his love for her? Did some psychic recognition of this in Othello render Iago's work that much the easier? By such hints and speculations the knot of central passions is slowly tightened, and by such subtle preparation as this early planting of the handkerchief coincidence is elevated to a disturbing and dramatic fatalism. Not even the willow song is avoided, despite the threat it can clearly present to realism on the screen. Youtkevich has already shown us a Desdemona who loves to sing, and the first seeds of suspicion are sown to the sound of her singing as her boat drifts across the bay. Later, when her happiness is already overshadowed, she is still heard singing sadly.

The first scene of treachery is a typical example of Youtkevich's invention. A conception that, given a less than impeccable feeling for the total shape of the action, might have defied control or remained merely bleakly abstract, here amplifies the scene with a striking dramatic symbolism. As the two men walk along the beach (the same scene in Welles' film was also shot on the move), and Iago's hints assume their meaning for Othello, they pass through a tangle of fishing nets. The nets hang more densely, Othello's perturbation mounts, and physical and mental claustrophobia commingle. In their next scene together, the seeds have taken root; the treachery is already a complex growth, and a note of fearful intimacy is struck. Convinced finally of Desdemona's guilt, Othello sinks to his knees on the shore, oblivious of the waves dashing against him. Iago kneels beside him: and as Othello's head sinks on his breast, there is something of a lover's ecstasy in Iago's thrill of possessive triumph:

> *Othello:* Now art thou my lieutenant.
> *Iago:* I am your own forever.

There are interesting uses of soliloquy throughout *Othello*. The key speech, "O now, for ever . . . Farewell the tranquil mind" is extracted from the scene with Iago and treated as a soliloquy. Othello walks through the camp at night, speaking his distracted thoughts aloud, unaware of the amazed concern of his men. On the occasion of Othello's arrival in Cyprus, Iago is seen in close-up, backed by the festive fireworks. His thoughts are heard on the sound track but his lips (as in Olivier's *Henry V*) remain motionless. Later, Iago addresses another soliloquy to his reflection mirrored in a well. This captures effectively the quality of dramatic dialectic inherent in soliloquy, its essential function as an inner dialogue between brain and spirit. Othello also addresses his own reflection in the same pool, but here the need is for an assuagement of his torment, a desperate attempt to rediscover a remembered peace in the mirrored face.

I have already mentioned Youtkevich's remarkable visual sense. Sovcolour, in its latest development of the Agfa process, serves this with beautiful subtlety. Much of the action takes place out of doors, but the passions lose none of their intensity when exposed to the bright sunlight backed up by the blue sea. Iago is seen alone in foreground shadow while Othello is teased by a skittish Desdemona under clustering sundrenched vines; Othello reels in his first onrush of anguish against a burning white wall. It is only towards the end that the clouds gather, the candles are lighted, and the drama darkens to climax. Here Sergei Bondarchuck rises finely to the tragedy's demands, presenting a naturally noble spirit fearfully wracked in its battle against baffling and malignant odds. After the murder, particular mention should be given to A. Maximova's Emilia. Her horrified inability to grasp the enormity of her husband's offence is a powerful and true interpretation of a challenging scene. A. Popov's Iago is a plausible villain, generally withdrawn and watchful, but enough of the extrovert to sing a lusty soldier's song at a celebration. Competent enough to serve the director's main intention, this is not, though, a performance that attains any great subtlety.

Youtkevich has defined the tragedy's climax as follows:

I believe that after the murder of Desdemona the Moor remains calm. The tragedy only attains its climax at the moment when Emilia reveals her husband's lie. . . . The treachery of "honest Iago" is what finally plunges Othello into chaos. Iago is calm; he has lost the game, but as long as Othello lives he is the victor. When Othello raises his dagger, it is Iago who leaps forward to stop him, having understood his intention. Othello's death negates the victory of Iago. The Moor pays for his crime with blood. His courage and his honesty elevate him above Iago. The final wave of Iago's envy breaks forth: he has lost the last round.

The moral implications which Youtkevich discovers in the v
make his Othello an authentically tragic hero; his collapse is a di
integration from the highest spiritual refinement. And in the final
scenes Othello's calm re-assumption of his lost nobility—his with-
drawal from earthly chaos—lends the tragedy a deeply moving dying
fall. An elevating and intensely satisfying exposition of the play, this
Russian *Othello* must rank with the best of filmed Shakespeare.

Richard III
1955

DIRECTION	Sir Laurence Olivier
SCRIPT	Sir Laurence Olivier and Alan Dent
PHOTOGRAPHY	Otto Heller
MUSIC	Sir William Walton
ART DIRECTION	Carmen Dillon and Roger Furse
COSTUMES	Roger Furse
EDITING	Helga Cranston
SOUND	Bert Rule

A London Films Production

CAST

Richard III	SIR LAURENCE OLIVIER
Edward IV	SIR CEDRIC HARDWICKE
Edward V	PAUL HUSON
Henry VII	STANLEY BAKER
Buckingham	SIR RALPH RICHARDSON
Clarence	SIR JOHN GIELGUD
Norfolk	JOHN PHILLIPS
York	ANDY SHINE
Cardinal Bourchier	NICHOLAS HANNEN
Rivers	CLIVE MORTON
Dorset	DOUGLAS WILMER
Grey	DAN CUNNINGHAM
Hastings	ALEC CLUNES
Stanley	LAURENCE NAISMITH
Lovel	JOHN LAURIE
Ratcliff	ESMOND KNIGHT
Catesby	NORMAN WOOLAND
Tyrrel	PATRICK TROUGHTON
Brackenbury	ANDREW CRUICKSHANK
Lord Mayor	GEORGE WOODBRIDGE
Queen Elizabeth	MARY KERRIDGE
Anne	CLAIRE BLOOM
Jane Shore	PAMELA BROWN
Duchess of York	HELEN HAYE
Dighton	MICHAEL GOUGH
Forrest	MICHAEL RIPPER

Olivier's RICHARD III:
A Reevaluation
CONSTANCE BROWN

❖❖

At about the same time that Laurence Olivier was producing his first two films, John Mason Brown deliberately applied "that precious, dangerous final adjective 'great'" to Olivier's performance as Oedipus.[1] Since then Olivier has been the subject of two biographies (one in Italian), the occasion of numerous spreads in the popular magazines, a frequent interviewee—as an actor. And still no one has published a critical study of his films.

The omission seems odd for a man who has created acknowledged classics such as *Henry V, Hamlet,* and *Richard III.* Yet the only critical material available on the films is contemporary reviews and occasional passing references—although, these provide a few clues as to why Olivier's work has attracted relatively little interest from film critics. Olivier's films have been dismissed as stagey in their restriction of space and use of sets, as actor's films, as adaptations (which Agee implied made them intrinsically inferior).[2] Still, none of these qualities, or all of them put together, necessarily diminishes a film's value, as anyone acquainted with film history must freely grant. Certainly there is no good reason why Olivier's films do not merit a close critical analysis—especially since they lend themselves to it so readily.

Richard III in particular offers as much as can reasonably be expected of a film. In Olivier's hands, one of Shakespeare's better plays (certainly not one of his best) is transformed into an intricate, subtle, coolly ironic plunge into one of those recesses of human nature that are generally avoided through the same fastidious impulses that make the manufacture of sewer covers a profitable business. In its rather

From Film Quarterly *20, no. 4: 23–32.* © *by The Regents of the University of California. Reprinted by permission of The Regents.*

[1] Felix Barker, *The Oliviers* (London, 1953), p. 242.
[2] James Agee, review of *Henry V* in *Time* XLVII (April 8, 1946), 58. Reprinted in *Agee on Film.*

stylized way, *Richard* is an extraordinarily honest film, and requires proportional honesty from anyone who hopes to assess it correctly— which may partly account for the fact that so far no one has bothered. It is a great deal of trouble to shuck off prejudices about what films should be like, and even more trouble to rinse the mind of conventional notions of what people are like; but perhaps it can be demonstrated that *Richard* is well worth the price of admission.

There is an advantage to beginning a discussion of Olivier's *Richard* with reference to his handling of the text, primarily because it provides some concrete and illuminating clues to his intention. Olivier's alterations of *Richard III* are so numerous that it would be virtually impossible (and pointless) to enumerate them all. It is in the major changes, in any case, that the interest lies, and they are fairly easily accounted for. The pattern of Olivier's major alterations suggests the operation of two basic principles which work together almost inextricably, the first being one of economy and cinematic expediency. He slashes out half-a-dozen of the lengthy cast of characters—most notably Queen Margaret—who clutter the stage when the play is performed in its entirety (which is almost never); and he consequently reduces the parts of many more. Every ounce of linguistic fat is removed, leaving a lean, swiftly moving plot (slightly rearranged to make it more comprehensible and effective as a film) with its central characters still intact.

The second principle is an interpretive one, involving judgment as to the relative importance of various parts of the play, and right at the heart of it is the removal of Queen Margaret. Margaret and her prophetic curses must necessarily seem a little quaint to modern audiences. A prophetic curse is a rather mechanical device for structuring a rambling history and heightening dramatic irony—the sort of effect an audience would appreciate fully only when superstition was a way of life. It is a device which a modern production of *Richard* can do without, especially since there are other possibilities in the play which can be more profitably developed—as Olivier apparently felt there were.

During an interview with Kenneth Tynan on the BBC in 1966, while discussing the stage performance of *Richard III* which preceded his film by ten years, Olivier remarked: "I had a lot of things on my side, now I come to think of it, from the point of view of timeliness. There was Hitler across the way, one was playing it definitely as a paranoiac; so that there was a core of something to which the audience would immediately respond." [3] There is no evidence that Olivier intended his audience to make a connection between Richard and Hitler when he performed the role on the stage in 1944. His film, how-

[3] *The New York Times,* Sunday, August 21, 1966, Sec. 2, p. 6.

ever, seems to insist that some such connection be made. The removal of Margaret and the reduction of other parts forces particular attention on the psychology of Richard—who in any case dominates the play. Besides, the structure placed on the action of the play by Margaret's curses is replaced in Olivier's film by another structure, visual rather than linguistic, which forcibly suggests how his Richard is to be taken.

As in Olivier's earlier films, the form in *Richard* is achieved through a complex imagistic structure with one dominant parabolic formal device. In *Henry V*, the device is the Globe Theater, which begins and ends the film. In that case, the device came about more or less by accident. Olivier had been concerned with preserving the speeches of the chorus, which express eloquently Shakespeare's longing to escape from the limitations of the Elizabethan stage. He had toyed with the idea of a disembodied voice, until it occurred to him that he might begin on the stage, interspersing the chorus speeches as he gradually worked out into wider space and freer film technique, thereby simultaneously introducing stage and film audiences to the idea of film adaptation of Shakespeare. *Henry V* is often criticized for beginning on the stage, which is attributed to Olivier's fancied theatrical orientation—but actually it works, and works brilliantly. The device which began as a textual expedient provided the film with a framework for the kind of tight structure Olivier compulsively seeks, and turned what might have been only another strategy film into a dynamic essay on the power of the camera as an extension of the imagination.

Similarly, the visual structure of *Hamlet* is provided by the labyrinthine Elsinore, into which the camera descends at the beginning of the film and from which it does not fully emerge until the end. In the case of *Richard III*, the central device of coherence is the crown.

The crown imagery is built around three coronations, a structure facilitated by the incorporation of the coronation of Edward IV from *Henry VI, Part 3* (the play immediately preceding *Richard* in Shakespeare's history cycle) into Olivier's film script. Olivier added the coronation partly to elucidate for modern audiences Shakespeare's version of the political situation existing in England before Richard achieved the crown, but its formal function is also evident. The first coronation is that of Edward, certainly not an outstanding king but more or less a legitimate one. The coronation of Edward is followed by the coronation of Richard, the "Red King," the tyrant, the king of misrule. The third coronation is that of Richmond, representing the restoration of order and the return of authority to its proper place.

The parabolic curve from legitimate king to tyrant to legitimate king is clearly defined through the use of crown images. The crown motif is hurled at the audience immediately. As the last words of the creeper title, "the Crown of England," fade from the screen, the first object which appears is an ornamental crown hanging in the air, suspended from slender wires. The scene is the coronation of Edward IV, and the crown, the symbol of divinely sanctioned authority, dominates the coronation sequence.

Richard's coronation is closely paralleled to that of Edward, with the suspended crown once more beginning the sequence, while the third coronation, an implied coronation, takes place on Bosworth Field after Richard's body has been carted off on the back of a horse. Stanley, walking to join Richmond, discovers the crown, which has fallen from Richard's head earlier in the battle, lying, symbolically, in a bramble bush. He retrieves it, brushes it off reverently, then lifts the crown as he walks as if to place it on Richmond's head. The camera isolates the crown, which dominates the screen as the ornamental crown dominated it at the previous coronations. The crown then dissolves to a painted red crown over which the closing credits are superimposed.

The film is concerned, then, with the nature of kingship and tyranny, which sets Olivier's *Richard* at some distance from the play. Although Shakespeare's play, to a degree, shares this concern, the primary focus is on plot and character per se. It is only necessary to evoke *Hamlet* to see to what extent *Richard III* is plot-oriented. Both plays deal with sensationalistic material, murder and court intrigue, but *Hamlet* is by far the greater play because the plot is eclipsed by the concern with meaning. Had Olivier tried to adapt *Richard III* simply by snipping out some of its less inspired passages, he would have accomplished little. Instead, by giving predominance to a theme obscured in the play, he has given his film a significance that the play does not have. Olivier's film, like the play, is a portrait of an individual tyrant. Unlike the play, Olivier's film surpasses melodrama to become a portrait of tyranny.

That Olivier's film is concerned with tyranny is obvious; exactly what it has to say about tyranny is more difficult to define. There are elements of *Richard* (besides the crown motif) which suggest that the film takes the orthodox libertarian line on tyranny—that tyranny is an immoral infraction of human freedom, and that inevitably, human dignity will assert itself and the tyrant will be overthrown. One of these is the consistent use of Richard's shadow, and those of his conspirators, to trace and comment on the development of Richard's plot. The shadow is one of the most overworked cinematic devices, but Olivier's employment of it is fresh and sophisticated—symbolic and metaphorical rather than horrific. Richard's shadow plays freely through the film like a familiar demon, assuming different aspects as the action progresses.

After the initial scene with Anne, in the abbey, Richard declares: "Clarence beware! Thou keepest me from the light. But I will plan a pitchy day for thee." As he speaks, the camera wanders away from him to his shadow stretched over the stone steps of the abbey. He starts to move down the steps as he speaks, and the shadow occupies more and more of the screen until, on his last words, it swallows up the screen completely—just as Richard's tyranny will swallow up England; just as every tyrant swallows up the country he rules.

From this point on, the shadow reappears intermittently. After Richard has finally succeeded with Anne, his new influence over her is symbolized through his shadow. He kicks open the door of the room she has just entered, and the train of Anne's white dress becomes visible in the upper part of the screen. Richard's shadow stretches across the floor as he steps into the doorway, overlapping her train.

When Buckingham begins to incline toward Richard, shadows are used to symbolize their union. To Buckingham's suggestion that he and Richard go with Rivers and Grey to Ludlow to fetch the prince, Richard replies, with an air of discovery, "My other self." As they walk out of the room, the camera lingers on their shadows which, side by side, are stretched out across the floor.

Reinforcing Olivier's use of shadows is his persistent weaving of religious references into the fabric of his film. Generally, religious episodes and symbols are placed in ironic juxtaposition to Richard's acts —thus, by implication, condemning Richard's conduct as immoral. In Olivier's film script, the text of the play is augmented with religious chants which serve as an ironic comment on the action. As Richard maneuvers Edward into suspecting Clarence, two monks in the background recite Psalm 51 in church Latin: "Against thee, thee only, have I sinned . . . and thou mayst be clear when thou judgest; behold, I was shapen in iniquity."

Conventional religious symbols, like the chants, are employed by Olivier to suggest Richard's satanic aspect. Clarence and Hastings are both sacrificed to Richard's ambition, so both are associated with saintly images. While Clarence tells Brackenbury of his nightmares, he wanders to the recessed window of his cell. A crucifix hangs on the right side of the window, and Clarence leans against the wall to the left of the window, facing the crucifix, as he speaks. As he delivers the line "Seize on him, Furies, take him to your torments!" Clarence flings his arms back and up against the wall. The parallel of Clarence's position to that of the crucified Christ on the facing wall is unmistakable.

Hastings is likewise associated with religious images. When he is betrayed at the tower, he sits alone at the end of a long table, the rest of the coronation committee having removed themselves to a safe distance at the far end. The camera shoots down the table at him. Above him is a wall painting of winged angels. The camera moves in close enough to include only Hastings and the painting, so that the angels seem to hover over him.

Olivier employs the same technique to make another kind of comment on tyranny. Richard is not only placed in opposition to religion, but his subordination of religion, his exploitation of religion to achieve his own ends, is made clear in the film through the interaction of Richard and religious trappings. Richard's most notable misuses of religion occur when he and Buckingham taunt the Archbishop into violating sanctuary, and when Richard extracts a mandate from a group of citizens at Baynard's Castle, appearing with a pair of clergymen in order to create a favorable impression.

The film places heavy emphasis on the scene at the castle. As in the play, the entire sequence is built around the basic discrepancy between the reluctance of the assembled citizens to accept Richard and the favorable attitude which Richard's henchmen try to instill by pretending that it already exists. Richard, feigning reluctance, accepts the crown. As one of the monks takes a bell-rope hanging by the balcony where he and Richard are standing and starts to ring the bell, presumably to sound an entrance into meditation, Richard snatches the rope away and spins down it to the street. Richard walks up to Buckingham and thrusts out his hand for Buckingham to kiss while the bell, still spinning, clatters deafeningly. When Buckingham starts to kiss the hand, Richard lowers it, forcing Buckingham to his knee. At the point when the action reaches its climax, the film reaches an imagistic climax. Richard throws back his head, savoring his power. The camera cuts to the madly swinging bell, then dissolves to the bells of Richards' coronation.

Certainly Richard's descent of the bell rope is a concrete representation of his intense lust to put his new power into immediate force, but it is much more than that. The essence of Richard's tyranny, and the tyranny of every man who ever mobilized religion to gain his own ends or had an insane lust to see someone on his knee, are packed into a single visual image.

Still another aspect of Olivier's interpretation of *Richard III* which tends to support the notion that the film is an anti-tyranny apologue is the way Olivier has chosen to represent Richard's psychological make-up. He does indeed, as he has said, play Richard as a paranoiac —an interpretation which the play invites. Some of Richard's waspish diatribes take on a new significance when they are viewed as being partly inspired by self-indulgent delusions of persecution. Part of Richard's long soliloquy from *Henry VI, Part 3,* incorporated by Olivier into the "winter of our discontent" speech, is particularly suggestive of Richard's paranoiac conviction that he is the victim of a conspiracy so cosmic that all nature is a party to it:

> Why love forswore me in my mother's womb:
> And, for I should not deal in her soft laws,
> She did corrupt frail nature with some bribe,
> . . . To disproportion me in every part,
> Like to a chaos. . . .[4]

But Richard is portrayed as a special kind of paranoiac—one whose resentment finds its supreme expression (and its chief compensatory device) in sadistic aggression and a lust for power that is quite literal and physical as well as figurative and psychological.

The progress of Richard's logic in his first speech suggests that his quest for power is a substitute for normal sexual activity:

> But I, that am not shap'd for sportive tricks,
> Nor made to court an amorous looking-glass;
> I that am rudely stamp'd, and want love's majesty
> To strut before a wanton, ambling nymph;
> . . . Have no delight to pass away the time
> . . . And therefore, since I cannot prove a lover
> . . . I am determined to prove a villain.

The particular form which Richard's quest for power takes is suggested in a few lines from *Henry VI, Part 3*:

> And I, like one lost in a thorny wood,
> That rends the thorns and is rent with the thorns,
> Seeking a way and yet straying from the way;
> . . . Torment myself to catch the English crown,
> And from that torment I will free myself,
> Or hew my way out with a bloody axe.

The passage certainly exhibits a curious selectivity. Thorns are a common symbol of sterility. They were used as such by Christ in the parable of the sower, and the next line, "Seeking a way and yet straying from the way," seems to be an ironic reinforcement of the Biblical echo. The entire figure used in the passage has strong sado-masochistic

---

[4] All quotations are reproduced as they appear in Olivier's film script, except the one beginning "But I." In this case, Richard's logic exhibits a similar pattern in an earlier speech from *3 Henry VI*, and Olivier's text omits the last three lines of the passage as it appears in *Richard III*, substituting those representing the logical turn in *3 Henry VI*. I chose to use the speech from *Richard III* here, in order to avoid the appearance of misrepresenting the play. I have not provided references to the lines in the plays to which the passages in the film script correspond, because sometimes there is no exact correspondence due to Olivier's rearrangement of lines and coining of connectives.

implications, and the last lines do somewhat more than imply. That Olivier went out of his way to incorporate these lines into both his stage and screen performances, along with the passage referring to bribery of nature, on the ground that they "helped to explain Gloucester's character" should come as no surprise.[5]

Olivier seems to have been thoroughly aware of this implicit aspect of Richard's character, and he has incorporated ample suggestions of sadism and power as a sexual object into his film. Richard's relationship to his throne is one way Olivier chooses to represent Richard's concept of power. After his coronation, Richard snatches Anne's hand and swoops into the throne room, followed by a train of nobles. He stands in front of the throne and stares up at it for a moment then snaps, "Stand all apart." The nobles give him space, Richard releases Anne's hand and slowly and deliberately mounts the steps, one at a time. As he reaches the top, he turns around and sinks slowly, inch by inch, into the seat, staring fixedly into space. At length he seems to relax, and his eyelids droop slightly. Anne falls to the floor. When her attendants have helped her to her feet, she looks up at Richard and puts her fingers to her lips, perhaps apprehensively, perhaps as if to blow him a kiss. Then her hand drops limply and she walks slowly away. She is not seen in the film again. When Richard possesses the throne he possesses it in the fullest sense of the word—and the throne admits of no rivals.

Richard's sadism is more readily apparent. From the beginning he has a marked penchant for kicking doors (Brackenbury's and Anne's), human beings (a guard in the Abbey), and, presumably, whatever else may lie within range. Once Richard sits on the throne, his indulgence in violence is intensified. "What's o'clock?" Richard asks, in an attempt to discourage Buckingham's petitioning. "Upon the stroke of ten," Buckingham replies. "Well let it strike," Richard shrieks, smashing the scepter down fiercely on the arm of the throne. The camera cuts back of the throne just in time to catch the scepter as it strikes the arm. The closeness of the camera to the throne and the suddenness of the cut contribute to a subjective impression of violence and emphasize the narrowness with which the scepter misses smashing Buckingham's hand, which he pulls off the throne just in time.

The violent use of the scepter, with its implication of abuse of power, is repeated when Buckingham persists in his petitioning. "Thou troublest me. I am not in the vein," Richard snaps, planting the scepter in Buckingham's chest and shoving him away from the throne, none too gently. Shortly afterward, instead of merely telling Tyrell to smother Edward's children, Richard chooses to demonstrate by clap-

[5] Barker, p. 235.

ping a red cushion from his throne over Tyrell's face for a few seconds, then releasing it and whispering, "There is no more but so."

Olivier evidently considered this aspect of Richard's character of some importance, for he chose to suggest it again in Richard's death scene. Olivier has become noted for sensational and violent death scenes in Shakespeare, and he is sometimes inclined to recall an element of his interpretation which he wants to stress at this point in his performance as a device of emphasis. In *Richard III,* several of the film's major motifs recur in the death scene. The soldiers cluster around Richard to kill him, pull off his armor and stab him. Suddenly their faces assume an expression of horror, and they back away. Richard lies still for an instant and then begins to thrash and twitch convulsively. The motion accelerates, and finally he extends his left arm, with his sword in his deformed hand, upward, stares for a moment at the cross formed by the hilt of the sword, and dies.

The hilt of the sword, of course, provides the last ironic contrast of religion and Richard. The physical horror of his death, which is historically accurate, following More's version rather than Shakespeare's, forms a powerful comment on the fate of tyrants.[6] The difficulty of killing him also bears implications about the nature of tyranny. Yet there is something distinctly sensual about the way he dies. The convulsive twitching, which may pass for technical accuracy at first, has none of the irregularity associated with spasms. It is movement that is distinctly structured and rhythmed, a kind of grotesque ballet. In fact, it is rather overtly suggestive—an orgastic consummation to a life characterized by the identification of love and violence. The fact that, this time, Richard is on the receiving end only intensifies the raw power of the effect, introducing an element of poetic justice and implying, as does the play, that a portion of Richard's destructive impulse is self-directed.

All of these elements of Olivier's interpretation—the crown imagery, the shadow, the use of religious reference, the portrayal of Richard's psychology—constitute a strong temptation to conclude that Olivier's film is an anti-tyranny moral fable. But *Richard* is designed to squeeze somewhat more meaning than this out of the concept of a tyrant, an undertaking which necessarily involves, in the interest of telling the truth, a certain amount of willful failure to assume any moral position whatsoever.

If *Richard III* were a moral fable, it would be natural to expect that some attractive alternative to Richard's tyranny would be pre-

[6] "King Richard himself . . . slain in the field, hacked and hewn at his enemies' hands, carried on horseback dead, his hair in despite torn and tugged like a cur dog. . . ." *The History of Richard III* from *The Complete Works of Sir Thomas More,* I, ed. W. E. Campbell (New York, 1931), p. 451.

sented in the film. However, this is clearly not the case. Often Richard is described as having disrupted an idyllic situation in order to jack himself into a position of command. Actually, King Edward's court is far removed from any semblance of established virtue. The nobles are all factious, and the dissension is not even remotely superficial. Moreover, it is clear that Edward is a weak king, and that his wife and brothers-in-law, who have engineered the imprisonment of Hastings, take advantage of his weakness.

The corruption in the court is by no means restricted to Richard. Buckingham's description of Edward "lolling on a lewd love-bed" is not inaccurate, and Richard's many contemptuous references to Mistress Shore are completely justified. Moreover, there is an aura of guilt still hanging over the throne, a guilt acquired during the Wars of the Roses. Only Clarence, whose nightmares reveal his sense of guilt, seems to feel pangs of conscience. The king who is old and sick as well as weak, is provided with an heir, but the heir is only a child. The court in *Richard III* is clearly in the state of political instability which invites a Hitler to move in, and, as seems often to be the case, a Hitler is available.

Olivier's film reflects the play's inherent absence of any satisfactory alternative to Richard in Edward's court. To visualize the corruption of the court Olivier added Mistress Shore, who is only alluded to in the play, to the cast of his film. She is always present in the court, ministering to the king or hovering in the background, and on the whole she is mute. Olivier has provided her with only a "Good morrow, my lord," for she needs no dialogue. Her presence speaks for itself. Edward's fondness for her is established almost at once. As he leaves the place of his coronation, he passes Mistress Shore, who is leaning in a doorway. As he passes through the doorway, Edward pauses to chuck her on the chin with the scepter. This shot sets up one misuse of the scepter which can later be contrasted to Richard's violence, and conveys a vivid impression of Edward's lasciviousness. Later, as Edward leaves for a triumphal procession through the city, he exits speaking of pastimes which "befit the pleasure of the court." The camera moves back to reveal Mistress Shore in the foreground of the screen, the recipient of an ironic glance from Richard.

Edward's inadequacy as a king, like Richard's tyranny, is elucidated through religious reference. After Edward has signed Clarence's death warrant, he exits leaning on the arm of Mistress Shore. The camera cuts back to the two monks (a permanent fixture of Edward's throne room) who gaze after them, still chanting, exchange mildly scandalized glances, and finally close their prayer book and fold their arms. In addition to religious chants, religious symbols are used to stress Edward's corruption. During the scene in which Edward tries to reconcile the factious nobles, he lies in bed clutching a rosary. At a moment when the queen's back is turned he kisses the hand of Mistress Shore, still clutching the rosary tightly in his hand.

Olivier also visualizes the inadequacy of the child, Prince Edward. When the prince arrives in London, Richard and Buckingham escort him into the throne room. The doors swing open and he runs in. He pauses abruptly, his back to the camera, looking up at the empty throne. The camera moves back and up until Edward, a small, solitary red smear against soft grey, is dwarfed by the room.

The established Church, which serves in Olivier's film partly as a contrast to Richard's villainy, fares no better as an alternative to Richard than Edward and his partisans (the second brother, Clarence, is not particularly promising as royal timber either, for he lacks the restrained unscrupulousness that characterizes Shakespeare's successful kings). In fact, the Church is subjected to a certain amount of oblique satire. Instead of serving as a moral bulwark, the Church joins the conspiracy of compliance that ultimately places Richard on the throne.

In Olivier's film, the conduct of the clergy is clearly presented as conforming to the general moral laxity which characterizes Edward's court. The two monks in the throne room may exchange scandalized glances, but they shrug and fold their arms. The Archbishop, similarly, not only allows Richard to bring the prince's brother, York, out of sanctuary, but also is portrayed as being an active advocate (probably out of fear) of Richard's decision to behead Hastings. When Richard accuses Mistress Shore of having caused his innate deformity and Hastings of treason for protecting her, the Archbishop remarks, "I never looked for better at his hands. After he once fell in with Mistress Shore." These lines are spoken by the Lord Mayor a scene later in the play (and repeated in the film), not by the Archbishop. By presenting them to the Archbishop, Olivier contributes to the impression that the Church is hardly fulfilling its function as a moral force.

Perhaps it is possible to contend that Richmond is the alternative to Richard, but the film does not particularly support this hypothesis. There is even less of Richmond in the film than in the play, and what there is of him is not overwhelmingly appealing. He has a certain forthright manliness which is attractive enough—but it is hard to be persuaded on the basis of forthright manliness that there is anything appealing about him. He is, as Richard calls him, "shallow Richmond," an utterly humorless being who bears no scars of psychological conflict, who apparently never engaged in a battle with his conscience. In Olivier's film he is endowed with a conventional square jaw, a melodious Welsh accent, and a head of blonde hair with not a curl out of place. He cannot even be credited for defeating Richard. It takes Richard to do that. Richmond has all the compelling properties of a vacuum.

It is in Richard alone that the power of the play, and, even more so, of Olivier's film lies. Buckingham is the craftsman, the technician, the super-subtle instrument, Richard the master designer and driving force. He is utterly unscrupulous (which in itself is attractive enough —for the human fascination with powerful men can hardly be denied), but there is a great deal more to him than that. He has the attributes tyrants often possess—a sharp intellect, an enviable way with words, and sufficient sex appeal, in spite of his deformity, to woo successfully a woman whose husband and father-in-law he has murdered.

The essential ambivalence of Olivier's film is most evident in his portrayal of Richard. There are, as might be expected two extreme ways to play Richard. At one pole he can be underplayed, so that he resembles Iago—sinister and clever, but about as amusing as a vial of undiluted sulphuric acid. At the other pole, he can be overplayed to the point where he becomes a lovable buffoon with an unfortunate tendency towards homicide. Olivier's interpretation lies somewhere between the two extremes, leaning slightly towards the latter in the first part of the film, and then taking a significant swing towards the former during the scene at Baynard's Castle.

The Richard of the first part of the film limps up to the camera as soon as he is left alone with it, gazes into it with a pair of sharp, incessantly blinking eyes, smiles, wags his head, and tells the audience all about the murders he has planned. His manner is smooth, professional, beguiling. "We'll do it together, you and I," he seems to suggest, making sleepy eyes at the camera, looking it up and down as some men contemplate a prospective lover. It was the first time a cinematic character addressed himself to the audience so directly and personally, much less invited them to participate in a conspiracy. It is a delightfully brazen sort of behavior, characteristic of the audacity people admire in powerful men.

As the phases of his plot, one after another, are successfully completed, Richard pauses to comment on his own villainy with obvious relish, and the audience is encouraged to rejoice with him. It seems a harmless enough sort of indulgence, for Richard lends to the proceedings the aspect of an amusing game. He is, himself, amusing enough, inclined to droll self-denunciation:

> And if King Edward be as true and just
> As I am subtle, false, and treacherous,
> This day should Clarence closely be mew'd up.

Richard's confidential communications regarding his sentiments and motivation, combined with a can-do briskness of diction which Olivier exploits to the utmost, is frequently comic:

He cannot live, I hope, and must not die
Till George be pack'd with post-horse up to heaven.
Which done, God take King Edward to his mercy
And leave the world for me to bustle in.

He is a master of irony, the pregnant pause, the after thought. "A sweeter and a lovelier gentleman/ This spacious world cannot again afford," he remarks parenthetically of Edward Lancaster, rolling his eyes in mock piety. Of the King he observes that "he hath kept an evil diet long/ And overmuch consumed his royal—person," taking advantage of the pause to cast a long, speculative glance at Mistress Shore. Olivier's Richard has a scalpel for a tongue, and he handles it masterfully.

In addition to his comic bent for self-congratulation and his rhetorical dexterity, Olivier's Richard has certain idiosyncracies of behavior which are innocuous and rather charming. He tackles his projects with a hand-rubbing enthusiasm which almost belies their sinister nature. At times he is disarmingly absent-minded. He stops on the brink of confusing the king's revocation of Clarence's death warrant with the warrant itself, and as he enters the balcony at Baynard's Castle he almost forgets about pretending to read his prayer book. He is a Duke of Very Little Elegance. The kisses he bestows are sometimes conspicuously audible. His voice has a way of cracking at strategic moments, as when, after successfully wooing Anne, he croaks, "Shine out, fair sun."

It is difficult to believe that this funny fellow has just joked Clarence into a butt of malmsey wine. Of course, Olivier's Richard is unmistakably deadly. The impression is reinforced from the beginning by his high-pitched, brittle precision of speech and his curious, reptilian appearance—hard, thin lips and an incessant, lizard-like blink. Also, there are times when the clown forgets to wear his mask. As Clarence enters the tower, Richard's face assumes an expression of cold hatred; at another point he turns on his nephew, York, with a pulverizing glare. Yet the audience can hardly avoid being taken in to a degree (anyone who laughs is taken in), as it was meant to be. After all, enough people are taken in that Richard becomes king.

The shift in Olivier's characterization occurs during the scene at Baynard's Castle. After accepting the kingship, Richard holds out his black-gloved hand for Buckingham to kiss. He thrusts it forcibly toward the camera, and holds it extended in the air like a huge, black claw. The hand is extended toward the audience as much as toward Buckingham. For the first time, the audience is advised that what it has approved by laughter and condoned in the earlier part of the film is its own destruction. From this point on, Richard's tyranny is no longer so purely amusing.

Once Richard is exposed as a threat to the audience, he might be expected to lose his appeal entirely. Instead, after the scene at Baynard's Castle, he begins to take on some of the stature of a tragic hero, so that the basis for sympathy shifts markedly but is nevertheless retained. Richard's triumph is succeeded immediately by the paranoiac conviction that he cannot continue to reign unless he destroys his nephews and disposes of his wife in order to marry their older sister, and it is precisely at this point that his character begins to work against him like an over-corrected skid. When he has Buckingham most firmly in hand, he alienates him over the issue of murdering Edward's children, and, at the same time, loses all hope of winning the support of Stanley, whom he further antagonizes by threatening his son's life. It is the familiar pattern of the tragic hero committing a decisive act which sets him irrevocably on a path of self-destruction.

Richard retains his ferocity and personal force, even when the consequences of his acts begin to close in on him. After he learns that Buckingham has joined forces with Richmond, he towers on the platform near his throne and roars, as the messengers cringe in terror, "Out on you, owls!/ Nothing but songs of death!" Olivier has omitted from his film the patently tragic "recognition" scene in which Richard, after being visited by the ghosts of his victims, reviews his past actions and is afflicted by an attack of conscience and moral revulsion, teetering precariously between self-love and self-loathing. Richard's horror is conveyed effectively enough, however, for the speech is replaced in the film by a grisly howl that brings Richard's attendant running.

Richard also shares the tragic hero's ultimate comprehension and acceptance of his fate. The lines which convey Richard's attempts to maintain a semblance of confidence once he reaches the battlefield are delivered with a forced jauntiness that betrays his underlying despair. When he learns that Stanley has withheld his forces, and consequently that he is beaten, Richard first surrenders to an irrational impulse ("Off with his son George's head!"), then turns back towards Richmond's forces and utters a lie that is at once a manifestation of dogged pride and genuine bravery: "A thousand hearts are great within my bosom/ . . . Upon them! Victory sits on our helms." After he has been unhorsed and is virtually defenseless, his only response to Catesby's offer of assistance is monumental contempt: "Slave, I have set my life upon a cast/ And I will stand the hazard of the die." And die he does.

Thus Richard remains the powerful figure of Olivier's film. A delicate ironic balance is maintained between condemning Richard as a tyrant and loving him for it, which reflects the ambivalence of the human attitude toward tyrants and, by extension, the intrinsic ambivalence of tyrants themselves. Perhaps Olivier's surest asset as a director is this ironic poise, this wry detachment, this "curious, amoral strength," as Kenneth Tynan puts it.[7] The only ideal Olivier seems committed to is telling the truth, and telling it as excellently as possible, but as long as sensationalism, pseudo-artistic jive, sermonizing, schmalz, and pure inanity are so prevalent, that is no mean commitment. Films must be judged, ultimately, by how close they come to realizing this ideal, and few of them have come closer than *Richard III.*

[7] *The Observer Magazine,* December 12, 1965, p. 8.

Hamlet
1964

DIRECTION	Grigori Kozintsev
SCRIPT	Grigori Kozintsev, after the translation by Boris Pasternak
PHOTOGRAPHY	I. Gritsyus
MUSIC	Dmitri Shostakovich
ORCHESTRA DIRECTION	N. Rabinovich
ART DIRECTION	E. Ene and G. Kropachev
COSTUME	S. Virsaladze
EDITING	E. Makhankova
SOUND	B. Khutoryanski

A Lenfilm Production

CAST

Hamlet	INNOKENTI SMOKTUNOVSKI
Ophelia	ANASTASIA VERTINSKAYA
Claudius	MIKHAIL NAZWANOV
Gertrude	ELIZA RADZIN-SZOLKONIS
Horatio	V. ERENBERG
Laertes	S. OLEKSENKO
Polonius	YURI TOLUBEYEV
Fortinbras	A. KREVALD
Rosencrantz	I. DMITRIEV
Guildenstern	V. MEDVEDEV
Gravedigger	V. KOLPAKOR
First Player	A. CHEKAERSKII

HAMLET
MICHAEL KUSTOW

◆◈◈◆

Shakespeare no longer belongs to us: he is the greatest national poet of a dozen European countries. In France, Gide, in Hungary, Aranyi, in Germany, Schlegel, and in Russia, Pasternak have translated *Hamlet*, and over and above their individual contributions, something of each nation's sensibility (elusive quality) plays across Shakespeare's spectrum. One of the best things in Grigori Kozintsev's film (Lenfilm Sovexport) is the first appearance of the Ghost. Dusk. A giant figure in glinting armour, his black cloak flaming and fluttering like a turbulent storm-cloud, his face shadowed by a vizor—all these elements seem to call up the worst kind of Beerbohm Tree romanticism. And yet, linked with Shostakovich's deep brass sounds, and the crowning shots of horses neighing and bolting with fear, the Ghost becomes as telling as the Grand Inquisitor. A specifically Russian sensibility instinctively illuminates an area of Shakespeare's play. Where Olivier's Ghost was really romantic, an out-of-focus vaporous apparition, Kozintsev chances his arm and achieves something precise, firm and genuine. Those bolting horses have the true Shakespearean feel of natural order tottering.

Kozintsev's film is full of these illuminations. "Denmark's a prison" —shots of a massive portcullis, a vast drawbridge, guards with muskets, and a harsh iron corset into which Ophelia is strapped as she dresses in black to mourn Polonius. Claudius' court is emphatically *there*—indeed the film spends ten minutes placing the court and the Fortinbras business before the Ghost appears at all. There is a threatening circular council-room in which Claudius' central committee meet to decide on Hamlet's trip to England. No one can be alone in this castle: Hamlet's "O that this too too solid flesh" is spoken "voice over," while we see him picking his way through a crowded room of smiling, posturing courtiers. Ophelia's mad scene takes place in a similarly crowded assembly, and the embarrassment and discomfort it generates are true and apt. The guards just don't know where to look as this pale, high-born girl wanders among them distributing twigs.

From Sight and Sound *33, no. 3 (Summer 1964): 144–45. Reprinted by permission of the author and* Sight and Sound.

Shostakovich's score lifts the film on to a plangent, epic plane. He almost makes you believe that "His cockle hat and his sandal shoon" is really an old Serbian folksong; and the presentation of Ophelia is a good example of director and composer working together. When we first meet her, she is being given a dancing lesson. Shostakovich's music is played on a cembalo, insidiously sweet and tinkling. In Ophelia's madness, her dancing gestures return, and so does this crystal tune, now slightly awry and tragic in its incongruity.

This all goes to indicate that the style of Kozintsev's film is realistic-operatic. All the effects we see underline and deepen the main emotional line of the story. The interpretation—blunt, serious Hamlet versus sophisticated inhuman society—has obviously been deeply thought through, but its execution often surprises us by employing conventions that seem old-fashioned. There is little counterpoint or multiplicity. This seems to be a *Hamlet* (as far as I can judge by tempo and shape alone) that is passionate, but lacks quicksilver.

Thus the obverse of Kozintsev's full-blooded expansiveness is a tendency to overplay certain evocative symbols. After Ophelia's death, for example, there are long shots of a seagull pregnant with meaning. The omnipresent shots of the sea surrounding the castle are impressive in giving the film an overall rhythm, but by the end of the film tend to become a bit inert, and one realises how deft the cinema must be to make its images as potent as those of language. (Conversely, the arid, rifted rocks which enclose Hamlet for "To be or not to be" allow the inner eye full scope.)

Smoktunovski as Hamlet is foursquare, strong, and direct, though Kozintsev places him too often in Burne-Jones positions for my liking. It's hard to tell, without knowing the language, whether he gets the wit of the part; one suspects not, though he has one delicious gag (almost the only one in the film) where he brings the guards leading him to England to a standstill while he takes off his shoe to remove a stone. Michal Nazwanov is a proud, full-fleshed Claudius; he brings off a great *coup* in the Play scene. Petrified by the enacted murder, he rises from his throne. Suddenly, with immense effort, he forces himself to applaud dutifully before cracking up and rushing out in confusion. Gertrude is dignified and sensuous; Kozintsev has interpolated a scene after her set-to with Hamlet in which she says No to Claudius in the bedchamber. Anastasia Vertinskaya gives a beautifully judged screen performance as Ophelia, and Polonius (mercifully shorn of "To thine own self, etc.") is sober and muted and respectable. There is a fat, ripe Gravedigger.

One may quibble at some of the excisions ("Now might I do it pat" has gone completely, and Claudius, instead of praying, communes with himself in a mirror), one may find the film's tempo and decor occasionally monolithic, but one forgives a lot for those passages where

Kozintsev's imagination catches fire and he sends his figures hurtling across the screen with the true Shakespearean energy. Laertes' irruption into the castle on the news of his father's death brings in his wake what seems like half the population of Denmark. Laertes and his followers range through the castle corridors, he plucks an Excalibur-like sword from a chest, and solemnly offers it up to an altar before bursting in on the court. All this adds up to a real re-creation of the primitive pulse of Elizabethan revenge; and a similar authentic rhythm infects Hamlet's killing of the king—"King!", the word breathed from Laertes' lips, and Hamlet leaps across the room, thrusts his sword in like a javelin, and sends Claudius teetering through the castle, bellowing like a bull to his death. At such moments, and at many other points in this rich film, Kozintsev clutches the real thing.

HAMLET
DWIGHT MACDONALD

◆◆◆

The new Soviet *Hamlet* is a successful though not a great movie. The chief trouble is that it is staged in the academic style as was Olivier's *Hamlet* (from which it has borrowed freely, as the device of having Hamlet's soliloquies take place in his head, or rather on the sound track, a gimmick perhaps but not a bad one; but I wish those roaring seas around the castle hadn't also been borrowed). It opens with three riders, their long Sir-Henry-Irving–David-Belasco cloaks streaming behind them, furiously galloping up to the drawbridge of a picturesquely sinister castle as dark clouds scud across a stormy sky. One of them turns out to be Hamlet. The change in the play is all too typical; this is a Hamlet who rides and duels a lot more than he reflects; he is so much the man of action, indeed, that the long-debated mystery of the play—what keeps Hamlet so long from revenging his father's murder? —becomes more mysterious than ever, especially as the soliloquies in which he himself reflects on the reasons for his inability to act have

From Dwight Macdonald on Movies *by Dwight Macdonald (Englewood Cliffs, N.J.: Prentice-Hall, Inc., 1969), pp. 271–73. Reprinted by permission of Prentice-Hall, Inc.*

been cut drastically ("To be or not to be" is reduced to half-a-dozen lines) or omitted completely. (In a *Hamlet* recently staged in Poland *all* the soliloquies were left out.) Innokenti Smoktunovski looks a little like Richard Burton and plays the part in the Burton style, only better, as a vigorous type who is much more at home with horses and women than with ideas. As the *Corriere della Sera* put it in a head-line: "[The Venice Film Festival Closes with] *un 'Amleto' anti-amletico*."

The translation is Pasternak's, the fruit of his long eclipse in the Stalin period when he translated poetry instead of writing it. The music is by Shostakovich and is as conventional as the *mise-en-scène:* quite good as movie-music rhetoric, but hollow and overdramatic. The director is Grigori Kozintsev. Could this be *the* Kozintsev, I wondered, the founder, with Leonid Trauberg, in the early twenties of the super-experimental FEKS group (Factory of the Eccentric Actor) which ap-plied slapstick, vaudeville and circus techniques to serious drama, often using acrobats in the lead parts, and who, again with Trauberg, made in the late twenties *The New Babylon,* an extraordinary movie about the Paris Commune that made brilliant use of surrealist stylization to express a social theme? Indeed it is *the* Kozintsev, still alive and if not kicking at least continuing to produce movies: he looked extraordi-narily young, not a day over fifty when I saw him at the Venice Film Festival a few years ago. While his *Hamlet* "works" in its own terms, being coherent, well-acted, and handsomely photographed, there is something depressing about the founder of FEKS and the codirector of *The New Babylon* now turning out such a conventional work—and taking eight years to do it. True, there are two flashes of the old FEKSian fire: the play within a play was excitingly stylized (but this seems to be foolproof; it was well done even in the Burton-Gielgud *Hamlet*) and, more original and important, the concept of Ophelia as an automaton, carried out with many fine touches such as the iron corset and brassiere her maids put on her after her father's death, which solves many problems in this difficult part. But such flashes are, after all, rather depressing, like the last flareups of a dying fire.

Screened Culture—Letter from Venice
GABRIEL PEARSON and ERIC RHODE

❖◆❖

Mr. Rhode takes up Kozintsev's Hamlet *after having described a rather lustreless group of films shown at the 1964 Venice Film Festival.*

But there was one exception: the Russian *Hamlet,* directed by Grigori Kosintsev. It may have been academic, but it had passion. Everything was on the greatest possible scale: the widest of screens, three opening sequences (two of them false), and long moments when the camera lingered on rock faces or followed the flight of a tedious seagull while Shostakovitch's music played, so that you began to wonder whether the film was stretched to fit the music, rather than the music composed to fit the film. Kosintsev's reading of the play is all nineteenth-century characterisation at the expense of language. Speeches are cut heavily; little humour, no ribaldry. The emphasis is on action: and the first shot of Hamlet, oddly moving, is of a distant figure on horseback galloping across a beach towards Elsinore. Whatever verbal imagery remains, such as the sea or the state as prison, tends to be stressed visually with the insistence of a poster.

And yet on a third viewing—and never mind the rock faces and the tedious seagull—this *Hamlet* still excites. Kosintsev, you feel, has lived through this plot; he doesn't sheer away from the risk of melodrama. At the first appearance of his father, Hamlet really does show terror—and not without reason. We only need to see this chilling ghost once and the point is made; enough that we have a repetition of Shostakovitch's ghost theme as Hamlet leans over Gertrude. Kosintsev has had a number of brilliant ideas: Ophelia goes mad shrouded in the draperies of mourning; Polonius, dying, pulls down a curtain to reveal rows upon rows of dresses swollen up by frames; Claudius, apparently amused, applauds the players before shrieking for lights. Kosintsev's inspiration is sometimes halting, but he has no scruples about lifting ideas from Eisenstein or Olivier when his own ideas run dry. His technique is often clumsy and his styles confused. All the same, the

From Encounter *23, no. 5 (November 1964): 62. Excerpted and reprinted by permission of Gabriel Pearson, Eric Rhode, and* Encounter.

play comes over, and it comes over, I think, because the action is made credible.

One believes in this court. Kosintsev has an understanding of the totalitarian atmosphere: no one smiles unless Claudius smiles—or, rather, stretches lips across his teeth. Jokes are made in earnest; the wrong one may cost you your life. Huge busts of the king block your path from door to door. Eyes shift, sometimes cunningly, sometimes in fear. These effects are less stylised than similar ones in Eisenstein's *Ivan the Terrible,* but you feel the source of the experience to be just as authentic.

The acting is all substance; no trickery. The actors know how to wear their costumes and move like aristocrats. Polonius is not played for sniggers; he is garrulous but he is also shrewd—a man to be reckoned with. Even the lesser parts have weight. Osric may be euphuistic, which doesn't mean he is camp. Fortinbras really does give the impression of having fought epic battles. Hamlet is played by Innokenti Smoktounovski, who is pigeon-chested, sharp-nosed and stumpy, yet who *is* Hamlet in a way I have never seen before.

Why does this heroic/realistic style of acting work so well here, and yet fall so flat when used by actors in the West? In no other film did we have such a sense of solid, realised people. Characters became emblems, hints, were fragmented into effects. The one thing *Hamlet* had in common with two of the other films was a theme: what an existential psychologist might call the ambiguity of madness.

Othello
1965

DIRECTION	Stuart Burge, based on John Dexter's stage production
PHOTOGRAPHY	Geoffrey Unsworth
ORCHESTRA DIRECTION	Richard Hampton
ART DIRECTION	William Kellner and Jocelyn Herbert
EDITING	Richard Marden
SOUND	John Cox and Dickie Bird

A B.H.E. Production

CAST

Othello	SIR LAURENCE OLIVIER
Desdemona	MAGGIE SMITH
Iago	FRANK FINLAY
Emilia	JOYCE REDMAN
Cassio	DEREK JACOBI
Roderigo	ROBERT LANG
Lodovico	KENNETH MACKINTOSH
Brabantio	ANTHONY NICHOLLS
Bianca	SHEILA REED
Gratiano	MICHAEL TURNER
Montano	EDWARD HARDWICKE
Duke of Venice	HARRY LOMAX
Clown	ROY HOLDER

Pearl Throwing Free Style
JOHN SIMON

◆◆◆

Not long ago, Sir Tyrone Guthrie deplored Sir Laurence Olivier's wasting his energies on the British National Theatre, work that "could be done equally well by several other people, none of whom could play Othello, Macbeth, Lear, Faustus . . . which, at present, he has no time to think about." Soon thereafter, Sir Laurence found time to think about *Othello,* at any rate—to co-direct and play it at the National Theatre, without relinquishing the managerial reins. Sir Laurence seems actually to have had too much time to think: his Moor, though exceedingly black, is sicklied o'er with the pale cast of thought.

Before getting into the specifics of the movie version, let me discuss certain problems of the underlying stage production, which I caught two years ago at Chichester. Olivier and John Dexter, the co-directors, fell into three traps. First, they were influenced, as Dexter has declared, by F. R. Leavis' essay "Diabolic Intellect and the Noble Hero, or The Sentimentalist's Othello," one of the master's shriller pieces, which, considering his talent for shrillness, is no mean piece of stridency. It is also not a little foolish.

Overreacting to Bradley's established interpretation of a superhumanly noble Othello and an arch-fiendish Iago, Leavis tried to reduce the Moor to a forceful, valiant, but far from magnificent or even maturely loving fellow, and Iago to a verminous, but hardly especially inspired, villain. According to Leavis, it takes Iago a ludicrously short time to undermine a supposedly immortal love, and Othello, in his quick collapse, is revealed as more bloated than great. If Bradley's view was indeed swooningly sentimental, Leavis' corrective is nonetheless worse than the offense. Fortunately, John Holloway, in *The Story of the Night,* makes mincemeat of Leavis' arguments, even to the point of catching the master out in some quite unscholarly sleight-of-hand,

and restores, without going all the way back to Bradley, the play's dignity and magnitude.

The second trap, related to the first, was, I think, an attempt to play a classic in the modern way, that is, in the manner of Brecht or Beckett —if not, indeed, of Jan Kott—and, rather as in Peter Brook's recent *Lear,* to play down all heroic and romantic values. The third trap was the opportunity to capitalize rather meretriciously on contemporary racial problems, to make this Moor *plus catholique que le pape,* which is to say blacker than black, almost blue, so as to milk (if I may be allowed to mix my colors) Othello's *négritude* for all it is worth—or, rather, for all that it isn't.

Let it be said that Olivier plays this misconceived Othello spectacularly, in a way that is always a perverse joy to behold. The make-up (it took Olivier two hours each day to get into it) gives us a handsome jet-black Jamaican with incarnadined lips, palms, soles, and with a melismatic Calypso accent: What he does with the vowels A and O alone introduces an exotic marimba into Shakespeare's orchestration. But already he is in trouble: at moments when the poetry must swell, soar, or subtilize itself, Olivier is forced to abandon the accent.

Whenever remotely conceivable, the actor is barefoot, indulging in that swaying, lilting, almost prehensile walk of jungle-dwellers—which, too, must be jettisoned in scenes of courtly or tragic splendor. Again, he is the black man inconclusively converted to Christianity, and still prey to fetishistic impulses; around his neck hangs an oversize cross that he fondles or kisses on the slightest provocation—though he kisses with equal alacrity any number of tokens of the Doge's authority. When the stress finally becomes unbearable, he tears off the cross, and reverts to prostrations and abasements suggestive of Mohammedan ritual or voodoo. All this is fascinating, but diverts our attention from what the play is about, when it does not downright clash with it: The Othello solicitous for Desdemona's salvation ("I would not kill thy soul.") conflicts with the image of a regressive barbarian.

But contradictions of all kinds are common to this Othello who combines in himself the psychic geographies of Barbados, Aleppo, and Senegal. Thus, for example, after sanguinely referring to "men whose heads/ Do grow beneath their shoulders," Olivier suddenly and unaccountably waxes skeptical and looks at the Venetians with amused complicity, as if to say, "We know that such creatures don't exist." Or, upon discovering the bottomlessness of his tragic error, Othello, having jumped into bed with the dead Desdemona, passionately rocks back and forth with her body, and erotic overtones coupled with frenetic emphasis on blackness embracing blonde whiteness run riot— or should I say race riot? It is an awesome sight, but unmoving.

Here let us stop and state what ought to be a truism but—such **is** the power of capricious reinterpretation—may sound inflammatorily reactionary: *Othello* is a play about jealousy, about loving passion turned to hatred, about the ineffable fragility of goodness, intelligence, love. Desdemona is goodness, but how weak that is; Iago is intelligence, but how corruptible and corrupting that is; Othello is love, but, once its molecular structure has been disturbed, how like its opposite that is! True, these people are no Bradleyan saints and devils; but not even a host of thundering Leavises or rampaging liberals can turn this tragedy of love gone bitter into a drama of gullibility or of a noble savage victimized by white Venetian cunning. Granted, Shakespeare makes Othello a Moor, to add some precariousness to his prominence and make his downfall more credible, but to forfeit the emphasis on the pitiful morality of love "were such perdition/ As nothing else could match."

Actually the best Othello I remember seeing was the late Aimé Clariond's at—of all places—the Comédie Française about fifteen years ago. Clariond modeled himself on some archetypal Bedouin chieftain, a figure in whom prideful grace and cruel animality calmly cohabit; moreover, Clariond's schizophrenic voice, like a superb bell with a sinister crack in it, carried the split in Othello into his farthest-flung syllables. Which is not to say that Olivier's Othello is not impressive— as impressive as he is wrong.

The supporting cast does well enough, with three reservations: Frank Finlay's Iago is very good, if you can accept the Ancient as a clever little Cockney snake in the grass; Maggie Smith's Desdemona is fine, if you like your *Othello* with two Emilias in it, and can see this Venetian pearl as one of the horsier daughters of Albion, say, a field hockey coach at St. Trinian's; and Derek Jacobi's Cassio is just plain bad—priggish, doltish, and effete.

Now there are, curiously, some ways in which this filmed version of a stage play—usually anathema to sophisticated and demotic movie-goers alike—turns out to be superior to the stage production. On stage, Olivier dominated the proceedings to an uncanny extent; Finlay, whose elocution is a bit moss-overgrown anyway, tended to disappear altogether. Film, what with close-ups and recorded sound, acts as a leveler in this respect. Again, by transferring Jocelyn Herbert's sets to a movie studio, the production acquired a profitably increased acting area in which to stretch its legs; the linking together of scenes was also facilitated. Incidentally, the dominant color of this *Othello* is a kind of purplish brown, to be found in Venetian painting from Gentile Bellini to Carpaccio, which creates an atmosphere of appositely somber foreboding; it also, regrettably, tends to make Olivier's face merge with the décor. Much use is made of backlighting, presumably to create the illusion of sea and open skies around Cyprus without having to resort to backdrops, but the effect is only that of very theatrical back-lighting.

There is value in the film's experimental poking around at the frontier where the realms of film, theatre, and television meet: three Panavision cameras were used with television-style editing of shots, and the whole venture was filmed in three weeks, incorporating much of the original stage blocking. However, one does become aware of the somewhat limited range of shots for the film director, Stuart Burge, to choose from, and the entire *mise en scène* seems, some of the time, to vacillate in a no-man's-land between stage and screen. Certain features, like the crowd movements, seem too stagily conventionalized for film; others, like an unexpected and incongruous overhead shot, too cinematic for what is still largely photographed theatre. Geoffrey Unsworth, the photographer, has brought a refined discretion to his color work, though I wish he could have found a way around the shadow-play effects the backlighting often elicited.

No doubt about it, this is the best filmed *Othello* so far, vastly preferable to such a previous version as Orson Welles's, despite the exquisite Desdemona of Suzanne Cloutier. Indeed, as filmed Shakespeare, this *Othello* is surpassed only by Olivier's own *Henry V* and *Richard III*. Even so, with talent such as Olivier's and the British National Theatre's, what a chance was here for a definitive version of this tautest, swiftest, most concentrated of Shakespeare's major tragedies. The production, however, is "one whose hand,/ Like the base Indian, threw a pearl away/ Richer than all his tribe." Still, it is throwing away in the grand style. The thing is worth watching—not so much for the pearl as for the technique of the throwing hand.

The Taming of the Shrew
1966

DIRECTION	Franco Zeffirelli
SCRIPT	Franco Zeffirelli, Paul Dehn, and Suso Cecchi D'Amico
PHOTOGRAPHY	Oswald Morris and Luciano Trasatti
MUSIC	Nino Rota
ORCHESTRA DIRECTION	Carlo Savina
ART DIRECTION	Giuseppe Mariani, Elven Webb, Dario Simoni, and Carlo Gervasi
COSTUMES	Irene Sharaff and Danilo Donati
SOUND	David Hildyard and Aldo De Martino

A Royal Films International (N.Y.) F.A.I. Production

CAST

Petruchio	RICHARD BURTON
Katherina	ELIZABETH TAYLOR
Baptista	MICHAEL HORDERN
Grumio	CYRIL CUSACK
Lucentio	MICHAEL YORK
Tranio	ALFRED LYNCH
Bianca	NATASHA PYNE
Gremio	ALAN WEBB
Hortensio	VICTOR SPINETTI
Vincentio	MARK DIGNAM
Pedant	VERNON DOBTCHEFF

THE TAMING OF THE SHREW
CAREY HARRISON

Watching the edges of a Zeffirelli production is always a delight. His tableaux are exquisitely composed, his use of movement imaginative, and for once the extras are energetic and enthralled. You can even imagine that these people inhabit the sets, with their children and their dogs. But this is not the imaginative condition of watching an Elizabethan play. True, this is a film, not a play, and must be judged on its own terms, but no one with an understanding of the relation of the parts to the whole in a successful work could effectively hope to make a good film using the playwright's words in so significantly altered a setting.

It must be said that were it not for Shakespeare's lines (without which the scriptwriters would be "at a loss," the credits tell us) this *Taming of the Shrew* (BLC Columbia) could be a most engaging trifle. Far from being at a loss, the film's most successful moments in fact come between the lines, when Zeffirelli explores a storybook Padua, full of charming pageantry. But when all this is consigned to the background, it takes Zeffirelli's good taste with it, and in the foreground we are treated to the other aspect of his productions, weary farce, tasteless caricature, and a hysteria of grimaces. The central relationship fails because Elizabeth Taylor's Kate is too shallow to make a worthwhile conquest for even the most penurious Petruchio (though the production stresses apologetically that he is only doing it for the money). It is a shrill performance, offering Burton no challenge. By way of balance, Burton undermines the wit of the piece, playing Petruchio as a drunken peasant who owns land but sups with his slaves, rather than a swain fallen on bad times. The poetry and the flamboyance are not wholly missing, merely a little damp. Of the supporting cast, the young lovers are dull, and the comics more hysterical than funny. Only Michael Hordern as Baptista sustains the grotesquerie with success. But even these successes, verse from Burton, farce dotage from

From Sight and Sound *36*, no. 2 (Spring 1967): 97–98. *Reprinted by permission of* Sight and Sound.

Hordern, are no kin of the material *mise-en-scène*, the detail of the sets, the extras with faces out of Renaissance portraiture.

And yet, if the film had offered a Shrew with character, it would have been an entertaining story, disorganised and often vulgar, but very pretty to watch. . . . This is hardly a re-creation of the 16th century, Padua warts and all, but it is imaginative, and permits one to dream about the Renaissance with renewed excitement. Zeffirelli's next film project is *Romeo and Juliet* as a cinéma-vérité documentary (his words) on Renaissance Verona. Which takes us back to the very first point: one can't help feeling that only a man without a concept of the way parts of an art work relate to the whole could cherish this ambition; or a man who neither understands nor profoundly likes Shakespeare for what he is.

Chimes at Midnight
1966

DIRECTION AND SCRIPT	Orson Welles
PHOTOGRAPHY	Edmond Richard
MUSIC	Francesco Lavagnino
ORCHESTRA DIRECTION	Carlo Franci
ART DIRECTION	José Antonio de la Guerra and
	Mariano Erdorza
EDITING	Fritz Mueller
SOUND	Peter Parasheles

An Internacional Films Española/Alpine Production

CAST

Sir John Falstaff	ORSON WELLES
Prince Hal	KEITH BAXTER
Henry IV	SIR JOHN GIELGUD
Mistress Quickly	MARGARET RUTHERFORD
Doll Tearsheet	JEANNE MOREAU
Henry Percy	NORMAN RODWAY
Kate	MARINA VLADY
Shallow	ALAN WEBB
Poins	TONY BECKLEY
Worcester	FERNANDO REY
Silence	WALTER CHIARI
Pistol	MICHAEL ALDRIDGE
Child	BEATRICE WELLES
Westmoreland	ANDREW FAULDS
Northumberland	JOSÉ NIETO

CHIMES AT MIDNIGHT
PIERRE BILLARD

❖❖

The new film which Orson Welles is just completing in Spain has been shot in conditions of maximum secrecy: its title, *Chimes at Midnight*. The scenario may be regarded as a collaboration between Welles and Shakespeare. To be more precise, it follows his stage *Chimes at Midnight,* presented at Belfast in 1960, as a drama constructed around the history of Falstaff. Welles has drawn on the plays in which Falstaff appears (both parts of *Henry IV, The Merry Wives of Windsor*), on the references in *Henry V,* and on *Richard II* and also Holinshed's *Chronicles,* for the further light they throw on actions and motives. The focal point of the theme which he has shaped out of all this marvellous data is Falstaff's friendship with Prince Hal, and its betrayal.

A few weeks before he started shooting, Welles described his intentions: "Falstaff is the best role that Shakespeare ever wrote. He is as outsize a character as Don Quixote. I've always wanted to play him, which is unusual, as there are very few characters who really tempt me as an actor. *Chimes at Midnight* will be a dark comedy, the story of the betrayal of a friendship. It will concentrate on the actors and there are going to be a lot of close-ups: in fact, it will be my close-up film. The number of sets available to me is so restricted that the film must be anti-baroque, and must work essentially through the faces. When the camera moves away from the faces, it uncovers period settings and actors in costume who are only going to distract from the real thing. But the closer we keep to the faces, the more universal the story becomes."

That was before. During the course of shooting, the sleeping *cinéaste* in Welles was awakened, and he forgot these modest resolves. The kind of "period" settings which Welles found in the little villages of Castille have remained more or less unchanged since the Middle Ages.

From Sight and Sound *34, no. 2 (Spring 1965): 64–65. Reprinted by permission of* Sight and Sound.

He had no trouble in collecting the right extras locally, exercising that extraordinary flair which remains one of the characteristics of his genius. Where the resources at his disposal did prove unequal to the demands of the script, any shortcomings on the part of sets or players will be dissolved in the dark, poetic shadows so conveniently cast by smoky torches. Little by little, the actor gave ground to the director, as the heat of action quickened his invention. In one daring scene, when Falstaff and Doll Tearsheet (Jeanne Moreau) are in bed together at Mistress Quickly's tavern in Eastcheap, he found an appropriately central position for the camera by letting it take the place of the bolster. For the scene of Henry V's coronation, shot in Cordova Cathedral, he had them build an immense platform across the cathedral, allowing him to play with perspectives and contrasts of lighting and to compose images which irresistibly recall Eisenstein. When it came to Falstaff's burial, Welles wanted the biggest coffin that could be found. They brought an old coffin about ten feet long, and when he didn't seem happy with it, they asked if perhaps it was too big. "Oh no," he answered with his huge laugh. "It's just that I would have liked one on wheels."

This verve, and this gluttonous appetite for effects, are characteristic of Orson Welles as he rediscovers the delights of creation. Tireless on the set, he moves about with disconcerting agility, even in the bulky padding which he wears for Falstaff's girth, and develops his *mise-en-scène* as changes of lighting bring him new ideas. For the few scenes not made on actual locations, Welles rejected studio help and had an old garage fitted up as a temporary studio, thus saving several thousand pounds. But these economies were soon swallowed up. Faithful to his reputation, which at this point at least makes contact with historical fact, Welles improvised to such an extent that he has been shooting twice as long, and has spent twice as much, as was allowed for in the initial budget. But who, in the circumstances, is likely to sympathise with the luckless producers?

On occasion, however, Welles' creative independence can begin to look like a caprice. So, feeling that his own American accent would grate on the perfect Shakespearean diction of actors such as John Gielgud (Henry IV), Margaret Rutherford (Mistress Quickly) and Keith Baxter (Prince Hal), Welles didn't want to play his dialogue scenes directly with them. While they were there, he filmed only those shots in which he doesn't appear, or reaction shots in which he doesn't speak. Then, after they had gone, he went back to the same locations, to shoot his dialogue on his own.

At the same time, Welles has begun work on a version of *Treasure Island,* adapted by himself, in which he plays Long John Silver. Jesus Franco, his Spanish assistant on *Chimes at Midnight,* is directing, and they plan to complete the film this summer. Simultaneously, the presence in Madrid of the Mexican actor Francisco Regueira has enabled him to shoot some new sequences for his *Don Quixote,* begun ten years ago and never completed. All of which is encouraging news for *cinéastes:* the young lion of the cinema hasn't lost his roar.

Filmography

The entries give, in order, the date of release, the title, the director (d.), the stars (s.), the producer when especially significant (p.), the country in which the film was made, the producing company, and the length uniformly converted to feet. Occasionally the length of a silent film is given in reels; one reel contained approximately 900 to 1,000 feet. It should be remembered that most silent films ran at sixteen or eighteen frames per second (approximately 1,000 feet each seventeen minutes), whereas sound film runs at twenty-four frames per second (approximately 1,000 feet each eleven and one-half minutes). Release dates may occasionally be confused with production dates, and the footages are not too reliable, especially for silent films. Where two or more footage figures were available, I chose the larger on the presumption that it represents an uncut version.

I have excluded from this list the dozens of modern short films based on excerpted scenes from the plays (usually intended for classroom use), and television productions not subsequently released as commercial films or shown in commercial theaters. I have included only the most significant adaptations and only a representative selection of the many, many parodies and burlesques.

My principal sources have been, for the silent era, Robert Hamilton Ball's *Shakespeare on Silent Film* (New York, 1968) and, for the sound era, the Wiesbaden brochure (see Bibliography), the *Monthly Film Bulletin* of The British Film Institute, and the *New York Times* film reviews. There are undoubtedly some errors and, more unfortunately, some omissions in the following list. I have placed question marks wherever there seemed reason to doubt any date, name, or length.

For those wishing to rent 16-mm, prints of these films, I have listed the distributors, if any, at the end of each entry, employing the following abbreviations:

AUD   Audio-Brandon/ 512 Burlington Ave./ LaGrange, Illinois 60525.

BUD   Budget Films/ 4590 Santa Monica Blvd./ Los Angeles, California 90029.

COL   Columbia Cinemathèque/ 711 5th Ave./ New York 10022.

CONT   Contemporary Films, McGraw-Hill/ 828 Custer Ave./ Evanston, Illinois 60076.

CUL   Cultural Films, Inc./ 1564 Broadway/ New York 10036.

CW   Clem Williams Films/ 2240 Noblestown Road/ Pittsburgh, Pennsylvania 15205.

EG   Em Gee Film Library/ 4931 Gloria Ave./ Encino, California 91316.

FCE   Film Classic Exchange/ 1926 South Vermont Ave./ Los Angeles, California 90007.

FINC   Films Incorporated/ 4420 Oakton St./ Skokie, Illinois 60076.

ICS   Institutional Cinema Service, Inc./ 29 E. 10th St./ New York 10003.

MMA   Circulation Director/ Dept. of Film/ The Museum of Modern Art/ 11 W. 53rd St./ New York 10019.

MSP   Modern Sound Pictures, Inc./ 1410 Howard St./ Omaha, Nebraska 68102.

SIII   Sigma III/ 444 Madison Ave./ New York 10022.

SFS   Standard Film Service/ 14710 W. Warren Ave./ Dearborn, Michigan 48126.

TWF   Trans-World Films, Inc./ 332 S. Michigan Ave./ Chicago, Illinois 60604.

TWY   Twyman Films, Inc./ 329 Salem Ave./ Dayton, Ohio 45401.

UA   UA/16 United Artists Corp./ 2904 Woodburn Ave./ Cincinnati, Ohio 45206.

UF   United Films/ 1122 S. Cheyenne/ Tulsa, Oklahoma 74119.

WB   Warner Brothers, Inc./ Non-Theatrical Division/ 4000 Warner Blvd./ Burbank, California 91505.

WP   Willoughby-Peerless/ 115 W. 31st St./ New York 10001.

WR   Walter Reade 16/ 241 E. 34th St./ New York 10016.

ANTONY AND CLEOPATRA

1908 *Antony and Cleopatra,* d. Charles Kent; s. Betty Kent, Charles Chapman. U.S.A., Vitagraph. 995 ft.

1912 *Cleopatra* (adapt.), d. Charles L. Gaskill; s. Helen Gardner. U.S.A., Helen Gardner Co. 6 reels. *AUD.*

1913 *Marcantonio e Cleopatra* (adapt.), d. Enrico Guazzoni; s. Amleto Novelli, Gianna Terribili Gonzales. Italy, Cines. 11 reels. *FCE, EG, AUD.*

1917 *Cleopatra* (adapt.), d. J. Gordon Edwards; s. Theda Bara, Fritz Leiber. U.S.A., Fox Film Corp. 10 reels.

AS YOU LIKE IT

1908 *As You Like It,* d. Kenean Buell. U.S.A., Kalem Co. 915 ft.

1912 *As You Like It,* d. Charles Kent; s. Rose Coghlan, Maurice Costello. U.S.A., Vitagraph. 3 reels. *FCE.*

1916 *Love in a Wood* (adapt.), d. Maurice Elvey; s. Elizabeth Risdon. G.B., London Film Co.

1936 *As You Like It*, d. Paul Czinner; s. Elizabeth Bergner, Laurence Olivier. G.B., 20th-British-Fox/ Inter-Allied-Film. 8,626 fa.

A COMEDY OF ERRORS

1940 *The Boys from Syracuse* (adapt.), d. A. Edward Sutherland; s. Allan Jones, Martha Rayt. U.S.A., Universal Pictures. 6,560 ft.

CORIOLANUS

1963 *Coriolano, Eroe Senza Patria/ Thunder of Battle* (adapt.), d. Giorgio Ferroni; s. Gordon Scott, Lilla Brignone. Italy/ France, Explorer Film 58/ Dorica Film/ Comptoir Francais du Film Prod. 101 min.

CYMBELINE

1913 *Cymbeline*, d. Frederic Sullivan; s. Florence LaBadie, James Cruze. U.S.A., Thanhouser Co. 2 reels.

1925 *Cymbeline,* d. Ludwig Berger. Germany, U.F.A.

HAMLET

1900 *Le Duel d'Hamlet* (the duel scene), d. Clément Maurice; s. Sarah Bernhardt, Pierre Magnier. France, Marguerite Chenu's Phono-Cinéma Théâtre.

1907 *Hamlet*, d. George Méliès. France. 570 ft.

1908 *Amleto,* p. Giuseppe de Liguoro? Italy, Cines. 855 ft.

Amleto, d. Luca Comerio? Italy, Milano.

1910 *Hamlet,* d. Wm. Barker; s. Charles Raymond. G.B. 1,325 ft.?

Hamlet, d. Henri Desfontaines; s. Jacques Grétillat, Colonna Romano. France, Eclipse Film.

Amleto, d. Mario Caserini; s. Dante Capelli. Italy, Cines. 1,066 ft.

Hamlet. France, Lux. 950 ft.

Hamlet, d. August Blom; s. Alwin Neuss, Emilie Sannom. Denmark, Nordisk. 1,200 ft.?

1913 *Hamlet* (sepulchre scene), d. André Calmettes; s. Mounet-Sully. France, Film d'Art?

Hamlet, d. Hay Plumb; s. Forbes-Robertson, Gertrude Elliot. G.B., Hepworth Mfg. Co. for British Gaumont. 6,000 ft.

1917 *Amleto,* d. Eleuterio Rodolfi; s. Ruggero Ruggeri, Elena Makowska. Italy, Cines. 3 reels.

1920 *Hamlet* (adapt.), d. Svend Gade and Heinz Schall; s. Asta Nielsen, Lilly Jacobsson. Germany, Art-Film. 7,764 ft. *MMA, FCE.*

1930 *The Royal Box* (excerpt), d. Bryan Foy; s. Edmund Kean. U.S.A., Warner Brothers. 8,000 ft.

1933 *Hamlet* (screentest, color, Act I.v; II.ii), d. Robert Edmund Jones and Margaret Carrington; s. John Barrymore. U.S.A., RKO. 900 ft.? *MMA.*

1935 *Khoon Ka Khoon*, d. Sohrab Modi; s. Modi. India, Minerva Movietone.

1948 *Hamlet*, d. Sir Laurence Olivier; s. Olivier, Jean Simmons, Basil Sidney, Eileen Herlie. G.B., Two-Cities Films/ Olivier/ Rank. 13,924 ft. *UF.*

1954 *Hamlet*, d. Kishore Sahu; s. Sahu, Mala Sinha. India (in Hindustani).

1959 *Der Rest ist Schweigen* (adapt.), d. Helmut Käutner; s. Hardy Krüger, Ingrid Andree. W. Germany, Freie Filmproduktion. 9,309 ft.

1960 *Hamlet*, d. Franz Peter Wirth; s. Maximillian Schell, Dunja Movar. W. Germany, Bavaria Atelier Gmb H. 14,485 ft. *AUD.*

1961 *Ophélie* (adapt.), d. Claude Chabrol; s. André Jocelyn, Juliette Maymal. France, Boréal. 9,439 ft.

1964 *Hamlet*, d. Grigori Kozintsev; s. Innokenti Smoktunovski, Anastasia Vertinskaya. USSR, Lenfilm. 16,170 ft. *UA.*

     Hamlet (for television), d. Sir John Gielgud; s. Richard Burton, Linda Marsh. U.S.A., Electronovision Prod. 17,384 ft.

1969 *Hamlet*, d. Tony Richardson; s. Nicoll Williamson, Marianne Faithfull. G.B., Woodfall. 10,573 ft. *COL.*

HENRY IV 1, 2

1966 *Chimes at Midnight* (also includes scenes from *Henry V* and *The Merry Wives of Windsor*), d. Orson Welles; s. Welles, Sir John Gielgud, Keith Baxter. Spain/ Switz., Internacional Films Española/ Alpine. 10,350 ft.

HENRY V

1944 *Henry V*, d. Sir Laurence Olivier; s. Olivier, Renée Asherson, Robert Newton. G.B., Two-Cities Films. 12,572 ft. *UF*

HENRY VIII

1911 *Henry VIII*, d. Wm. G. B. Barker; s. Sir Herbert Beerbohm Tree, Arthur Bourchier. G.B., Barker Motion Photography. 30 min.?

1912 *Cardinal Wolsey* (adapt.), d. Larry Trimble; s. Tefft Johnson, Clara Kimball Young. U.S.A., Vitagraph. 1,000 ft.

JULIUS CAESAR

1907 *Le Mort de Jules César*, d. George Méliès; s. Méliès. France. 344 ft.
1908 *Julius Caesar*. U.S.A., Lubin.
    Julius Caesar, d. Wm. V. Ranous?; s. Ranous. U.S.A., Vitagraph. 980 ft.
1909 *Giulio Césare*, d. Giovanni Pastrone. Italy, Itala Film. 836 ft.
1910 *Brutus* (adapt.), d. Enrico Guazzoni. Italy, Cines. 1,187 ft. *FCE*.
1911 *Julius Caesar*, d. Sir Frank R. Benson; s. Benson, Guy Rathbone, Murray Carrington. G.B., Co-operative Cinematograph Co. 990 ft.
1913 *Julius Caesar* (scene with Brutus and Cassius). U.S.A., Edison Kinetophone.
    Giulio Cesare. Italy, Gloria Films.
1914 *Giulio Cesare*, d. Enrico Guazzoni; s. Amleto Novelli, Gianna Terribili Gonzales. Italy, Cines. 7,328 ft. *FCE, AUD*.
1950 *Julius Caesar*, d. David Bradley; s. Bradley, Charlton Heston. U.S.A., Avon Prod. 9,437 ft. *AUD, TWF*.
1953 *Julius Caesar*, d. Joseph Mankiewicz; s. Sir John Gielgud, Marlon Brando, James Mason. U.S.A., MGM. 10,765 ft. *FINC*.
1970 *Julius Caesar*, d. Stuart Burge; s. Charlton Heston, Sir John Gielgud, Jason Robards, Jr. G.B., Commonwealth United Entertainment, Inc. 10,437 ft.

KING JOHN

1899 *King John*, d. Sir Herbert Beerbohm Tree; s. Tree and the cast of His Majesty's Theatre. G.B.

KING LEAR

1909 *King Lear*, d. Wm. V. Ranous?; s. Ranous, Thomas H. Ince. U.S.A., Vitagraph. 960 ft.
1910 *Re Lear*, d. Giuseppe de Liguoro. Italy, Milano. 1 reel?
    Re Lear, d. Gerolamo Lo Savio; s. Ermete Novelli, Giannina Chiantoni. Italy, Film d'Arte Italiana. 1,072 ft.
1911 *Le Roi Lear au Village* (adapt.), d. Louis Feuillade. France, Gaumont. 1,235 ft.
1912 *The Jewish King Lear*. G.B., filmed at the Pavilion Theatre.
1916 *King Lear*, d. Ernest Warde; s. Frederick B. Warde, Lorraine Huling. U.S.A., Thanhouser-Pathe. 5 reels. *FCE*.
1923 *Success* (excerpt), d. Ralph Ince; s. Mary Astor, Brandon Tynan. U.S.A., Metro Pictures. 6,800 ft.

1935 *The Yiddish King Lear* (adapt.), d. Harry Thomashefsky; s. Maurice Krohner, Jeanette Paskevitch. U.S.A., Lear Pictures, Inc. 7,669 ft.

1954 *Broken Lance* (adapt.), d. Edward Dmytryk; s. Spencer Tracy, Richard Widmark. U.S.A., 20th Century Fox. 8,782 ft. *FINC*.

1969 *King Lear*, d. Peter Brook; s. Paul Scofield, Irene Worth. Denmark.

1971 *King Lear*, d. Grigori Kozintsev; s. Yuri Jarvet, Elsa Radzin. USSR.

MACBETH

1905 *Duel Scene From Macbeth.* U.S.A., American Mutoscope and Biograph Co. 53 ft.

1908 *Macbeth*, d. Wm. V. Ranous; s. Ranous, Paul Panzer. U.S.A., Vitagraph. 835 ft.

1909 *Macbeth*, d. Mario Caserini; s. Dante Cappelli, Maria Gasperini. Italy, Cines. 1,460 ft.

1910 *Macbeth*, d. André Calmettes; s. Paul Mounet, Jeanne Delvair. France, Film d'Art. 1,000 ft.

1911 *Macbeth*, d. Sir Frank R. Benson; s. Benson, Lady Benson, Guy Rathbone. G.B., Co-operative Cinematograph Co. 1,260 ft.

1913 *Macbeth*, d. Arthur Bourchier; s. Bourchier, Violet Vanbrugh. Germany, Film Industrie Gesellschaft, Heidelberg. 4,700 ft.

1916 *Macbeth*, s. Madame Georgette Leblanc-Maeterlinck. France, Eclair.

Macbeth, d. John Emerson; supervised D. W. Griffith; s. Sir Herbert Beerbohm Tree, Constance Collier. U.S.A., Triangle-Reliance.

1917 *Lady Macbeth* (adapt.?), d. Enrico Guazzoni. Italy, Palatino-Film.

1922 *Macbeth*, d. Heinz Schall. Germany, Elel-Film/ Filmindustrie, Heidelberg. 3,005 ft.

1946 *Macbeth* (16 mm), d. Thomas Blair; s. David Bradley, Jain Wilimovsky. U.S.A., Willow Prod. 2,624 ft.

1948 *Macbeth*, d. Orson Welles; s. Welles, Jeannette Nolan, Dan O'Herlihy. U.S.A., Republic Pictures-Mercury Films. 9,525 ft. *FCE, AUD, CONT, BUD, CW, MSP, SFS, TWF, TWY*.

1950 *Macbeth* (16 mm, color), d. Katherine Stenholm; s. Bob Jones, Jr., Barbara Sowers. Unusual Films, Bob Jones Univ. 2,808 ft.

1952 *Le Rideau Rouge (Ce soir, on joue Macbeth)*, d. André Barsacq; s. Michel Simon, Pierre Brasseur. France, Cinéphone–S.N.E. Gaumont. 8,102 ft.

1955 *Joe Macbeth* (adapt.), d. Ken Hughes; s. Paul Douglas, Ruth Roman. U.S.A., M. J. Frankovich for Columbia. 8,072 ft.

1957 *Kumonosu-Djo/ The Throne of Blood* (adapt.), d. Akira Kurosawa; s. Toshiro Mifune. Japan, Toho Co., Ltd. 9,879 ft. *AUD*

1960 *Macbeth*, d. George Schaeffer; s. Maurice Evans, Judith Anderson. G.B., Grand Prize Films, Ltd. 9,630 ft. *AUD*.

1961 *Sibirska Ledi Magbet/ A Siberian Lady Macbeth* (adapt.), d. Andrzej Wajda; s. Oliver Marković, Ljuba Ladić. Yugoslavia, Avala Film. 8,318 ft.

1971 *Macbeth,* d. Roman Polanski; s. Jon Finch, Francesca Annis. G.B., Playboy Prod.

MEASURE FOR MEASURE

1913 *Dente per Dente* (adapt.?), s. Mignon Vassallo, Lidia Gauthier. Italy, Latium Film. 2,788 ft.

1942 *Dente per Dente,* d. Marco Elter; s. Carlo Tamberlani, Caterina Boratto. Italy, F.E.R.T. Studios, Turin.

THE MERCHANT OF VENICE

1905 *Le Miroir de Venise (Une Mésaventure de Shylock)* (adapt.?), d. George Méliès. France. 217 ft.

1908 *The Merchant of Venice,* d. Wm. V. Ranous?; s. Florence Turner. U.S.A., Vitagraph. 995 ft.

1910 *Il Mercante di Venezia,* d. Gerolamo Lo Savio; s. Ermete Novelli, Francesca Bertini. Italy, Film d'Arte Italiana. 890 ft. *FCE.*

1912 *The Merchant of Venice,* d. Barry O'Neill?; s. Wm. J. Bowman, Florence LaBadie. U.S.A., Thanhouser. 2 reels.

1913 *Shylock, ou le More de Venise* (adapt.), d. Henri Desfontaines; s. Harry Baur. France, Eclipse. 2,106 ft.

1914 *The Merchant of Venice,* d. Lois Weber, Phillips Smalley; s. Weber, Smalley. U.S.A., Universal Pictures. 3,998 ft.

1916 *The Merchant of Venice,* d. Walter West; s. Matheson Lang, Hutin Britton. G.B., Broadwest Film Co. 4,000–5,000 ft.?

1922 *The Merchant of Venice* (trial scene), s. Sybil Thorndike, Ivan Berlyn. G.B., Masters Films. 1,000 ft.?

1923 *Der Kaufman von Venedig* (adapt.), d. Peter Felner; s. Werner Krauss, Henny Porten, Max Schreck. Germany, Peter Paul Felner-Film-Co. 9,224 ft.

1952 *Il Mercante di Venezia/ Le Marchand de Venise,* d. Pierre Billon; s. Michel Simon, Andrée Debar. France/Italy, B.U.P. Prod./Venturini Elysées Prod. 9,168 ft.

THE MERRY WIVES OF WINDSOR

1910 *The Merry Wives of Windsor.* U.S.A., Selig-Polyscope Co. 1,000 ft.

1911 *Falstaff* (adapt.), d. Henri Desfontaines; s. Denis d'Inès, Louise Willy. France, Urban-Eclipse. 1,066 ft.

1917 *Die Lustigen Weiber von Windsor* (adapt.), d. Wm. Wauer. Germany, Beck-Film.

1923 *John Falstaff* (adapt.), s. Roy Byford. G.B., British and Colonial. 2 reels.

1935 *Die Lustigen Weiber von Windsor* (Nicolai's opera-comique), d. Carl Hoffmann; s. Leo Slezak, Magda Schneider. Germany, Cine-Allianz/ T. K. Tonfilm. 7,898 ft.

1940 *Falstaff in Wein* (based on Nicolai's opera-comique), d. Leopold Hainisch. Germany, Tobis-Filmkunst. 8,495 ft.

1950 *Die Lustigen Weiber von Windsor* (Nicolai's opera-comique), d. Georg Wildhagen; s. Paul Esser. E. Germany, VEB Defa Studio für Spiel filme. 8,426 ft.

1964 *Die Lustigen Weiber von Windsor* (adapt. of Nicolai's opera-comique by Norman Foster), d. Georg Tressler; s. Norman Foster, Lucia Popp, Igor Gorin. Liechtenstein, Norman Foster Prod. 9,184 ft. *SIII, AUD*.

A MIDSUMMER NIGHT'S DREAM

1909 *A Midsummer Night's Dream*, d. Charles Kent?; s. Maurice Costello, Gladys Hulette. U.S.A., Vitagraph. 994 ft.

1909 *Le Songe d'Une Nuit d'Été*, s. Footit (Tudor Hall), Stacia Napierkowska. France, Le Lion. 1,014 ft.

1913 *Ein Sommernachtstraum* (adapt.), d. Stellan Rye; s. Carl Clewing, Grete Berger. Germany, Deutsche Bioscop Gmb H. 4 reels? *FCE*.

A Midsummer Night's Dream, s. Socrate Tommasi, Bianca Hübner. Italy, Gloria Films. 33 min.?

1917 *Elfenzene Aus Dem Sommernachtstraum*. Ballet of the Deutschen Opernhauses, Berlin. Germany, Harmonie-Film.

1925 *Ein Sommernachtstraum*, d. Hans Neumann; s. Werner Krauss, Theodor Becker. Germany, Neumann-Prod. Gmb H. 8,295 ft.

1935 *A Midsummer Night's Dream*, d. Max Reinhardt; s. Mickey Rooney, Olivia de Havilland, James Cagney. U.S.A., Warner Bros. 12,169 ft. (Presently withdrawn from circulation.)

1957 *Sen Noci Svatojanské/ A Midsummer Night's Dream* (puppets), d. Jiří Trnka. Czechoslovakia, Studio loutkového a kresleného filmů. 6,724 ft.

1967? *A Midsummer Night's Dream* (ballet), d. Dan Eriksen (orig. choreography George Balanchine); s. Suzanne Farrell, Edward Villella. U.S.A., Oberon Prod., Ltd. 93 min.

1968 *A Midsummer Night's Dream*, d. Peter Hall; s. Diana Rigg, David Warner. G.B., Royal Shakespeare Co./ Filmways Prod. 11,160 ft. *AUD*.

MUCH ADO ABOUT NOTHING

1956 *Mnogo Shuma Iz Nichego/ Much Ado About Nothing*, d. L. Samkovoi. USSR, Mosk. kinstud. nauch-pop. filmov. 8,462 ft.

1963 *Viel Lärm um Nichts*, d. Martin Hellberg; s. Christel Bodenstein, Horst Kube. E. Germany, VEB Defa-Studio für Spielfilme. 8,410 ft.

OTHELLO

1907 *Otello*, d. Mario Caserini?; s. Ubaldo Del Colle. Italy, Cines. 540 ft.

1908 *Othello* (operatic?), s. Erik Schmedes. Austria, Pathé Frères. 277 ft.

    Othello, d. Wm. V. Ranous; s. Ranous, Julia Swayne Gordon. U.S.A., Vitagraph.

1909 *Otello*, d. Gerolamo Lo Savio; s. Ferruccio Garavaglia, Vittoria Lepanto. Italy, Film d'Arte Italiana-Pathé. 1,105 ft.

    Otello, d. Mario Caserini. Italy, Cines.

    Otello (parody), d. Yambo (Giulio Novelli). Italy, Società Anonima Pineschi.

1911 *Desdemona* (adapt.), d. August Blom; s. Valdemar Psilander. Denmark, Nordisk. 1,797 ft.

1912 *Lo Spettro de Iago* (adapt.). Italy, Aquila Films. 2,624 ft.

1914 *Otello*, d. Arrigo Frusta; s. Colaci, Léna Lenard. Italy, Ambrosio. 4,215 ft.

1918 *Othello* (adapt.), d. Max Mack; s. Beni Montano, Ellen Korth. Germany, Max Mack-Film.

1921 *Carnival* (excerpt), d. Harley Knoles; s. Matheson Lang, Hilda Bayley. G.B., Alliance. 6,500 ft.

1922 *Othello*, d. Dmitri Bukhovetski; s Emil Jannings, Werner Krauss. Germany, Wörner Film. 8,731 ft. *AUD.*

1936 *Men Are Not Gods* (adapt.), d. Walter Reisch; s. Gertrude Lawrence, Miriam Hopkins, Sebastian Shaw. G.B., London Film Prod. 8,046 ft. *FCE, AUD.*

1946 *Othello*, d. David MacKane; s. John Slater, Luanna Shaw. G.B., Marylebone Prod. 4,100 ft.

1947 *A Double Life* (excerpt), d. George Cukor; s. Ronald Colman, Signe Hasso. U.S.A., Universal Pictures. 9,807 ft. *BUD.*

1951 *Othello*, d. Orson Welles; s. Welles, Suzanne Cloutier, Micheál Mac-Liammóir. Italy, Mogador Films (Mercury). 8,325 ft.

1955 *Jubal* (adapt.), d. Delmer Daves; s. Glenn Ford, Rod Steiger, Ernest Borgnine. U.S.A., Columbia Pictures Corp. 9,069 ft. *MSP, BUD.*

    Othello, d. Sergei Yutkevich; s. Sergei Bondarchuk, Irina Skobzeva. USSR, Mosfilm. 9,833 ft. *AUD.*

1956 *Kean* (excerpt), d. Vittorio Gassman; s. Gassman. Italy, Lux-Vides. 7,469 ft.

1960 *Wenecianski Mawr/ Venetian Moor* (ballet), d. M. Chebukiani. USSR, Gruzia-Film.

1961 *All Night Long* (adapt. with jazz score), d. Basil Dearden; s. Paul Harris, Marti Stevens. G.B., Rank Organization Film Prod., Ltd. 8,170 ft.

1965 *Othello,* d. Stuart Burge; s. Sir Laurence Olivier, Maggie Smith, Frank Finlay. G.B., B.H.E. 14,940 ft. *WB.*

RICHARD III

1908 *Richard III,* d. Wm. V. Ranous; s. Thomas H. Ince, Julia Swayne Gordon. U.S.A., Vitagraph. 990 ft.

1911 *Richard III* (adapt.), d. Sir Frank R. Benson; s. Benson, Moffat Johnston. G.B., Co-operative Cinematograph Co. 1,385 ft.

1912 *Richard III,* d. André Calmettes; s. Philippe Garnier. France, Film d'Art.

1913 *The Life and Death of King Richard III,* d. M. B. Dudley; s. Frederick B. Warde. U.S.A., Sterling. 4,400 ft.

1919 *Richard III,* d. Max Reinhardt; s. Conrad Veidt and the Reinhardt Co.

1929 *Show of Shows* (excerpt), d. John Adolfi; s. John Barrymore. U.S.A., Warner Bros. 11,634 ft. *UA.*

1939 *Tower of London* (adapt.), d. Rowland V. Lee; s. Basil Rathbone, Boris Karloff. U.S.A., Universal Pictures. 8,252 ft. *UA.*

1954 *Prince of Players* (excerpt), d. Philip Dunne; s. Richard Burton. U.S.A., 20th Century Fox. 9,168 ft. *ICS, TWY, MSP.*

1955 *Richard III,* d. Sir Laurence Olivier; s. Olivier, Claire Bloom, Sir John Gielgud, Sir Ralph Richardson. G.B., London Films. 14,344 ft.

1962 *Tower of London* (adapt.), d. Roger Corman; s. Vincent Price, Bruce Gordon. U.S.A., Admiral Pictures. 7,143 ft.

ROMEO AND JULIET

1908 *Romeo and Juliet,* d. Wm. V. Ranous; s. Paul Panzer, Florence Lawrence. U.S.A., Vitagraph. 915 ft.

Romeo e Giulietta, d. Mario Caserini. Italy, Cines, 738 ft.

1909 *Romeo und Julia* (operatic), s. Luiza Tetrazzini. Germany, Deutsche Vitascope. 203 ft.

1911 *Romeo and Juliet,* s. George A. Lessey, Julia M. Taylor. U.S.A., Thanhouser Co. 2 reels.

Giulietta e Romeo, d. Gerolamo Lo Savio; s. Gustavo Serena, Francesca Bertini. Italy, Film d'Arte Italiana-Pathé. 2,342 ft.

1914 *Roméo et Juliette.* France, Société Cinématographique des Auteurs et Gens de Lettre.

1916 *Romeo and Juliet,* d. John Noble; s. Francis X. Bushman, Beverly Bayne. U.S.A., Metro Pictures. 7,997 ft.

Romeo and Juliet, d. J. Gordon Edwards; s. Theda Bara, Harry Hilliard. U.S.A., Fox Film. 5 reels.

1917 *Romeo and Juliet* (animation), created Helena Smith Dayton. U.S.A., S.S. Film Co.

1919 *Romeo and Juliet* (animation), created Anson Dyer. G.B., Hepworth. 1 reel.

1920 *Romeo und Julia Im Schnee* (adapt.), d. Ernst Lubitsch; s. Gustave von Wangenheim, Lotte Neumann. Germany, Maxim-Film. 3,109 ft.

Romeo and Juliet (burlesque), d. Vin Moore; s. Walter Hiers, Dorothea Wolbert. U.S.A., Universal Film Mfg. 1,699 ft.

1921 *Doubling for Romeo* (burlesque), d. Clarence Badger; s. Will Rogers, Sylvia Breamer. U.S.A., Goldwyn Pictures. 5,297 ft.

1922 *A Pasteboard Crown* (excerpt), d. Travers Vale; s. Evelyn Greeley, Robert Elliot. U.S.A., Playgoers Pictures. 4,468 ft.

1924 *Romeo and Juliet* (burlesque), s. Ben Turpin. U.S.A., Pathé Exchange. 1,873 ft.

Triumph (excerpt), d. Cecil B. DeMille; s. Rod La Rocque, Leatrice Joy. U.S.A., Famous Players Lasky Corp. 8 reels.

1926 *Wie Einst Im Mai* (excerpt), d. Willi Wolff, s. Karl Harbacher, Trude Hesterberg. Germany, Ellen Richter-Film Gmb H. 8,741 ft.

1929 *Hollywood Revue of 1929* (excerpt directed Lionel Barrymore), d. Charles Reisner; s. John Gilbert, Norma Shearer. U.S.A., MGM Pictures. 11,670 ft.

1936 *Romeo and Juliet,* d. George Cukor; s. Leslie Howard, Norma Shearer, John Barrymore. U.S.A., MGM Pictures. 11,391 ft. *FINC.*

1938 *Villa Discordia* (adapt.), d. Arturo S. Mom; s. Olinda Bozán, Paquito Bustos. Argentina. 7,118 ft.

1939 *Espoirs Ou Le Champ Maudit* (adapt. of the Gottfried Keller novel *Romeo und Julia auf dem Dorfe*), d. Willy Rozier; s. Constant Rémy, Jacqueline Roman. France, Sport Films. 8,288 ft.

1940 *Julieta y Romeo,* d. Jose Marie Castellvi; s. Marta Flores, Enrique Guitart. Spain, Cinedia. 8,200 ft.

1941 *Romeo und Julia auf dem Dorfe* (adapt. of the Gottfried Keller novel), d. Valerien Schmidely; s. Erwin Kohlund, Margit Winter. Switzerland, Pro-Film-Prod.

1943 *Romeo y Julieta* (parody), d. Miguel Delgado; s. Cantinflas (Mario Moreno), Maria Elena Marqués. Mexico, Posa Films. 11 reels.

1944 *Romeo et Juliette,* d. Kamal Selim; s. Ibrahim Hamouda, Leila Mourad. Egypt, Les Films el Nil.

1946 *Bodas Tragicas* (adapt.), d. Gilberto M. Solares; s. Roberto Silva, Miroslava. Mexico, Closa Films Mundiales.

1948 *Anjuman,* d. Akhtar Hussein; s. Jairaj, Nargis. India, Nargis Art Concern. 12,595 ft.

Les amants de Vérone (adapt.), d. A. Cayatte and J. Prévert; s. Serge Reggiani, Anouk Aimée. France, CICC-Borderie. 9,568 ft.

1954 *Romeo and Juliet,* d. Renato Castellani; s. Laurence Harvey, Susan Shentall. Italy/ G.B., Verona Prod./ Universal Cine. 12,612 ft. *UF.*

1955 *Romeo and Juliet* (ballet), d. Lev Arnshtam and Leonid Lavrovski; s. Yuri Zhdanov, Galina Ulanova. USSR, Mosfilm. 8,344 ft.

1960 *Romanoff and Juliet* (adapt.), d. Peter Ustinov; s. Ustinov, Sandra Dee, John Gavin. U.S.A., Pavor S.A., Zurich. 9,253 ft. *UF, UA.*

1961 *West Side Story* (adapt.), d. Robert Wise; s. Richard Beymer, Natalie Wood. U.S.A., Beta Prod. (Mirisch Pictures, Seven Arts Prod.) 13,651 ft. *UA.*

1962 *Mondo Sexy di Notte* (excerpt in Japanese), d. Mino Loy. Italy, Documento Film. 8,705 ft.

1965 *Romeo and Juliet,* s. Royal Academy of Dramatic Art. G.B., Royal Academy and the Regent Polytechnic Inst., London. 105 min. *CONT.*

1966 *Romeo and Juliet* (ballet), d. Paul Czinner; s. Margot Fonteyn, Rudolf Nureyev. G.B., Poetic Films. 11,350 ft. *AUD.*

1968 *Romeo and Juliet,* d. Franco Zeffirelli; s. Leonard Whiting, Olivia Hussey. G.B./ Italy, B.H.E./ Verona Prod./ Dino de Laurentis Cinematografica. 13,680 ft.

The Taming of the Shrew

1908 *La Bisbetica Domata,* d. Lamberto and Azeglio Pineschi. Italy, Società Italiana Fratelli Pineschi. 613 ft.

The Taming of the Shrew, d. D. W. Griffith; s. Florence Lawrence, Arthur Johnson. U.S.A., American Mutoscope and Biograph Co. 1,048 ft.

1911 *La Mégère Apprivoisée,* d. Henri Desfontaines; s. Cécile Didier, Denis D'Inès. France, Eclipse. 1,020 ft.

The Taming of the Shrew, d. Sir Frank R. Benson; s. Benson and the troupe of the Shakespeare Memorial Theatre at Stratford. 1,120 ft.

1913 *La Bisbetica Domata* (adapt.), d. Arrigo Frusta?; s. Eleuterio Rodolfi, Gigetta Morano. Italy, Ambrosio Films. 2,000–3,000 ft.

1915 *The Taming of the Shrew* (excerpt), s. Arthur and Constance Backner. G.B., British and Colonial.

1921 *Enchantment* (excerpt), d. Robert Vignola; s. Marion Davies, Forrest Stanley. U.S.A., Paramount Pictures. 6,982 ft.

1923 *The Taming of the Shrew,* d. Edwin J. Collins; s. Lauderdale Maitland. G.B., British and Colonial. 2,056 ft.

1929 *The Taming of the Shrew,* d. Sam Taylor; s. Mary Pickford, Douglas Fairbanks. U.S.A., The Pickford Corp./ The Elton Corp. 6,202 ft.

1933 *You Made Me Love You* (adapt.), d. Monty Banks; s. Banks, Thelma Todd, Stanley Lupino. G.B., British International Films. 6,422 ft.

1942 *La Bisbetica Domata* (adapt.), d. Fernando Poggioli; s. Lilia Silvi, Amadeo Nazzari. Italy, Excelsa Film.

1953 *Kiss Me Kate* (adapt.), d. George Sidney; s. Howard Keel, Kathryn Grayson. U.S.A., MGM. 9,843 ft. *FINC.*

1955 *La Mégère Apprivoisée, La Fierecilla Domada,* d. Antonio Roman; s. Carmen Sévilla, Alberto Closas. France/ Spain, Vascos-Interproduction/ Benito Perojo. 8,538 ft.

La Mégère Apprivoisée, d. Abdul Rashid Kardar. India.

1959 *Mas Fuerte Que El Amor* (adapt.), d. Tullio Demicheli. Mexico, Jorge Garcia Besné. 7,026 ft.

1961 *Ukroshchenie Stroptivoi/ The Taming of the Shrew,* d. Sergei Kolossov; s. Ludmila Kasatkina, Andrei Popov. USSR, Mosfilm. 9 reels.

1966 *The Taming of the Shrew,* d. Franco Zeffirelli; s. Elizabeth Taylor, Richard Burton. U.S.A./ Italy, Royal Films International F.A.I. Prod. 10,942 ft. *COL.*

THE TEMPEST

1905 *The Tempest* (excerpt), d. Sir Herbert Beerbohm Tree; s. Tree and the troupe of His Majesty's Theatre, London. G.B., Urban. 100 ft.

1908 *The Tempest.* G.B., Clarendon Co. 780 ft.

1911 *The Tempest,* d. Edwin Thanhouser? U.S.A., Thanhouser Co. 1 reel.

1912 *La Tempête.* France, Eclair. 1,885 ft.

1955 *Forbidden Planet* (adapt.), d. Fred McLeod; s. Walter Pidgeon, Anne Francis. U.S.A., MGM. 98 min. *FINC.*

TWELFTH NIGHT

1910 *Twelfth Night,* s. Julia Swayne Gordon, Florence Turner. U.S.A., Vitagraph. 970 ft.

1947 *Noche de Reyes* (adapt.), d. Luis Lucia; s. Fernando Rey, Carmen de Lucio. Spain.

1955 *Dwenatzataja Notch/ Twelfth Night,* d. Yakov Fried; s. Klara Luchko, Alla Larionova. USSR, Lenfilm. 8,108 ft. *AUD.*

The Winter's Tale

1910 *The Winter's Tale,* d. Barry O'Neill?; **s.** Martin Faust, Rosemond.
     U.S.A., Thanhouser Co. 1,000 ft.

     Racconto d'Inverno. Italy, Cines. 947 ft.

1914 *Novella d'Inverno,* d. L. Sutto; **s.** V. Cocchi, Pina Fabri. Italy, Milano
     Film. 3,000 ft.?

     Das Wintermärchen, **s.** Senta Söneland, Albert Paulig. Germany, Belle
     Alliance.

1966 *The Winter's Tale,* d. Frank Dunlop; **s.** Laurence Harvey, Moira Red-
     mond, Jane Asher. G.B., Cressida/ Hurst Park. 13,581 ft.

Selected Bibliographies

1. BOOKS, REVIEWS, AND ARTICLES

*Agee, James. [A review of *Henry V.*] *Agee on Film.* New York: McDowell, Obolensky, Inc., 1958.

*Alexander, Peter. "From School in Wittenberg." *Hamlet: Father and Son.* Oxford: Clarendon Press, 1955.

Ashworth, John. "Olivier, Freud and *Hamlet.*" *Atlantic Monthly* 183 (May 1949): 30–33. Argues against Olivier's Oedipal reading of *Hamlet.*

Barbarow, George. "*Hamlet* Through a Telescope." *Hudson Review* 2 (Spring 1949): 98–117. Elaborated costume and set distract from the text; Olivier has produced "neither drama nor cinema."

*Bazin, André. [A review of *Othello.*] *Cahiers du Cinéma* 13 (June 1952): 18–19.

Bentley, Eric. [A review of *Othello.*] *The New Republic* (October 3, 1955): 21–22. Finds Welles's *Othello* a "precise example of formalistic decadence."

*Beylie, Claude. "*Macbeth* ou la Magie des Profondeurs." *Études Cinématographiques* 24–25 (1963): 86–89.

*Billard, Pierre. "*Chimes at Midnight.*" *Sight and Sound* 34 (Spring 1965): 64–65.

Blumenthal, J. "*Macbeth* into *Throne of Blood.*" *Sight and Sound* 34 (Autumn 1965): 190–95. Suggestive, if somewhat overpowered analysis of Kurosawa's sensitive "distillation" of the essence of Macbeth's character and world.

*Brown, Constance. "Olivier's Richard III—A Re-evaluation." *Film Quarterly* 20 (Summer 1967): 23–32.

———. "Othello." *Film Quarterly* 19 (Summer 1966): 48–50.

Cobos, Juan, and Miguel Rubio. "Welles and Falstaff." *Sight and Sound* 35 (Autumn 1966): 158–62. An excellent interview with Orson Welles on the subject of *Chimes at Midnight.*

Cross, Brenda. *The Film "Hamlet": A Record of Its Production.* London: Saturn Press, 1948. Includes short essays by Olivier, Roger Furse (design), William Walton (music), Alan Dent (script), and others.

*Crowther, Bosley. "*Henry V.*" *The Great Films: Fifty Golden Years of Motion Pictures.* New York: G. P. Putnam's Sons, 1967.

* Items marked with an asterisk are included in the text of this volume.

Dent, Alan. *Hamlet, the Film and the Play.* London: World Film Pub., 1948. Complete text of *Hamlet* with cuts in brackets and studio directions.

Diether, Jack. *"Richard III:* The Preservation of a Film." *The Quarterly of Film Radio and Television* 11 (Spring 1957): 280–93. The film was cut even before it was distributed; the only record of the original version is the RCA Victor complete sound track (Victor LM–6126).

*Harrison, Carey. *"The Taming of the Shrew."* Sight and Sound* 36 (Spring 1967): 97–98.

Houseman, John. *"Julius Caesar:* Mr. Mankiewicz' Shooting Script." *The Quarterly of Film Radio and Television* 8 (Winter 1953): 109–124. Valuable excerpt from Mankiewicz's script, with camera directions.

Houseman, John. "This Our Lofty Stage." *Theatre Arts* 37 (May 1953): 26–28. Houseman, speaking as producer of Mankiewicz's *Julius Caesar,* discusses conceptions behind casting, sets, and so forth.

*Jorgensen, Paul A. "Castellani's *Romeo and Juliet*: Intention and Response." *The Quarterly of Film Radio and Television* 10 (Fall 1955): 1–10.

*Kustow, Michael. *"Hamlet."* Sight and Sound* 33 (Summer 1964): 144–45.

*Lambert, Gavin. *"Romeo and Juliet."* Sight and Sound* 25 (Autumn 1955): 85–86.

*Lemaitre, Henri. "Shakespeare, Le Cinéma Imaginaire et le Pré-cinéma." *Études Cinématographiques* 6–7 (1960): 383–96.

*Macdonald, Dwight. *"Hamlet."* Dwight Macdonald on Movies.* Englewood Cliffs, N.J.: Prentice-Hall, Inc., 1969.

*MacLiammóir, Micheál. *Put Money in Thy Purse.* London: Methuen & Co. Ltd., 1952.

*McCarthy, Mary. "A Prince of Shreds and Patches." *Sights and Spectacles, 1937–1956.* New York: The Noonday Press, 1956.

*Nicoll, Allardyce. "Film Reality: Cinema and the Theatre." *Film and Theatre.* New York: Thomas Y. Crowell Co., 1936.

*Pasinetti, P. M. *"Julius Caesar:* The Role of the Technical Adviser." *The Quarterly of Film Radio and Television* 8 (Winter 1953): 131–38.

Phillips, James. "Adapted from a Play by Shakespeare." *Hollywood Quarterly* 2 (October 1946): 82–90. Analysis of the cuts made in Olivier's *Henry V.*

*Prouse, Derek. *"Othello."* Sight and Sound* 26 (Summer 1956): 30.

*Reeves, Geoffrey. "Finding Shakespeare On Film: From an Interview with Peter Brook." *The Tulane Drama Review* 11 (Fall 1966): 117–21.

*Rhode, Eric. "Screened Culture—Letter From Venice." *Encounter* 23 (November 1964): 61–65.

Shakespeare, William, and Laurence Olivier. *"Hamlet*: The Play and the Screenplay." *Hollywood Quarterly* 3 (Spring 1948): 293–300. Reprints parallel texts of the "get thee to a nunnery" scene from the play and the screenplay.

Tyler, Parker. *"Hamlet* and Documentary." *The Kenyon Review* 3 (Summer 1949): 527–32. Finds *Hamlet* bad because it is "traditional cinema" dominated by a narrow Freudian interpretation of what is really an "ironic comedy."

Walker, Roy. "Bottled Spider." *Twentieth Century* 159 (January 1956): 58–68. Good, slashing attack on Alan Dent as adaptor and Olivier as interpreter of *Richard III.*

*———. "In Fair Verona." *Twentieth Century* 156 (November 1954): 464–71.

*Watts, Richard. "Films of a Moonstruck World." *The Yale Review* 25 (December 1935): 311–20.

Wilson, Richard. *"Macbeth* on Film." *Theatre Arts* 33 (June 1949): 53–55. Interesting account of the Utah stage production that preceded the filming of Welles's *Macbeth.*

2. Filmographies

Ball, Robert Hamilton. *Shakespeare on Silent Film.* New York: Theatre Arts Books, 1968. The definitive work on the subject. All references to silent films should be checked against Ball's text *and* notes.

Gauthier, Guy. "Shakespeare au Cinéma." *Europe* No. 417 (January 1963–64): 193–200. Incomplete and error-filled filmography.

Lippman, Max, ed. *Shakespeare im Film.* Wiesbaden: Saaten-Verlag, 1964. The best and most complete filmography of both silent and sound films, but must be checked against Ball, *Shakespeare on Silent Film,* for errors in the silent entries.

Montague, Arthur. *Shakespeare en el cine.* Madrid: Ateneo, 1958. Pages 31–33 contain a list of 72 films; there are numerous errors.

Morris, Peter. *Shakespeare on Film.* Ottawa: Canadian Film Institute, 1964. A discursive filmography apparently not intended to be thorough. Contains passages from reviews of major films.

Redi, Riccardo and Roberto Chiti. "Shakespeare e il Cinema." *Bianco e Nero* 43 (1957): 80–91. The filmography is inferior to those of Ball and the Wiesbaden brochure, but the bibliography is extensive for Italian sources —and annotated.

Viani, Alex. "Notas para una Filmografia de Shakespeare." *William Shakespeare* 61. I have not located this publication.

Index